Priestly Celibacy Today

THOMAS McGOVERN

Priestly Celibacy Today

SCEPTER PUBLISHERS • PRINCETON
FOUR COURTS PRESS • DUBLIN
MIDWEST THEOLOGICAL FORUM • CHICAGO

This book was typeset by Woodcote Typesetting, Burnley
in 11 on 13 point Bembo for

SCEPTER PUBLISHERS, INC.
20 Nassau Street
Princeton, NJ 08542

FOUR COURTS PRESS
Fumbally Lane, Dublin 8, Ireland
e-mail: info@four-courts-press.ie

MIDWEST THEOLOGICAL FORUM
712 S. Loomis St., Chicago 60607
e-mail: jsocias@msn.com.

A catalogue record for this title
is available from the British Library.

ISBN 1-890177-07-5 (MTF edition)
ISBN 1-85182-352-2 (FCP edition)

First American Edition 1998.
Printed in the United States of America.

Contents

Preface

To write a book about celibacy at the present time could be regarded as a foolhardy enterprise. Over recent years the impression has been created by the media that this is a discipline of the Catholic Church more honoured in the breach than in the observance. In addition, there seems to be a widespread expectation that optional celibacy, despite what John Paul II may say, is inevitable and, indeed, long overdue.

However, current discourse on this topic suggests that there is a confused understanding of the historical development of this charism in the Church, which inevitably leads to erroneous judgements and conclusions. There are also, it would appear, large gaps in the scriptural and theological appreciation of celibacy which result in a reductionist approach to it, causing people to see it primarily from a human and sociological perspective.

What I am attempting in this book is to try to present again the wisdom of the Church and the memory of a tradition about a particular aspect of the Catholic priesthood. Recovering this tradition is important if priests are going to have a sense of conviction about their commitment, and be able to offer reasons for the hope that they have for the future. They also need a sense of discrimination to recognise the shallowness and ideological bias which characterise much of contemporary comment about celibacy. Indeed, Pope John Paul II refers to 'a systematic propaganda which is hostile to celibacy' and 'which finds support and complicity in some of the mass media'.[1]

A theological and historical study of celibacy explains many basic ideas about this discipline. Still, this is never a substitute for the witness of celibacy as lived by priests who have been faithful to their calling, both in times when they were revered for doing so, and at other times, as now, when perhaps they feel they are regarded as freaks. The lives of such priests are the best advertisement for celibacy, and it is their example, more than anything else, which will continue to inspire young men to respond to the Master's invitation.

1 Address, 27 October 1990. All the papal addresses referred to in the text are available in the English language weekly edition of *Osservatore Romano*, usually about one week after the event. Since these are easily accessible, to avoid overloading the footnotes we will omit the actual dates of publication.

In 1992 I gave a seminar for diocesan priests to commemorate the twenty-fifth anniversary of Paul VI's encyclical *Sacerdotalis caelibatus* on priestly celibacy (1967). In the intervening years much has happened, and a lot has been written or said on this topic, both in the documents of the Magisterium and in public discourse. As a contribution to the ongoing debate, I have developed my original seminar paper to look in more detail at the historical, scriptural and theological basis for celibacy, as well as dealing with its ascetical consequences. In *Pastores dabo vobis*, which contains the most recent statement of the Magisterium on priestly celibacy, there is an appeal that this charism be 'presented and explained in the fullness of its biblical, theological and spiritual richness'.[2] This volume is an effort to respond, even if only in an outline way, to this concern.

In doing so, it will become clear that I draw heavily on John Paul II's teaching on celibacy as he has developed it over the twenty years of his pontificate. His clarity, theological penetration, and supernatural optimism when he speaks about this topic should be an inspiration for every priest.

As a result of researching and writing this book three fundamental ideas have crystallised in my mind. In the first place, to study priestly celibacy is, to paraphrase Newman, to be deep in history. And, without an awareness of the historical tradition related to celibacy, it is impossible to appreciate or understand it fully.

Secondly, it is not feasible to penetrate the meaning of this charism, or to justify it, without a deep appreciation of the virtue of chastity. Here, I am referring to a chastity, not in the diminished or anaemic sense in which it is perceived by a sensate culture, but to one which has all the vigour and freshness of a Christian virtue.

Finally, and at first sight paradoxically, only the person who grasps the greatness of the Christian vocation to marriage will be able fully to appreciate the call to priestly celibacy. The interdependence of these three ideas will be a recurring theme of the chapters ahead.

This volume is not meant to be an academic treatise about celibacy. It has a different objective. Its purpose is to draw attention to some basic considerations related to the charism of celibacy which are frequently absent from current discourse about it, and thus enable people come to a more balanced judgement regarding this gift of the Spirit. It is also my hope that a fuller presentation of the supernatural richness of this commitment will help to reinforce in priests their conviction and pride in the gift that is theirs. If it achieves this aim, I will feel that this effort has been well worthwhile.

2 Apostolic Exhortation, 25 March 1992, no. 29.

I would like to express my gratitude to Fr Brendan Purcell for his encouragement to complete this study. In addition he read through the entire text and made many helpful suggestions. My thanks also go to Fr Jimmy Gavigan, Fr Pat Gorevan, Fr Gerry Healy, and Fr Tom O'Toole for reading through the typescript and eliminating a number of obscurities in the text. Fr Gerry Hanratty read three of the chapters and helped me at many points to articulate more clearly what I was trying to say. They don't necessarily agree with everything I have written, so any deficiencies that appear in the final form of this book are ultimately my responsibility.

In memory of my parents

Maura McLoughlin

and

Thomas McGovern

who kept the Faith and passed it on to their children

Introduction

Priestly celibacy has been a topic of active discussion for a number of years. In the past it rarely drew attention to itself because it was accepted as a normal part of the lifestyle of the priest. However, for different reasons it has become a subject of keen media interest, not least because of some recent high profile failures in commitment to this discipline.

Several questions are being asked about celibacy at the present time. It is suggested that it creates a barrier between priest and people, especially married people with whose difficulties, we are told, he can have little empathy. Some contend that celibacy leads to emotional and psychological isolation. Others see it as a repression of natural feelings and inclinations, with a stunting of the normal growth of personality.

It is frequently affirmed that celibacy is a burden for most priests, a cause of loneliness and lack of fulfilment. Indeed one newspaper editorial quoted with approval 'research' which suggested that 'a mere two percent who pledge celibacy achieve it'.[1] In any case, it is asserted, since celibacy is not a precept of divine law but rather a matter of ecclesiastical discipline, it can be changed at any time.

Many consider it the main cause of the significant drop in candidates for the priesthood, and thus a barrier to attracting the right kind of young men into seminaries. For all these reasons it is affirmed that the Church should make celibacy an optional requirement for ordination, because otherwise it will have to face serious manpower difficulties in the future. As a backdrop to this scenario the shadow of John Paul II is seen to be cast over the present impasse because of his strongly traditionalist brand of Catholicism and his refusal to accommodate law to 'reality'.

From another perspective it is affirmed that, with the development of the theology of marriage since Vatican II, it is no longer tenable to consider priesthood as a 'higher' calling, and that there is, therefore, a need to 'demythologise' the traditional concept of ministry to bring it into line with the requirements of modern society.

For some, the Catholic priesthood, as at present constituted, is seen as a privileged position characterised by the exercise of 'power' without re-

---

[1] Cf. *Irish Times*, 21 September 1996.

sponsibility. It is also claimed that, precisely through the insistence of the Church on a celibate priesthood, this 'power' is perpetuated for the domination of the rest of the Christian faithful.

Some of these objections at first sight may seem to have a certain validity and consequently they need to be confronted. But there are others which betray a patent ideological bias. It is clear too that underlying many of the arguments against what is sometimes referred to as 'compulsory' celibacy, there is an understanding of priesthood which differs in varying degrees from the traditional concept of ministry which developed in the first millennium and a half of the Church's life, and as articulated by the Council of Trent and Vatican II. It is also evident that current perceptions of the priesthood have not been uninfluenced by different philosophical and theological attitudes which have surfaced over the past thirty years. Consequently we need to review what has been happening in the Church over this period in order to try to identify the causes of what many would consider to be a crisis in the priesthood today.

This is essential if we are to begin to understand why in one generation the status of the priesthood has been devalued in the minds of people, as reflected in the dramatic fall-off in vocations, and why celibacy, which was previously an object of reverence, is frequently now a cause of misunderstanding, if not of downright hostility. Even five years ago it would have been inconceivable that a serious newspaper would carry the headline, 'Is Celibacy a Perversion?',[2] as was recently the case.

CHURCH TEACHING ON CELIBACY

Let us first of all briefly define what the Church teaches at present about celibacy, as background to our analysis of the influences which have brought about change in the perception of priesthood. Vatican II affirmed the tradition of celibacy in the Western Church.[3] Based on this teaching, Paul VI developed a rich theology of celibacy in his 1967 encyclical, *Sacerdotalis caelibatus*.[4] Although this document didn't receive an enthusiastic reception in some quarters, four years later his teaching was reaffirmed by the 1971 Synod of Bishops:

> Because of the intimate and multiple coherence between the pastoral function and a celibate life, the existing law is upheld: one who

2 *Irish Times*, 25 November 1996.   3 Cf. *Presbyterorum ordinis*, 16.   4 Published on 24 June 1967.

freely wills total availability, the distinctive character of this function, also freely undertakes a celibate life. The candidate should feel this form of living not as having been imposed from outside, but rather as a manifestation of his free self-giving, which is accepted and ratified by the Church through the bishop. In this way the law becomes a protection and a safeguard of the freedom wherewith the priest gives himself to Christ and it becomes 'an easy yoke'.[5]

The same position was adopted in the 1983 revised Code of Canon Law:

Clerics are obliged to observe perfect and perpetual continence for the sake of the Kingdom of heaven, and are therefore bound to celibacy. Celibacy is a special gift of God by which sacred ministers can more easily remain close to Christ with an undivided heart, and can dedicate themselves more freely to the service of God and their neighbour.[6]

In the build-up to the 1990 Synod of Bishops, and subsequently, there was a lot of pressure to introduce optional celibacy. The mind of the Church on priestly celibacy today was stated very clearly in the synodal document on priestly formation, *Pastores dabo vobis*, published on 25 March 1992. As if anticipating the current speculation and unrest, John Paul II affirmed that 'The Synod does not wish to leave any doubts in the mind of anyone regarding the Church's firm will to maintain the law that demands perpetual and freely chosen celibacy for present and future candidates for priestly ordination in the Latin rite.'[7] This, in outline, is the status of celibacy in Church teaching at present.

THEOLOGICAL INFLUENCES ON PRIESTHOOD

Vatican II devoted two of its sixteen documents to the topic of priests; one related to the formation of future priests,[8] the other was the decree on the ministry and life of priests.[9] These are theologically rich and well developed statements of the mind of the Church on the Catholic priesthood, and, with good reason, they gave rise to considerable hopes for a renewal of the spiritual life and the pastoral effectiveness of the clergy.

5 Synodal document, *The Ministerial Priesthood*, Part Two, Section I, no. 4c.   6 Canon 271, §1.   7 John Paul II affirming *Propositio* no. 11 of the 1990 Synod of Bishops in *Pastores dabo vobis*, 29.   8 *Optatam totius*, 28 October 1965.   9 *Presbyterorum ordinis*, 7 December 1965.

However, considering what has happened in the interim, I think it is
true to say that many of these hopes were not realised. On the contrary,
the priesthood has suffered serious setbacks during the past few decades.
This is reflected particularly in two areas. In the years since the Council
priests have abandoned their vocation by tens of thousands.[10] In the past
quarter century there has been a veritable haemorrhage from the ranks of
the priesthood which perhaps has no precedent in the history of the Church
except for the early decades of the Reformation. Indeed the present Holy
Father has referred to this exodus as one of the big set-backs to the great
hopes for renewal aroused by the Council.[11] It was largely a universal
phenomenon, affecting both secular and religious priests, but one which
was most marked in the developed countries of Western Europe and North
America. A second negative aspect is the significant decline in the number
of vocations to the priesthood in the post-Vatican II years, at least in the
more affluent West.

Concurrently with these developments there was a serious questioning
of the very identity of the Catholic priesthood. Was this loss of certainty
and confidence about the essence of the priesthood one of the main reasons why so many abandoned their vocation? Did it undermine the traditional Catholic perception of the priesthood to such an extent that considerably fewer young men were now able, or prepared, to see it as a vocation worthy of a life-long commitment? There is no doubt that the debate
about priestly identity did undermine commitment, with the subsequent
departures from the ranks of the clergy and the increasing reluctance of
young men to see the priesthood as a viable option.

Cardinal Ratzinger analysed this phenomenon in depth in his opening
address to the 1990 Synod of Bishops on the Formation of Priests,[12] and
returned to it again in a paper delivered to mark the thirtieth anniversary
of the proclamation of Vatican II's *Presbyterorum ordinis* in 1995.[13] The
Council, he tells us, set out to produce a decree on the ministry and life of
priests conscious that at that time the traditional idea of the Catholic priesthood, in some quarters of the Church, was losing its validity. In ecumeni-

10 Different sources give different figures. Statistics in the 1995 Vatican Year Book for the
period 1964 to 1992 indicate that departures from the priestly ministry were 54,432 during
that period (cf. statistical summary by the Revd Professor Michael Nolan in the *Sunday
Business Post*, Dublin, 9 July 1995).   11 Cf. Address to Priests in Maynooth, 1 October
1979.   12 Cf. Address 'The Nature of Priesthood', 1 October 1990, published in *Osservatore
Romano*, 29 October 1990.   13 'The Ministry and Life of Priests', lecture at International
Symposium organised by the Vatican Congregation for the Clergy, 24 October 1995, in
Homiletic and Pastoral Review, August-September 1997, pp 7–18.

cal circles the seeds of a crisis were already evident in the concept of the Catholic priesthood, a crisis, he says, that after the Council would flare up with devastating effects on priestly life and vocations.

NEW INTERPRETATIONS OF PRIESTHOOD

Undoubtedly these consequences were to some extent provoked by reasons which had nothing to do with the Church. However, in Ratzinger's opinion, these extra-ecclesial reasons would not have been nearly so influential if the theological foundations for the priestly ministry had not been discredited among many priests and young people. The Prefect of the Congregation for the Doctrine of the Faith affirms that 'in the new cultural situation which has evolved since the Council, the old arguments of the sixteenth-century Reformation, together with more recent findings of modern biblical exegesis – which moreover were nourished by the presuppositions of the Reformation – acquired a certain plausibility, and Catholic theology was unable to respond to them adequately.'[14]

Other factors were also involved. On the one hand there was a change in the perception of the meaning of life, when the sense of the sacred gave way to new criteria of functionality. On the other hand theological ideas borrowed from Protestantism gave rise to a reinterpretation of the New Testament concept of priesthood, despoiling it of its unique sacral dimension, and breaking the continuity between the sacred offices of the Old Covenant and the ministries of the nascent Church.[15]

---

14 Address, 1 October 1990. For a deep analysis of the origins and development of the crisis about priesthood, see 'Priestly Ministry', in *International Theological Commission: Texts and Documents: 1969–1985*, San Francisco, 1989, pp 3–18. **15** What were these arguments which had such an influence on Catholic theology? In the analysis of the scriptural basis of priesthood it is claimed that there is a discontinuity between the ministries of the New Testament and the priesthood of the Mosaic Law. The fact that the early Church used the term 'elder' rather than 'priest', that there is a certain lack of definition about the variety of names used for ministries during the first century of the Church, that these ministries are nowhere linked with the Eucharistic celebration, and that the preaching of the Gospel appears as their primary function – these are the arguments from Reformation theology to the effect that in subsequent centuries the Church changed the role of the priest from its original definition in the New Testament. Thus it is affirmed that the ministries of the early Church were not at that time perceived as linked to sacramental ordination but in terms of function.

Another Reformation argument which has also influenced recent theology of the priesthood is the affirmation that, since at the death of Jesus the veil of the Temple was rent, there was no longer any separation between temple and world, between the sacred and the profane.

The Lutheran model of priestly ministry was making ground at the expense of the identity of the Catholic priesthood as defined by Trent. While initially these opposing views of priesthood were reflected primarily in theological literature, with time the trickle-down process caused the same ambivalence about priestly identity to be reflected not only in the lives of priests themselves but also in the public perception of it.

This change of perception of the essential nature of the priesthood is reflected in different streams of contemporary theology. It questions the idea of the priest as a man apart, as somehow 'different' from the rest of men, and who as a consequence acts independently of the Christian community. There is pressure to demythologise the priest, to have it recognised that lay people can do many of the priest's functions just as well as he does. Obviously if the identity of the priest can be reduced to that of a functionary, it follows that his celibacy is no longer a significant consideration. In addition, the current resurgence of neo-Arian Christology and the advocacy of optional celibacy would seem to go hand in hand.

These different ways of understanding the nature of priesthood were naturally paralleled by a change in the understanding of the priest's role. Traditional Catholicism saw the priestly ministry as oriented to the sacrifice of the Mass, and the administration of the sacraments. The functional perception of priesthood placed more emphasis on the preaching of the Word. Ratzinger says that Vatican II did not tackle these doctrinal problems specifically, problems which were just beginning to emerge. This is not surprising in view of the fact that Vatican II was an explicitly pastoral council. *Presbyterorum ordinis*, taking Trent as a point of departure, did however provide a comprehensive statement of the Church's vision of

---

A hermeneutical key used in recent Catholic writing about priesthood, which also has its roots in Protestant exegesis, is the perceived opposition between Law and Gospel deduced from Pauline theology. Because the Law was abolished by Christ it is opposed to the Gospel. And therefore since priesthood and cult (sacrifice) belong to the category of law they acquired a negative connotation because they lead man to the letter that kills and to works that don't justify. On the other hand, the essence of the Gospel consists in hearing the Word of God, and in faith, which is what alone makes a man just. Thus the understanding of the priest as prophet and teacher is the authentic interpretation of the New Testament. Related to this conception of ministry is a blurring of the essential distinction between the ministerial priesthood and the common priesthood of the laity, which Catholic Tradition has always taught.

Ratzinger says that it is this hermeneutical perspective which has dominated biblical exegesis, and which Catholic theology since the Council has accepted almost without argument, thus giving rise to the crisis already referred to. However, in the meantime the work of theologians is beginning to acquire a more balanced view of these questions, as indeed happened among Protestants after the Reformation (cf. Ratzinger, Address, 1 October 1990).

priesthood for modern times, achieving a profound synthesis of the prophetic, sanctifying, and pastoral aspects of the priestly ministry. The 1971 and 1990 Synods of bishops expanded on this conciliar teaching.

CELIBACY AFTER VATICAN II

As we have seen, Vatican II teaching on celibacy was developed a few years later in Paul VI's encyclical on the same topic. Despite the encyclical, there was considerable pressure from different sources to lift the requirement of obligatory celibacy for ordination to the priesthood. This was paralleled by a massive exodus from the ranks of the clergy. Indeed, many of those who left claimed that the issue of celibacy was the main cause of their departure.

In the wake of the encyclical the celibacy crisis was so exacerbated by the statements and actions of a number of Dutch priests that Paul VI felt compelled to issue a personal statement about it in 1970. Recent public declarations in Holland, the Pope said, had 'profoundly afflicted' him, because of the 'grave attitude of disobedience' to the law of the Latin Church which they implied.[16] Paul VI was concerned not only because of the negative effects these statements would have on the Church in Holland as a whole, but in particular because of the scandal they would cause for young men preparing for the priesthood. These declarations, he said, created a great deal of uncertainty. What he found particularly unconvincing in the arguments of the Dutch priests was the diminution in the authentic concept of the Catholic priesthood which they implied.

In some quarters it had been expected that the 1971 Synod would modify the Church's stance, and in the lead-up to it a campaign for a married clergy had been conducted, as one commentator describes it, 'with an almost prophetic fervour'.[17] A report of the International Theological Commission, published before the Synod, suggesting that celibacy should be optional, had perhaps fuelled these expectations. While maintaining that celibacy is the better way, the Commission affirmed: 'The hierarchy responsible for a proclamation of the gospel that is permanent, efficacious, and universal, as a word of truth and a sacramental instrument of grace, may choose for the exercise of the apostolic ministry both persons who

---

16 Paul VI, Letter, 2 February 1970, to Cardinal Villot, Secretary of State, published in *The Tablet*, 14 February 1970.   **17** Jean Galot, SJ, *Theology of Priesthood*, San Francisco, 1985, p. 243.

have been called to, and already live, the charism of virginity, and those who, after an experience of many years in marriage, have achieved human and professional maturity, domestic balance and above all apostolic worth in the sense indicated in the pastoral epistles.'[18]

The Synod refused to be pressurised and affirmed categorically that 'the law of priestly celibacy existing in the Latin Church is to be kept in its entirety'.[19] But the pressures to make celibacy an optional requirement for the priesthood have continued unabated.

CHANGING MORAL PERSPECTIVES

Up to the early seventies in Ireland vocations were still flowing into the seminaries. They reached a peak in the sixties but then started to decrease gradually. In the last five years there has been a rapid decline, and 1996 saw the lowest intake this century.

One has to ask: What is it that has brought about such a significant change? Why are vocations now reduced to a trickle by comparison with the steady stream of a generation ago? Why is it that the priesthood no longer seems to be regarded as an attractive, challenging life-style? Is it the so-called 'compulsory' celibacy which puts off young men aspiring to the priesthood, or are there deeper, structural reasons at work?

The last thirty years since Vatican II have been times of great change in the Church. This has given rise not only to a different perception of the faith but also to a diminished commitment to it, resulting in a dramatic fall-off in practice, especially in urban areas.

The findings of surveys of young people's attitudes to religion indicate a rejection of core elements of the faith. Significant aspects of Christian moral teaching have failed to be presented effectively to increasing numbers of the younger generations. This credibility gap, if one might so define it, relates particularly to sexual *mores*.[20] The reality of this change in

18 *Le Ministère sacerdotal* (Paris, 1971), p. 106, quoted by Galot, ibid., p. 249. Galot's assessment of the document is that, because the Commission took the position that celibacy was attached to the priesthood by ecclesiastical tradition, it failed to give adequate recognition to the commitment Jesus required of the Twelve, a commitment which included the renunciation of marriage (cf. ibid.).   **19** *The Ministerial Priesthood*, Part Two, I, 4c, p. 27.   **20** Cf. *Religious Belief, Practice and Moral Attitudes: A Comparison of two Surveys 1974–1984*, Council for Research and Development, Maynooth College, Report no. 21, with particular reference to the 18–30 age group, under headings of attitudes to: Use of Contraceptives, Pre-marital Sex, Abortion, and Divorce; Thomas F. Inglis, 'Di-

attitude is substantiated by the rapid growth in the levels of illegitimacy and abortion over the past twenty-five years.[21]

Because of the way chastity is trivialised in the media it is no longer highly regarded as a virtue. Thus for many people the idea of living the traditional demands of purity in thought and action is considered as scrupulosity or fastidiousness. Consequently promiscuity, or what is frequently referred to as recreational sex, is increasingly becoming 'normal' behaviour among teenagers.[22] Among married people changes in moral outlook are also reflected by the fact that a high proportion of couples are now using some form of artificial contraception.[23] In a society where such attitudes are becoming more pervasive it is inevitable that difficulties arise for understanding the very idea of celibacy, not to mention a personal commitment to it.

INTELLECTUAL AND CULTURAL INFLUENCES

We might ask what were the causes of this change of attitude to the faith, to priesthood and to chastity? What were the non-theological reasons which affected the perception of priesthood in the past thirty years? Like most other countries of the West, a number of different influences have impacted on the Irish social and cultural environment. These influences have operated in different ways but perhaps especially through the mass media, educational philosophy and legislation. Many of them have been positive, producing a greater openness to ideas, a deeper appreciation of

mensions of Irish Students' Religiosity', *Economic and Social Review*, 11, no. 4, July 1980, pp 237–56; Christopher W. Whelan, ed., *Values and Social Change in Ireland*, Dublin 1994; Julian MacAirt, 'Religion Among Irish University Students', in *Doctrine and Life*, 40, April 1990, pp 172–83. **21** Illegitimate births in the Republic rose from 1709 in 1970 to 12,484 in 1996, representing an increase from 2.6% to 24.8% of total live births. Abortions increased from 261 in 1970 to 4894 in 1996. Sources: annual reports of Central Statistics Office, Dublin, and Office for Population Census and Surveys, London. **22** Cf. Western Health Board study by E. MacHale, and J. M. Newell, *Sexual Behaviour and Sex Education in Irish School-going Teenagers* (forthcoming). See also Midland Health Board survey of secondary schools, reported in *Irish Independent*, 23 September 1997. **23** Cf. survey by the Economic and Social Research Institute, *Women and Health Care in Ireland*, Dublin, 1996; North Eastern Health Board Survey of Contraceptive Usage (*Irish Medical Times*, 31 May 1996); UCD Department of Sociology Survey of Family Planning (*Irish Independent*, 9 November 1995). However, perhaps the most revealing statistic in this context is the remarkable drop in the fertility rate – from 3.97 in the 1960s to 1.87 in 1995. In 1993 for the first time births dropped significantly below the replacement level of 2.1 (source: *Statistical Abstract* 1995).

other cultures, and more awareness of the needs of third world countries and of Ireland's contribution as a member of the international community.

Other influences of a less positive nature have also been at work. While one can attempt to identify them individually, because of the social dynamics of a culture, many will be seen to be not only interrelated, but also at times interacting with each other. Modern society and culture are multidimensional, and while common trends do emerge, different areas have shifting nuances of their own.

Still, I think it will be a useful exercise to try to distinguish some of the trends which underlie existing cultural attitudes. It will at least provide a perspective against which to evaluate the current outlook on priesthood and the vocation to celibacy, and, hopefully, it will help priests themselves understand why things have changed so much in the last thirty years or so.

FREEDOM AND TRUTH

The quest for personal freedom is one of the more defining characteristics of contemporary culture. It is generally regarded as a superior good to which other competing values should be subordinate, especially those which would seem to restrict freedom. Hence anything which is considered a taboo, or a relic of archaic prohibitions or fears, is seen as a fetter on human freedom and self-expression. Consequently the concept of a personal, permanent commitment to anything is increasingly regarded as an imposition, if not impossible of attainment.

The general cultural environment encourages people to feel free to determine their own moral code and not to accommodate themselves to any system which they consider imposed from outside.[24] This concept of freedom, the absence of any permanent or stable commitments, sees no obligation to maintain any bonding with the past, and thus precludes the possibility of providing any personal inheritance for those who come afterwards.

However, the increased affirmation of freedom does not seem to lead to a greater degree of happiness and self-fulfilment. Indeed there is much evidence to suggest that the opposite is the case when we consider the

24 Cf. John M. Haas, 'Crisis of Conscience and Culture', in *Crisis of Conscience*, New York, 1996, pp 21–49. This is a comprehensive analysis of the philosophical influences which underlie present trends towards subjectivism and moral relativism, and the increasing inability of consciences to distinguish between good and evil (cf. *Evangelium vitae*, 4). Haas illustrates the influence of Kant in particular on current moral attitudes.

rapid increase in crime, vandalism, drug addiction, family breakdown and sexual exploitation. This is because such a vision of freedom is selective and one-sided, and frequently at the expense of truth.

Psychoanalysts and behaviourists have divorced guilt from personal responsibility, the correlative of freedom, and declared that sin is the result of various forms of conditioning – hereditary, social, cultural etc. There is a radical loss of the sense of sin.[25] Man thus becomes less and less aware that he is in need of redemption, but his sense of alienation does not go away. On the contrary, it becomes more oppressive. And so, paradoxically, while sacramental confession has almost disappeared as a sacred ritual from the lives of many, psychiatry and other forms of secular counselling have become a growth industry.

RELATIVISM

The eighteenth-century Enlightenment had promised to get rid of what it saw as myth and taboo (especially the Faith), and to replace it with a humanistic ethic and a rational social equilibrium. It aimed at a contractual code of ethics based on consensus rather than conviction, expressly rejecting the notion of absolute truths, particularly in the area of morality. Ethical choices, according to this system, were personal ones rather than rational ones, and religious belief was regarded as a type of personal experience which should not overflow the bounds of personal conscience.

Thus it said that education should be value-free, untrammelled by religious influence. What such an attitude failed to recognise is that there is no such thing as a value-free educational policy; it is an illusion to think otherwise. The vacuum will always be filled by the ideology of the educational philosophers who determine the syllabus in the absence of a particular school ethos. An educational philosophy which emphasises values clarification and training for 'safe sex' sows the seeds for a subjectivist morality independent of objective moral criteria. The bitter fruits of this exercise have been reaped with disturbing consequences in the educational systems of other jurisdictions.

In Ireland, somewhat belatedly, we have embarked on our own Enlightenment project over the past three decades without, it would seem, learning very much from the negative experiences of other countries. We

25 Cf. John Paul II, Apostolic Exhortation *Reconciliatio et paenitentia*, 2 December 1984, no. 18.

have reproduced the consequences of this philosophy with a rapidity which has surprised our European neighbours. The level of crime, drug-taking, suicide, sexual assault, and family disintegration has escalated at a rate that now seems to be out of control. Many projects in social engineering have been tried to solve these problems, but with little apparent success. What is striking is the failure of public authority to invoke the idea of personal moral responsibility as the fundamental antidote to the breakdown of traditional values. It is perhaps part of the current malaise that there is a reluctance to talk about morals or the teaching of morals in public discourse.[26]

In public life there seems to be a fear of asserting the truth, of pointing out that a particular position – legal, political, or moral – is in opposition to it. This is perhaps indicative of how deeply moral relativism pervades contemporary culture, and of how much our own attitudes are influenced by it. If all truths are relative – the basic assumption of a pluralist philosophy – then nobody is prepared to articulate the idea of absolute ethical values, either out of lack of conviction or for fear of being ridiculed by the media.[27]

It is not surprising that in such a cultural context celibacy as a life-style would seem marginal and esoteric, not to mention the idea of considering such an option for oneself.

SCIENTISM AND UTILITARIANISM

In a world where the natural sciences provide the dominant paradigm of knowledge, and where sentiment and feelings have replaced philosophy and revelation as the key to reality, there is deep scepticism about establishing an adequate foundation for a coherent moral system.[28] From this perspective there is a restriction of the range of reason to facts verifiable by

---

26 Cf. Alasdair MacIntyre, *After Virtue: A Study in Moral Theory*, London, 1981, especially Chapter 5, 'Why the Enlightenment Project of Justifying Morality had to Fail', pp 49–59, and Chapter 6, 'Some Consequences of the Failure of the Enlightenment Project', pp 60–75.   27 In *Veritatis splendor* (6 August 1993), John Paul II speaks of '*the risk of an alliance between democracy and ethical relativism*, which would remove any sure moral reference point from political and social life, and on a deeper level make the acknowledgement of truth impossible' (no. 101; italics in original).   28 Recovery of this situation is, however, well under way through the work of Finnis and MacIntyre in the field of ethics, and that of García de Haro, Grisez, May and Pinckaers in moral theology. In addition, the encyclical *Veritatis splendor* of John Paul II has articulated a synthesis of the foundational principles of Catholic moral teaching in a way no previous Pope has attempted.

the methods of the natural sciences, and thus real knowledge is reduced to truths of the facts of such sciences.

Truth has also tended to become more subjective. It is what 'I' feel about things that makes them valid, rather than the correspondence of the mind with objective reality. Given these presuppositions it is not difficult to see how the utilitarian ethic takes precedence. In such a system, pleasure is equated with goodness and happiness, pain with evil, leading to a hedonistic morality. If goodness is the satisfaction of desires, then we don't have to look any further to justify sexual permissiveness.[29]

Utilitarianism is a philosophy of self-interest and thus contradicts the specifically Christian teaching that man's true good consists not in self-interest but in *self-giving* and service to others. Consequentialism and proportionalism are present-day forms of utilitarianism. They do not allow one to say that any actions are intrinsically bad, but only better or worse than others. This is an attitude which clashes head on with the idea of Christian happiness achieved by the total gift of self, especially in marriage or the betrothed love of celibacy.[30]

INDIVIDUALISM AND DEMOCRATISATION

The term 'individualism' encapsulates much of what is happening in contemporary culture. It is characteristic of some of the attitudes outlined above, but it is also evident in the creation of an apparent conflict between the individual and different forms of authority. One of the consequences of individualism is the loss of the notion of the common good, and of commitment to human solidarity.[31]

This attitude has had profoundly negative effects on the structure of the family. The bonding and coherence of the family has become diluted, showing signs of fragility as an institution as the traditional social and spiritual supports are undermined. The family, John Paul II tells us, is threatened today 'not only by external factors, such as social mobility and the new characteristics of work organisation, but first and foremost by an individualistic culture without solid ethical moorings, which misrepresents the very meaning of conjugal love and, challenging the connatural need for stability, undermines the family unit's capacity for lasting communion and peace'.[32] Since the family is the basic unit of stability in the

---

29 Germain Grisez, *The Way of the Lord Jesus I: Christian Moral Principles*, Chicago, 1983, p. 86. 30 Cf. ibid., pp 141–164. 31 Cf. ibid., pp 206–207. 32 Address, 8 November 1995.

social structure, and the context in which moral values, as well as traditional and cultural norms, are primarily transmitted to successive generations, any disintegration in this area is bound to have a negative effect on
the living of the faith and its transmission. This has, of course, knock-on
effects for vocations to the priesthood, since the Christian family is the
irreplaceable *locus* for the nurturing of such vocations.

Because the media judge and present the Church primarily in terms of
political categories, it is not surprising that many people would tend to
view Church authority from this perspective. A logical development of
this attitude is that the validity of particular teachings should somehow be
determined by democratic sanction. One can detect echoes of this perspective in areas such as contraception, divorce, and, more recently, in
relation to celibacy.

However, the Church is not a club where rules can be changed in
accordance with the preference of members. The Pope is not a manager
who should respond to the doctrinal or moral preferences of the faithful.
He is the keeper of the Scriptures and of a Tradition which are not his, but
which are guaranteed to bring man to redemption and salvation as no
other human wisdom is capable of doing. The Vicar of Christ is not a
facilitator or the president of a club, but the Successor of Peter to whom
has been guaranteed the special light and assistance of the Holy Spirit to
lead us into all truth (cf. Jn 14:26; 16:13).

Individualism and democratisation have, nevertheless, produced a trend
in the opposite direction – people searching more seriously for mystery
and a sense of the sacred. This is because the spirit of man needs to feed on
something more substantial than sentiment and ideology. There is an increasing flow of intellectual converts to Catholicism in USA, England,
and other countries, impelled by the search for an authoritative teaching
voice which will answer to the deepest needs of the human soul, a voice
which people are increasingly recognising to be that of John Paul II.

PRIVATISING MORALITY

Pluralism, as understood politically today, is the presumption to legislate
for freedom in different areas, but for a freedom emancipated from its
foundations in morality and truth. It is an approach which supposes there
is no grounding for absolute values outside oneself, that values are subjective and therefore private, and that all that can be achieved is to legislate
on the basis of a democratic consensus which is always changeable. Indeed

the logic of this presumption is that values should remain private to pre-serve democracy.

Those eloquent words in St John's Gospel, 'and you will know the truth, and the truth will make you free' (Jn 8:32) have, in the legal positiv-ism of our times, been largely reversed. The Gospel instructs us that free-dom results from our relationship with something outside of ourselves. Adapting our life-style, our ambitions, to objective truth is what gives us freedom. Yet the thrust of current social and political doctrine tries to reverse the relationship between freedom and truth, reducing it to a slo-gan without content.

Legislative proposals in favour of contraception, divorce, homosexual-ity, and abortion are purveyed as exercises in pluralism, and consequently as an advancement of freedom. Nowhere, however, are there to be found any clear definitions of what the legislators mean by freedom or pluralism. This process has also the effect of convincing people that what is legal is morally acceptable.

Yet authentic pluralism does not imply hiding our most profound dif-ferences. On the contrary it means accepting them within the bond of civility. Pluralism is not indifference with regard to the truth; it is a genu-ine respect for others and their convictions.[33]

RECOVERY

It is clear then that there are influences at work in our society which are often in direct competition with the precepts of the Gospel message and frequently hostile to them. This is the environment in which priests have to live, and in which they have to try to make their celibacy intelligible both to themselves and to others.

However, they should not be discouraged by the social and cultural pressures which create difficulties for the proclamation of Christ. The truth of the Master's teaching is always attractive and challenging, and is

33 John Paul II has argued, especially in his encyclical *Centesimus annus* (1 May 1991), that it is not agnosticism which guarantees a free and just society, but a religiously grounded respect for the person: 'Nowadays there is a tendency to claim that agnosticism and scep-tical relativism are the philosophy and the basic attitude which correspond to democratic forms of political life ... It must be observed in this regard that if there is no ultimate truth to guide and direct political activity, then ideas and convictions can easily be manipulated for reasons of power. As history demonstrates, a democracy without values easily turns into open or thinly disguised totalitarianism' (no. 46). See also Richard John Neuhaus, *The Naked Public Square: Religion and Democracy in America*, Grand Rapids, Mich. 1984.

ultimately the only vision of reality which will satisfy the deepest yearnings of the human heart. If the priest is motivated by a deep faith in the power of grace, and if he has the courage to present the full implications of the gospel for personal, family, and social life, he has no reason to doubt that the culture can be re-evangelised and recover its Christian roots again.

Because of the shadow which has been cast on the charism of celibacy in recent years due to clerical scandals, and the efforts to undermine it in sections of the media, there is a need for priests to recover personal conviction about the value of this gift and its perennial validity. The purpose of this book is to try to make a contribution to this process of recovery.

To do this we need to consider celibacy in its historical background. The constant commitment of the Church to remain faithful to a way of life, which was invariably a sign of contradiction, tells us much about the nature and the value of this charism. At all times it had to contend with human weakness and worldly opposition but, out of the conviction that it was being faithful to a norm of apostolic origin, the Church drew on the necessary supernatural resources and fortitude to renew the discipline of celibacy many times down through the centuries. The first chapter of our study examines the main elements in the ebb and flow of that history .

This background on the place of celibacy in tradition is followed by chapters on the scriptural foundations and the theology of this charism. As we have already noted, John Paul II, in *Pastores dabo vobis*, expressed a desire to see celibacy presented and explained more fully from a biblical, theological and spiritual perspective.[34] He is conscious that often it is badly explained, and has gone so far as to say that the widespread view that celibacy is imposed by law 'is the result of a misunderstanding, if not of downright bad faith'.[35]

While one can adduce practical arguments for celibacy, since it is an essentially supernatural charism, the theological, scriptural and spiritual reasons for it, as the Holy Father suggests, are the only adequate basis for its justification. In recent discussion little attention has been paid to these aspects of celibacy. One of the objectives of this book is to try to restate these arguments and to suggest why they have a profound importance for any real understanding of this discipline.

Nobody has done more than the present Holy Father to articulate the scriptural and theological foundations for celibacy. This he has developed in his weekly catechesis in Rome, in magisterial documents, and in his countless addresses to priests in every part of the world over the past twenty

34 Cf. no. 29.   **35** Cf. Holy Thursday Letter to Priests, 1979, no. 9.

years. A particular characteristic of John Paul's teaching on celibacy is that he invariably considers it in relation to the vocation to marriage. For him they are correlative states in life, one illustrative of the commitment involved in the other, both reflective of the one vocation to holiness. He comes to this conclusion as a result of a deep and prolonged study of the data which Revelation offers to enable us construct a valid anthropology. In his weekly catechesis on 'the nuptial meaning of the body', between 1979 and 1984, John Paul II developed a rich Christian anthropology based on Scripture and the reality of the Incarnation. As he graphically points out, consequent to the fact that the Word of God became flesh, 'the body entered theology through the main door'.[36] Thus to formulate an adequate theology of celibacy, as well as that of marriage, it is necessary to consider the fundamental anthropological implications of these commitments. This I hope to do in Chapter 4.

The Church, through the Pope's Apostolic Letter, *Pastores dabo vobis*, devoted its best efforts to charting a course for the effective formation of seminarians and priests. Education in celibacy is an important element in this programme, especially at present when the very *raison d'être* of celibacy is being contested, not just in the secular media, but even among some sections of the clergy themselves. However, formation in celibacy also implies, and requires, a profound awareness of the theology of conjugal love in marriage as a vocation to holiness. Indeed John Paul II makes the striking claim that a mature decision for celibacy can only derive from a full awareness of the potential for self-giving which marriage offers.[37] The seminarian needs this deeper formation also if he is to make the Church's teaching on human sexuality credible in a culture which is increasingly influenced by a utilitarian and materialistic ethic. Chapter 5 will review some of the more important elements involved in this formation.

Celibacy is a gift of the Holy Spirit, and thus an essentially supernatural charism. However, we bear this treasure in vessels of clay and, as we are forcefully reminded by St Paul, there is a constant battle between the desires of the flesh and the aspirations of the Spirit. To protect and nurture this gift requires a constant effort, an asceticism which is sustained by a daily incorporation into the paschal mystery of the death and resurrection of Christ. The pastoral experience of the Church over the centuries has given rise to a rich store of Christian wisdom about how to cultivate priestly celibacy as a means for deeper identification with Christ the Eternal High Priest, and how to offset the obstacles that can arise in this quest.

36 Address, 2 April 1980, no. 4. 37 Cf. Address, 5 May 1982, no. 2.

In Chapter 6 we review how the challenge of celibacy can be approached in a positive sense, and see how it is a means to personal holiness and effective pastoral activity.

As we have already seen, contemporary culture suggests a number of objections against the discipline of celibacy. In Chapter 7 I have tried to deal with the more common ones. At a time when celibacy has many critics, and is generally treated in a hostile way by the media, one could be forgiven for thinking that there is a lack of cogent testimony to the relevance and authenticity of this charism. That, however, is not the case. Support for celibacy comes from many different sources, and thus at the present time it is encouraging to read the testimonies of people who can affirm priests in the value of their commitment. The final chapter of the book gives a few examples of such testimonies.

RENEWAL

It is not surprising, given the way they have been bashed by the media in the past few years, that priests might feel insecure and uncertain about their identity and self-image. In addition, the prestige of the priesthood would seem to have lost some of its status in the eyes of people. As a consequence priests could be influenced to be more tentative in their pastoral outreach and more defensive in their preaching of the Gospel. They could be tempted to a lack of conviction about the validity of their vocation.

In the present circumstances priests need to rediscover their sense of the dignity and greatness of their calling. They will do this, not so much by considering it from a human point of view, as by reflecting more deeply on the mystery of Jesus Christ and their insertion into that mystery. This is essential for the priest at any time, but it is a particularly appropriate enterprise in these years of preparation for the Jubilee 2000.[38]

Through the sacrament of Order the priest is appropriated by Christ as his own. As a consequence he can do what he could never do on his own initiative – make present the sacrifice of Christ, confect the Eucharist, absolve from sin, impart the Holy Spirit. These are divine prerogatives which no man can acquire by his own effort or by delegation from any community.[39]

---

38 Cf. Apostolic Letter, *Tertio millennio adveniente*, 40, 10 November 1994.   **39** Cf. Ratzinger, 'The Ministry and Life of Priests', op. cit., p. 12.

At a time when there is much talk about freedom, the priest is the only man who can absolve people from the weight of their sins, and thus confer on them the greatest of all freedoms. Chesterton admitted that the ultimate reason he converted to Catholicism was because the Catholic Church was the only church that guaranteed him it would forgive him his sins. And it was in this that he saw the fundamental dignity of the Catholic priesthood.[40] Perhaps priests need to rediscover this truth for themselves.

The priesthood is a demanding commitment but, if it is exercised in true fidelity to the priesthood of Christ, it is the most fulfilling of all professions or human advocations. It offers a deep intellectual and theological formation. It encourages priests to be familiar with the great inheritance of Christian culture and wisdom, and all that the human sciences can offer to win the heart of man for Christ.[41] The priesthood is Christ's greatest gift to humanity, but it is offered to relatively few. Only to them has Christ said: 'As the Father has sent me, even so I send you' (Jn 20:21).[42] They have every reason to be immensely proud of their calling.[43]

Much has been written as part of the current debate about celibacy. One item struck me particularly, not least because it was penned by a convert who is the wife of a convert –a former Anglican minister. 'Priestly celibacy,' she affirms, 'is a jewel in the Catholic Church, which has only been questioned since we became obsessed with sexual fulfilment, rather than the other fulfilment that the priesthood offers. We need look no further than Pope John Paul to see a fully rounded person whose intellectual gifts and physical accomplishments are combined with deep compassion and sympathy which celibacy has enabled him to use for the benefit of the whole human race.'[44] The following pages are an effort to suggest why she is right, why celibacy is a unique gift that enables priests to live a life of total personal fulfilment in the service of the Master.

---

40 *Autobiography*, London, 1937, pp 329–30. **41** Cf. *Directory on the Ministry and Life of Priests*, 69–79, published by the Congregation for the Clergy, 31 January 1994. **42** While it is true that every Christian is called to the apostolate as a consequence of Baptism, only the priest can act fully *in persona Christi* in the work of evangelization. **43** 'When we grasp the greatness and the sacredness of the office of the priest, we understand that the sacrifice which the priest makes in accepting celibacy is small in comparison with the gift which he receives in being able to be a priest of the holy Church' : Dietrich von Hildebrand, *Celibacy and the Crisis of Faith*, Chicago, 1971, p. 35. **44** Pamela Nightingale, *Daily Telegraph*, 18 September 1996.

Celibacy – A Historical Perspective

In the current debate on celibacy, there is a considerable range of opinions about the origin and development of this charism in the Church. Some affirm that it became obligatory from the fourth century while, for others, the Second Lateran Council (1139) is the basic reference point. There is also disagreement as to its source, ranging from those who consider it to be of divine or apostolic origin, to the affirmation that it is merely a later expression of ecclesiastical discipline.

It is well known that the practice of the Latin Church, which requires of its priests an irrevocable commitment to celibacy, differs from the discipline of the Eastern Church. There is a commonly held belief that in the Eastern Churches (apart from special cases) no law of celibacy exists. There is also a perception that the Eastern tradition is the more ancient, and that the Latin discipline was imposed at a comparatively late date. In discussion about revising the tradition of celibacy in the West the discipline of the Eastern Churches is frequently offered as a point of reference.

Why is there a divergence in discipline between East and West, and how did this come about? How explain that the East insists rigidly on celibacy for bishops, but encourages a married clergy? Why in the East is it normal that there are married priests, but at the same time it was never permitted to a man to marry after he had been ordained?

That such a variety of opinion, and indeed contradictory affirmations, are the consequence of an inaccurate knowledge of the historical facts is confirmed by important publications in recent years on the history of ecclesiastical celibacy both in the Eastern and Western Church. In particular the detailed studies of Cochini, Cholij and Stickler open up new ground on the history and the theology of this charism and make a strong case for the apostolic origin of this discipline.[1]

---

1 Christian Cochini, *Apostolic Origins of Priestly Celibacy*, San Francisco, 1990; Roman Cholij, *Clerical Celibacy in East and West*, Leominister, 1988; Alfons M. Stickler, *The Case for Clerical Celibacy: Its Historical Development and Theological Foundations*, San Francisco, 1995. See also George W. Rutler, 'A Consistent Theology of Clerical Celibacy' in *Homiletic and Pastoral Review*, February 1989, pp 9–15, and the bibliography given there; Stanley L. Jaki, *Theology of Priestly Celibacy*, Front Royal, Va. 1997; J. Coppens, ed., *Priesthood and Celibacy*, Milan, 1972.

To understand the history of celibacy from today's perspective it is necessary to realise that in the West, during the first millennium of the Church, a large number of bishops and priests were married men, something which today is quite exceptional. However, a precondition for married men to receive orders as deacons, priests, or bishops was that after ordination they were required to live perpetual continence or the *lex continentiae*. They had, with the prior agreement of their spouses, to be prepared to forego conjugal life in the future.

Nevertheless, alongside the married clerics, there were always present in the Church, in varying proportions, many clerics who never married, or who lived in celibacy as we know it today. As time went on, the appropriateness of a celibate priesthood in the Western Church became clearer and the proportion of married men called to the priesthood decreased. With the institution of seminaries by the Council of Trent, the Church had sufficient candidates for a celibate clergy to meet all the needs of the dioceses. Accordingly, instances of married men being admitted to orders, through a dispensation of the Holy See, became less and less frequent.

In the early Church, as already indicated, ordination of married men was the norm. Sacred Scripture confirms this; St Paul prescribes to his disciples Titus and Timothy that candidates for ordination should only have been married once (cf. 1 Tim 3:2.12; Tit 1:6). We know that Peter was married and perhaps others of the Apostles. This seems to be implied in Peter's question to Christ 'We have left our homes and followed you'. And Jesus replied, 'Truly, I say to you, there is no man who has left house or wife or brothers or parents or children, for the sake of the kingdom of God, who will not receive manifold more in this time, and in the age to come eternal life' (Lk 18:28–30; cf. Mt 19:27–30).

Here we see the first obligation of clerical celibacy, that is continence in relation to the use of marriage after ordination. This was the original meaning of celibacy – the *lex continentiae* or absolute continence in relation to the generation of children. This is how it is defined in all the first written laws about celibacy, dating from the fourth and fifth centuries. Candidates for ordination could not commit themselves to live continence without the prior, express agreement of their spouses, since as a consequence of the sacramental bond they had an inalienable right to conjugal relations.

For several reasons, practical as well as ascetical, a preference developed in the Church for the ordination of celibate, unmarried men, a preference which subsequently became the normal requirement for all candidates for the priesthood in the Western Church. Hence, as has been pointed out, in the first millennium of the Church, celibacy meant either of two things: that ordained ministers did not marry, or, if those chosen to be ordained were already married, after ordination they had to commit themselves to a life of perpetual continence. The failure to distinguish between the *lex continentiae* and celibacy as we understand it today has given rise to a number of misunderstandings and misinterpretations about the history of this charism.

Up to recently, the general historical perception held that it was not until the fourth century that the Church articulated a law of celibacy. This view was established by Franz X. Funk, the well-known ecclesiastical historian, in the last century.[2] However, Funk's judgement was erroneous because of basing it on a document that has since been proved to be spurious.[3] In addition Funk was incorrect in one of his basic assumptions. If discourse on the question of celibacy is to advance scientifically from a theological and juridical point of view, there is a second fundamental presupposition which needs to be clearly understood. Historians of law have pointed out that it is a basic methodological error to identify the concepts of *ius* and *lex*, which is what Funk did.[4]

All obligatory juridical norms, both those handed down *orally* and transmitted through *custom*, as well as those expressed in writing, constitute the content of the idea of *ius*. On the other hand, law understood as *lex* is a narrower concept, since it refers only to dispositions which have been *written* down and legitimately *promulgated*. History confirms that all juridical ordinances began as oral traditions which were only slowly fixed in writing, as was the case, for example, with Roman and Germanic law.[5]

---

2 During the years 1878–80 a much publicised debate took place about the origins of clerical celibacy between two German scholars – Gustav Bickell, a convert, and author of important works on the sources of canon law, and Franz Xaver Funk, professor of history and theology at Tübingen university. Bickell, an expert in Oriental languages, defended the thesis that in the West the obligation of continence did not start with Pope Siricius in the fourth century, but went back to the apostles, appealing in particular to evidence from the East. In conjunction with this position, he affirmed that the same obligation existed in the East at the time of the apostles, but was progressively neglected from the fourth century. Funk rejected the idea of celibacy rooted in a law coming from the apostles, saying that it was only in the fourth century that a valid law of celibacy was established. After a few scholarly exchanges, Bickell, still convinced that he was right, for the sake of peace and convinced that Funk was intransigent, left him with the last word. Funk continued to publish his views which became the received wisdom among most leading scholars. See Stickler, op. cit., pp 15–16.   **3** This refers to one Paphnutius, a monk-bishop from Egypt, who supposedly intervened at the Council of Nicea (325) to reject any plan to impose the discipline of absolute continence on married clerics. Cf. Cholij, ibid., pp. 85–92, and Cochini, ibid., pp 195–200, for a discussion on this point.   **4** Cf. Stickler, ibid., pp 16–

The juridical constitution of the nascent Church consisted largely of provisions and obligations which were transmitted orally; all the more so since, during the first three centuries of persecution, it would have been difficult to have put any laws in writing. Certainly some elements of the primitive law of the Church were written down, yet St Paul also encouraged the Thessalonians to keep to the traditions which had been passed on orally (cf. 2 Thess 2:15). Funk made the basic error of dating the origin of celibacy from the first known *written* law about it, that is from the Council of Elvira. This is our starting point for a review of the significant developments in the Latin rite legislation up to the seventh century.

CELIBACY IN THE LATIN CHURCH

The Council of Elvira (Spain) is of particular significance for the legislative history of celibacy. Held at the beginning of the fourth century (*c.*305), the purpose of its eighty–one canons was to renew the life of the Church in the western part of the Roman empire, to reaffirm ancient disciplines and to sanction new norms. Canon 33 contained the first known written law about celibacy, applicable to bishops, priests, and deacons, (that is 'for all clerics dedicated to the service of the altar'), which proclaimed that they ought to keep complete continence in relation to their wives, and that anyone who had broken this rule should be excluded from the clerical state.[6] Canon 27 of the same Council prohibited women living with ecclesiastics, except for a sister or a daughter who was a consecrated virgin.

From these primitive and important legal texts, it can be deduced that most of the ecclesiastics in the Spanish church were *viri probati*, that is, men who were married before becoming ordained deacons, priests or bishops. All, however, were obliged, after receiving Holy Orders, to renounce completely the use of marriage, that is to live in total continence. Consequently Stickler can say that, in the light of the aims of the Council of Elvira, and of the history of law in the Roman empire, in no way can one see in canon 33 a statement of a new law. It was, on the contrary, a

19.   5 For several centuries the laws of these peoples derived from oral tradition only, but nobody would suggest that as a consequence these laws were not obligatory, or that their observance was left to the free choice of the individual.   6 'It has seemed good absolutely to forbid the bishops, the priests, and the deacons, i.e. all the clerics in the service of the ministry to have [sexual] relations with their wives and procreate children; should anyone do so let him be excluded from the honour of the clergy' (cf. Cochini, ibid., p. 159).

reaction to the extended lack of observance of a traditional and well-known obligation, to which at this time the Council added a sanction: either the delinquent ecclesiastics accepted the obligation of the *lex continentiae*, or gave up the clerical state. The fact that the legislation of Elvira was pacifically accepted confirms that no juridical novelty was being introduced, but that it was concerned primarily with *maintaining* an already existing normative discipline. This is what Pius XI meant when, in his encyclical on the priesthood, he affirms that this written law implied previous praxis.[7] To suggest, therefore, that Elvira is the origin of the law of celibacy in the Church, and that there is, consequently, a discontinuity in discipline between its introduction and what was the praxis beforehand, is, for the reasons already given, a fundamentally erroneous conclusion.[8]

COUNCIL OF CARTHAGE

At the end of the fourth century, legislation of the Synod of Rome (386) and the Second Council of Carthage (390) confirmed the *lex continentiae* as a discipline practised universally from the beginning of the Church, and related it explicitly to the teaching of the Apostles.[9] Canon 3 of Carthage stipulated that married clerics had to observe continence with their wives on the basis of a tradition originating with the Apostles:

> It is fitting that the holy bishops and priests of God as well as the Levites, i.e. those who are in the service of the divine sacraments, observe perfect continence, so that they may obtain in all simplicity what they are asking from God; what the Apostles taught and what antiquity itself observed, let us also endeavour to keep ... It pleases us all that bishop, priest and deacon, guardians of purity, abstain from conjugal intercourse with their wives, so that those who serve at the altar may keep a perfect chastity.[10]

7 'The earliest trace of a law of ecclesiastical celibacy – based, however, on long established custom – is found in the 33rd canon of the Council of Elvira, held at the beginning of the fourth century when Christians were still being actively persecuted. This law only made obligatory what the gospels and the apostolic preaching had already shown to be something like a natural requirement' (Encyclical, *Ad catholici sacerdotii*, *AAS* 28 [1936] 25).   8 Similar canons promulgated at the Council of Arles (314) confirm this; see Cochini, ibid., pp 161–9.   9 Cf. Stickler, ibid, pp 23–33. See also the discussion of *Codex canonum Ecclesiae Africanae*, canon 3, in Cholij, ibid., pp 118–24.   10 Cochini, ibid., p.5.

This canon became known, through different collections, to all the dioceses of the Roman Church, and in the East the Quinisext Council of Trullo (691) would refer to it explicitly as a sure link with Tradition. The law that was promulgated in 390 was officially inserted in the definitive legislative record of the African Church, the *Codex canonum Ecclesiae Africanae*, completed and promulgated in 419, while Augustine was bishop of Hippo.

At that time most, though not all, of the clergy were married men. They are asked by the African Synod to give up all conjugal intercourse, because it is deemed that this would prevent them from carrying out *simpliciter* their mediatory function. The import of the canon is that those who by consecration have now become sacred persons should in future manifest by their lives this new ontological reality. To be effective mediators between God and man, and the commitment to service at the altar, are the specific reasons for the continence they are asked to observe.

DECRETALS OF POPE SIRICIUS

Three other documents issued by the Magisterium at the end of the fourth century claim apostolic origin for clerical celibacy and the perpetual continence required of ministers of the altar. These were the two decretals of Pope Siricius, dating from 385 and 386, and a canon of the Synod of Rome of about the same time.[11]

In the first of these, the *Directa* decretal written in 385, the Pope is responding to news that clerics in major orders continued living with their wives and having children in violation of the traditional discipline, and that this was being justified with reference to the tradition of the Levitical priesthood of the Old Testament. He replies that these priests were under the obligation of temporary continence when serving in the Temple, but that with the coming of Christ the old priesthood had been brought to completion, and by this very fact the obligation of temporary continence became an obligation to perpetual continence.[12]

---

11 Cf. Stickler, ibid., pp 29–33. 12 'We have indeed discovered that many priests and deacons of Christ brought children into the world, either through union with their wives or through shameful intercourse. And they used as an excuse for the fact that in the Old Testament – as we can read – priests and ministers are permitted to beget children. Whatever the case may be, if one of these disciples of the passions and tutors of vices thinks that the Lord –in the Law of Moses – gives an indistinct license to those in sacred Orders so that they may satisfy their passions, let him tell me now: why does the Lord warn those who have the custody of the most holy things in the following way: "You must make your-

In the *Cum in unum* decretal, sent to the different ecclesiastical provinces in 386, Pope Siricius refers to the various Pauline texts (cf. Tit 1:15; 1 Tim 3:2; 1 Cor 7:7; Rom 8:8–9) as the scriptural foundation for the discipline of ecclesiastical celibacy, and in doing so gives an authoritative interpretation of the *unius uxoris virum* (man of one wife) text. If Timothy and Titus are to choose bishops, priests or deacons among 'men married once only', this does not mean that after ordination they can continue with their conjugal life. Rather it is seen as a requirement to guarantee the future continence (*propter continentiam futuram*) that the candidate for orders will be asked to practise. In other words, a man who had remarried after his first wife died could not be considered as a candidate for ordination, since the fact of his remarriage would indicate an inability to live the life of perpetual continence required of clerics in major orders.[13]

The legislation of Pope Siricius in 385 and 386, and the canons of the Council of Carthage (390), claim apostolic origin for the *lex continentiae*. It is worth noting that these are not the claims of mere individuals but are the view of those who carried hierarchical responsibility in the Church. In Carthage it was the unanimous view of the whole African episcopate which declared '*ut quod apostoli docuerunt, et ipsa servavit antiquitas nos quoque custodiamus*' (what the Apostles taught and what antiquity itself observed, let us also endeavour to keep). In Rome Pope Siricius was conscious of placing himself in the line of the same living tradition with his predecessors as bishops of the See of Peter.[14]

---

selves holy, for I am Yahweh your God" (Lev 20:7). Likewise, why were the priests ordered, during the year of their tour of duty, to live in the temple, away from their homes? Quite obviously so that they would not be able to have carnal knowledge of any women, even their wives, and, thus, having a conscience radiating integrity, they could offer to God offerings worthy of his acceptance. Those men, once they had fulfilled their time of service, were permitted to have marital intercourse for the sole purpose of ensuring their descent, because no one except the members of the tribe of Levi could be admitted to the divine ministry. This is why, after having enlightened us by his coming, the Lord Jesus formally stipulated in the Gospel that he had not come to abolish the Law, but to bring it to perfection; this is also why he wanted the beauty of the Church whose Bridegroom he is to shine with the splendour of chastity, so that when he returns, on the Day of Judgement, he will find her without stain or wrinkle, as his Apostle taught. It is through the indissoluble law of these decisions that all of us, priests and deacons, are bound together from the day of our ordination, and held to put our hearts and our bodies to the service of sobriety and purity; may we be pleasing to our God in all things, in the sacrifices we offer daily' (PL 13, 1138a–39a, as quoted in Cochini, ibid., p. 9). **13** Cf. Cochini, ibid., pp 11–13. For a fuller discussion of the significance of this text, cf. Chapter 2 on the Scriptural foundations for celibacy. **14** The authoritative confirmation of the African legislation on celibacy by Rome, and other evidence of seeking papal approval for this discipline, not only reflects a universal tradition but points to the importance of the position of the Ro-

Later in the eleventh century the promoters of the Gregorian Reform drew on the Carthaginian canons of 390 for their most solid historical argument. After the Reformation, when the German princes wrote to the Pope requesting the authorisation of a married clergy, Pius IV's negative reply was grounded in the first place on the same Carthaginian canons.

As we have seen, the Latin rite legislation of the fourth century did not represent an innovation in the sense of imposing sexual abstinence on clerics for the first time. It was rather a response to a difficult situation in the Church when the general atmosphere of moral laxity was threatening a discipline which was regarded as a tradition, the infraction of which was sanctioned by severe penalties. In an unfavourable situation Church authorities would not have imposed on clerics the heavy burden of continence if they did not have the conviction of being accountable to apostolic tradition for the fidelity of their teaching.

PATRISTIC EVIDENCE

Theologically, in the first four centuries of the Church's history, the validation of clerical continence is grounded on the Pauline teaching, linking it to availability for service at the altar and a greater freedom for prayer. Being permanently in God's presence, and because of the importance given to prayer, praise and adoration, the minister of the New Covenant does not have the leisure needed to fulfil the responsibilities of married life.[15]

Nevertheless, the catechesis of St Cyril of Jerusalem (313–86) had already affirmed that the discipline of clerical continence was anchored in the example of the Eternal High Priest, a living norm that was more convincing than all other justifications. By linking priestly continence closely to the virginal birth of Christ, in the mind of Cyril it is based on a foundation that goes far beyond mere historical conjecture.[16]

For St Jerome (347–419) continence is above all a matter of holiness. In his *Letter to Pammachius* he justifies continence on the authority of Scripture and the actual witness of priestly chastity. This latter is not offered as an ideal to be pursued but as a fact admitted by all. Chastity, he claims, is also the rule for selection of clerics: bishops, priests and deacons are all

man See on this question. The conciliar acts of the period underline and confirm an awareness of genuine unity and essential uniformity, made real and translated into practice by the principle of unity, the Roman primacy (cf. Stickler, ibid., pp 28–30; 32–7). **15** Cf. Cochini, ibid., pp 248–51. **16** Cf. ibid., pp 208–10.

chosen from one of the following: virgins (that is single men), widowers, or married men who, after ordination, will observe perfect continence.[17]

It is also significant that Jerome in his defence of the traditional discipline does not feel called on to make any distinction between the witness of the Western, Egyptian, or Eastern Churches in this matter. In his polemic with one Vigilantius from Gaul (406), who saw continence as nothing but heresy and an occasion for sin, Jerome reaffirms the practice which he knows to be traditional: the Church of Egypt, the East and the Apostolic See never accept clerics unless they are virgins or continent men, or, if they were clerics who had a wife, accept them only if they give up matrimonial life. In affirming this discipline he is offering as testimony the experience of the greater part of the Church of which he, through his many travels, had firsthand experience.[18] He also gives testimony to the apostolic origin of this discipline: 'The Apostles were either virgins or continent after having been married. Bishops, priests, and deacons are chosen among virgins and widowers; in any case once they are ordained, they live in perfect chastity.'[19]

St Jerome, considering the role of Christ and his mother in the origin and institution of the Church, finds in them the living principles of virginity and priestly vocation.[20] Now freely accepted by some, it is for priests the principle of the sanctity called for by their ministry, and at their level it is translated into the special demands of continence. The imitation of virginal purity, inaugurated by Christ and his mother, is from now on the rule of the new priesthood.

St Augustine participated in the Council of Carthage (419) where the general obligation to continence for major clerics had been repeatedly affirmed and traced back to the apostles and to a constant tradition. In his treatise *De conjugiis adulterinis* he asserted that even married men who were unexpectedly called to enter the ranks of the major clergy, and were ordained, were obliged to continence. In this they became an example to those laymen who had to live separated from their wives and who therefore were more liable to be tempted to commit adultery.[21]

---

17 Cf. ibid., p. 78.   18 Cf. ibid., p. 298.   19 Ibid., p. 297.   20 'The virgin Christ and the virgin Mary have consecrated for each sex the beginnings of virginity: the apostles were either virgins or continent after having been married' (*Letter to Pammachius*, quoted in Cochini, ibid., p. 297).   21 No 2, 22; PL, 40, 486.

SIXTH-CENTURY LEGISLATION

In the sixth century there were some significant pieces of legislation on celibacy. The *Breviatio Ferrandi* was a digest of Church legislation in Africa assembled about 550 which reaffirms earlier norms of priestly celibacy. In summary the main points were as follows:

- bishops, priests and deacons were to abstain from relations with their wives;
- any priest who got married was to be deposed; if he commits the sin of fornication he is to do penance;
- in order to safeguard the reputation of ministers of the Church and to help them observe chastity, clerics were not to live with women other than close family relations.

It is worth noting that this was a period of merciless persecution for the Church in North Africa when the Vandals invaded and eliminated the leaders of many of these Christian communities.[22]

The Third Council of Toledo (589) was convoked to remedy abuses that had penetrated the clergy arising from the Arian heresy. Bishops, priests and deacons, returning to the Catholic faith after abandoning Arianism, no longer considered continence an obligation of the priestly state. Matrimonial rights had reasserted themselves and, therefore, although Arianism had been officially defeated at the Council of Constantinople in 381, the negative effects of this heresy, as far as priestly chastity was concerned, were still being felt two centuries later. Canon 5 of Toledo III renewed the traditional discipline, indicating the sanctions which attended its infraction.[23]

---

22 Cf Cochini, ibid., pp 324–6. **23** 'It has come to the knowledge of the Holy Council that bishops, priests, and deacons, who were once heretics but returned to Catholicism, still gave in to carnal desire and united with their wives; so that it does not happen again in the future, we have ordered as follows, which had already been decreed by previous canons: that it not be permitted to these [clerics and their wives] to lead a common life favouring incontinence, but that while keeping conjugal fidelity toward each other, they watch to what is mutually beneficial to them both and not share the same room. With the help of virtue, it would be even better that the cleric find for his wife a new home, so that their chastity enjoy a good witnessing before both God and men. But if, after this warning, someone prefers to live in incontinence with his wife, let him be considered a lector; as to those who are still subject to the ecclesiastical canon, if they live in their cells, contrary to the elders' orders, in the company of women apt to raise suspicions harmful to their reputation, let those be struck with severe canonical penalties' (Cochini, ibid., p. 331).

In Gaul in the sixth century, councils held under the reforming and energetic St Caesarius of Arles reaffirmed legislation for the restoration of priestly celibacy, a discipline which had suffered as a result of the Visigoth invasions during the previous century.

ATTEMPTS AT REFORM IN THE WEST FROM THE SEVENTH TO THE TENTH CENTURIES

During the period of the early Middle Ages there were important historical factors which influenced the discipline of continence and celibacy. In the first place there was the gradual disintegration of the unity of the Roman Empire, giving rise to regional and national entities, which clouded the unity of vision of the various episcopates, and brought about a weakening of papal authority.[24]

The new races of barbarians, who overran the boundaries of the old empire, were often converted *en masse*. This meant that the full demands of Christian morality encountered serious difficulties among poorly instructed peoples, and even among the clergy who had to be recruited from them. Because these young states based several of their institutions on close collaboration with the Church, the result was that many pastors became temporal princes. Hence the interest of the state in the choice of the holders of ecclesiastical office, which was the origin of investiture by the secular powers. This resulted in important Church positions frequently being occupied by men who lacked the necessary moral and religious aptitudes. In addition, the crisis which affected the papacy during the Middle Ages diminished the vigour and effectiveness of its interventions over a long period.

The lower clergy were affected by the bad example of their superiors, but the principal cause of laxity regarding the law of continence arose from the system of conferment of benefices and the setting up of many private churches. This arrangement compromised the clergy by tying their ministry to the totality of material resources of which the Church could in future dispose. The material advantages of ecclesiastical positions were frequently more attractive than the pastoral responsibility, which often resulted in unsuitable and unworthy candidates entering the priesthood.

---

24 Cf. Alfons M. Stickler, 'The Evolution of the Discipline of Celibacy in the Western Church from the End of the Patristic Era to the Council of Trent', in Coppens, J. (ed.), *Priesthood and Celibacy*, Milan, 1972, pp 503–97.

With the resulting financial independence, economic security and free disposal of revenues, the ministerial function itself, as Stickler points out, became largely independent of higher authority. This inevitably led to worldly life–styles, which contributed to a deterioration in the practice of continence and celibacy as these had broadly established themselves at the end of the patristic era.

What was the response of Church authority to this situation of decadent morals among the clergy? The historical evidence shows that a number of disciplinary norms were laid down, which took on board the most significant patristic texts concerning continence and celibacy. These are to be found in the conciliar rulings of the African Church, of Gaul and Spain, as well as in the important decretals of Popes Siricius, Innocent I and Leo I, most of which we have already reviewed. They made their way into countless small collections of disciplinary norms which had a wide distribution.

Among these collections the *Penitential Books*[25] had a particular importance, containing as they did the whole of ecclesiastical discipline. They originated in Ireland and England and spread to the continent through missionaries from these countries. As regards the discipline of celibacy we read in one of these, dating from the second half of the sixth century, that a cleric who contracted marriage may not return to his wife after ordination and may no longer give her children, as this would be the equivalent of infidelity to the promise he had made to God.[26] Another penitential collection with Irish connections, the *Poenitentiale Bobiense*, laid down that a cleric in major orders, who after ordination renewed conjugal relations with his wife, should consider that he had committed a sin the equivalent of adultery, with severe penances attached.[27]

It is therefore true to say that, during those centuries of crisis for clerical morals, the Church never lost sight of the ancient tradition concerning the law of celibacy. From her memory she constantly affirmed the prohibition of marriage for clerics in major orders and the duty of a vow of perpetual continence for those married before ordination, even at times when these laws were being flagrantly violated. Apart from evidence in

---

25 Cf. Hugh Connolly, *The Irish Penitentials. Their Significance for the Sacrament of Penance Today*, Dublin, 1995, pp 80–96. **26** Cf. *Poenitentiale Vinniani*, no. 27, containing the ancient Irish-British norms on clerical continence, quoted in Stickler, ibid., p. 512. **27** 'Si quis clericus vel superior gradus, qui uxorem habuit, et post honorem iterum eam cognoverit, sciat se adulterium commisisse. Clericus quattuor, diaconus sex, sacerdos septem, episcopus duodecim, singuli in pane et aqua iuxta ordinem suum' (quoted in Stickler, ibid., p. 514, note 9).

the collections of disciplinary norms, this commitment is also attested to by the efforts of regional councils and diocesan synods. In France, for example, the Council of Metz (888) forbade priests to keep a woman in their homes; the Council of Rheims (909), noting the decadence in clerical conduct as regards continence, urged that association with women should be forbidden, and also cohabitation with them, both norms being related to the precept of continence. In Germany, the Council of Mainz (888) recalled that the prohibition on cohabitation with women even included the wife whom the cleric had previously married, that is, it confirmed the prohibition of canon 3 of the Council of Nicea (325). In England, Archbishop Dunstan of Canterbury, towards the end of the tenth century, made considerable efforts to reform the morals of the English clergy and restore the traditional discipline. His endeavours were resisted but he had no hesitation in replacing recalcitrant priests by monks.

During this period there were a number of papal rulings about celibacy despite times of decadence in the papacy itself. These consisted in instructions to bishops and princes of various countries, and decrees by Roman synods defending or restoring the tradition of celibacy. But it was not until the period of the Gregorian Reform in the eleventh and twelfth centuries that these instructions were given the canonical and disciplinary teeth necessary to be effective.

THE GREGORIAN REFORM

The Gregorian reform succeeded because it struck at the very root of the disorders which had become so widespread. The initiative for reform came from the monasteries and their objective was to re-establish the supreme authority of the papacy. The roots of the evil were not only recognised but eliminated. First there was a systematic attack against simony and Nicolaitism (the widespread violation of clerical celibacy), and this was followed by a courageous battle against the scourge of lay investiture. This led to a new era in the development of legislation concerning celibacy and, more importantly, its implementation. The basic inspiration of the Gregorian reform was not to innovate but rather to draw deeply on the wisdom of tradition and of the Fathers, and on the ancient and authentic discipline of the Church which it so desired to restore.

The ecclesiastical laws promulgated by Gregory VII (1073–85) reaffirmed the norms concerning continence of the clergy and the prohibition of marriage for clerics in major orders, as well as measures taken to forestall infringements, particularly in relation to cohabitation with women. Still, the programme for reform was not without opposition. The opponents of reform presented their own arguments, not only at the practical but also at the theoretical level. Their main argument was the scriptural one drawn from the Old Testament, which not only allowed priests to marry but mandated marriage to perpetuate the priestly caste. They also drew on the episode of Paphnutius whom, they claimed, opposed the idea of requiring absolute continence from married clerics at the Council of Nicea (325).

Ignoring all the historical documentation that supported the law of celibacy, they developed a whole series of supposedly moral and rational arguments against it. The renunciation of marriage, they claimed, could not be imposed but only recommended; it should be left optional. In any case the matter should be approached with benevolence and tact and not with Roman rigidity. Customs that the passage of time had made lawful should be accepted, and more charity and compassion shown towards human weakness.

They also made the point that an obligation as grave as that of continence could not be imposed universally as it did not come from God but from men, and presupposed in those who accepted it a charism which God only granted in individual cases. Thus, their argument continued, drawing on the Pauline admonition, it was better for a man to marry than to burn with impure desires. In any event, marriage was a sacrament instituted by Christ, hence something holy, and so marriage for a priest could not be described as wrong. It was therefore contrary to the holiness of matrimony to describe marital practice of priests lawfully united to a wife as *fornicatio* or *adulterium*. In the light of these considerations the opposition to the Gregorian reform deplored the new and severe measures decreed by Rome for infractions of the traditional discipline.[28]

The promoters of reform answered each of the objections raised by its opponents and then went on to elucidate the reasons for the new legislation. They draw on the scriptural arguments for continence, but it is to the witness of tradition that the main thrust of their arguments appeal. In this context the historical value of the Paphnutius incident at Nicea is rejected with convincing critical reasoning, an event which Gregory VII rejected as a falsification at the Synod of Rome in 1077.[29]

28 Cf. Stickler, ibid., pp 537–9. See also Jaki, op. cit., pp 128–147. 29 During the Gregorian reform there was sustained opposition to the traditional interpretation of canon

The partisans of reform strongly affirmed the primacy of the Pope as the governing authority for the whole Church, with the competence to lay down laws in respect of all the bishops in matters of universal ecclesiastical discipline. Gregory VII worked ceaselessly to bring about the implementation of the traditional discipline. He did this especially by way of regional synods presided over by his legates in collaboration with the bishops, and through countless letters made the new dispositions known. Another important consequence of the reform was the regulation decided by the Second Lateran Council (1139) that a marriage attempted by a bishop, priest, deacon or sub-deacon was not only illicit but invalid. This led to the misunderstanding, still widespread even today, that celibacy for the higher clergy was introduced only at Lateran II. In reality the Council declared invalid something that had in fact always been prohibited. As Stickler points out, this new sanction actually confirmed an obligation that had in fact existed for many centuries.[30]

From the time of Alexander III (1159–81) married men were not as a rule allowed to have ecclesiastical benefices, and a son of a priest was prohibited from succeeding to his father's benefice. Before the ordination of their husbands, young wives and the wives of bishops were to agree to enter a convent. Indeed, one of the factors which in the long run must have contributed to the ordination of unmarried men only would have

---

3 of the Council of Nicea (325)['This Great Council has strictly forbidden any bishop, priest or deacon, or any member of the clergy from having a subintroduced woman unless she be a mother, sister, aunt or person who is above suspicion'], and the supposed intervention of the Egyptian bishop, Paphnutius, at this Council was strongly canvassed to offset it. He is alleged to have risen during the Council to protest any plan to impose a discipline of total continence on married clerics, suggesting that it be left to the decision of the particular Churches. The argument runs that his advice is supposed to have been accepted by the assembly. The well-known Church historian, Eusebius of Caesarea, who was present at the Council and sympathetic to the Arians, does not make any reference to this episode. It is first recorded by the 5th century Greek historian Sozomen. As Stickler points out, there are several arguments against the authenticity of this episode, but the most telling one is that the Eastern Church itself, which should have had a great interest in it, either did not know of it or, because the Eastern Church leaders were convinced that it was false, did not have a record of it in any official document it used. None of the polemical writers on clerical celibacy made use of it, nor did the Council of Trullo (691) refer to it. And given the polemical tone of Trullo it would have served its purpose well to have referred to it if it was true. The story of Paphnutius was used against the Gregorian reform, and this was why Pope Gregory VII, at the Synod of Rome in 1077, condemned the episode as one of the two most important falsifications used by the opponents of the reform (cf. Cholij, ibid., pp 78–92, and Stickler, *The Case for Clerical Celibacy*, pp 62–5).   30 Cf. Stickler, ibid., p. 45.

been the assumption that the wife was not prepared to give up her marital rights.[31]

In summary we can say that, during this period, although the traditional discipline had not changed in its main features and was not forgotten, it had in practice, as Stickler points out, ceased to be observed. The Gregorian reform must take the credit for a total commitment to eradicating the principal disorders which sullied the Church. Nevertheless the level of resistance encountered indicated that practices contrary to the ancient discipline had become so ingrained as to be regarded as lawful. The means used to restore order were primarily the implementation of severe sanctions for infractions of the discipline of clerical continence, and the intervention of papal authority against which there was no appeal. Immediately subsequent to the period of the Gregorian reform, there was a notable development in the science of canon law during the twelfth, thirteenth and fourteenth centuries, the implementation of which facilitated the return to the traditional discipline of celibacy. In this way was developed the theology and the law for the basis of the obligation of celibacy. We will discuss later the reasons for the inherent limitations of this theology and jurisprudence.

DEVELOPMENTS LEADING UP TO THE COUNCIL OF TRENT

Despite all the efforts of the Gregorian reform the legislation on celibacy was still far from achieving the desired objectives. After the great Western Schism (1378–1417) the status of the papacy suffered a new decline and another reform was called for.

But the hoped-for reform did not materialise. This was due primarily to the economic organisation of the Church which was based on benefices that brought in considerable revenues. As we have seen already, the material advantages of these appointments attracted many men to the priesthood who had no vocation or aptitude for the priestly ministry. This situation, coupled with negligence by the competent authority, was the primary cause of decadence among the clergy. Given the abuses which were a reality in the Church, when the Protestant revolt started to take shape in the sixteenth century, it is not surprising that the question of celibacy was raised. Indeed many of the reformers had a strong aversion to

---

31 Cf. Roman Cholij, 'Priestly Celibacy in Patristics and in the History of the Church', in *For Love Alone: Reflections on Priestly Celibacy*, Maynooth, 1993, p. 46.

it, and with Luther and Zwingli it became one of the key issues of the Reformation.

Stickler summarises the situation as follows: 'The campaign waged against celibacy at both the theoretical and practical levels achieved notable success due to the violence, skill and literary talent with which all the old objections, whether psychological, social or even financial, were worked out and presented to the public. Furthermore – and this amounted to a revolutionary innovation – the abandonment of celibacy was placed in relation to a new concept of the priesthood. The denial of the sacramental character of the *ordo*, the emphasis on the priesthood common to all the faithful and the doubt thrown on the existence of the ministerial priesthood essentially distinct from that of ordinary believers – all this found its concrete expression in the wish to suppress celibacy.'[32]

The Protestant opposition to celibacy was also an opportunity to give testimony to their *sola scriptura* doctrine, in that their rejection of celibacy was, they claimed, based on finding no scriptural support for it. If Catholics appealed to tradition to justify the doctrine and practice of celibacy, this was a source which was totally rejected by the Reformers. Hence, in the context of the Reformation, celibacy now became much more than a disciplinary problem. It resulted in direct doctrinal confrontation and was raised almost to the level of a criterion of orthodoxy.

In England, after Henry VIII's break with Rome, Thomas Cranmer, whom he appointed archbishop of Canterbury, had already married secretly and prepared the ground for the abolition of celibacy under Henry's successor.[33]

---

32 'The Evolution of the Discipline of Celibacy', op. cit., p. 582.   33 Cranmer was the most completely subservient to Henry VIII of all the major players in the English Reformation. Although Thomas Cromwell was its chief political architect, it was Cranmer's religious ideas that became the beliefs of the fledgling *Ecclesia Anglicana*. He developed a deep antipathy to the Church and its sacraments, and especially to the Sacrifice of the Mass. It was he who drew up the arguments in favour of the divorce in Henry's appeal to the universities of Europe. He it was who was sent to Rome to plead the king's cause before the Holy See. He was chaplain to Anne Boleyn and through her influence was appointed archbishop of Canterbury in 1532, in which capacity he danced a canonical jig to Henry's tune. In 1533 he did what Rome would not do, giving sentence against the validity of the king's marriage to Catherine. He followed up by affirming the validity of Henry's marriage to Anne, whom he crowned queen of England on 1 June 1533. On 11 July the pope declared the king's marriage with Anne to be null and void. In September Anne gave birth to the future Elizabeth I. Nevertheless, on Mary's accession after the death of the boy king Edward VI in 1553, the laws relating to the marriage of clerics which Cranmer had championed were repealed, but only for a time, until Elizabeth eventually got round to reversing the situation again. See Diarmaid McCulloch, *Thomas Cranmer: A Life*, London, 1996.

Despite the monarch's well-known proclivity to taking wives, he was not prepared to countenance a similar arrangement for his clergy. Nevertheless, barely nine months after the king's death Convocation voted in December 1547 to abolish the laws which made the marriages of clerks in Holy Orders null and void *ab initio*, and a Bill to this effect was passed in the House of Commons in the 1548–9 session. All such marriages hitherto contracted, involving as many as eight or nine thousand clerics, were rendered good and lawful by the same Bill. Three years later a second Act was passed which legitimated the children born of such unions.[34]

In 1553 the new code of Canon Law for the Church of England condemned as heresy the belief that Holy Orders were an invalidating impediment to marriage.[35]

Following the elimination of celibacy in different countries, it is not surprising that many priests, diocesan as well as religious, abandoned their obligations. Sadly this was often the prelude to the abandonment of the faith as well.

RESPONSE TO THE REFORMERS

The revolutionary dimension of the opposition to celibacy at first evinced a political response from many civil authorities. The emperors Charles V (1519–56), Ferdinand I (1558–64) and Maximillian II (1564–76) all counselled a mitigation of the law at different stages during the Council of Trent. Humanists like Erasmus advised the same course. A change was admissible, even desirable they said, if it did not touch on the substance of the faith.

Some theologians and bishops rowed in with the humanists and were prepared for any accommodation which did not undermine the essentials of the faith. Still, the majority of bishops, convinced of the doctrinal and ascetical arguments for celibacy, refused to be railroaded into change. Since many of the priests who were living in compromised situations were already committed to heterodox theological positions, the bishops judged that a change in the law of celibacy would do little to win back these men to orthodoxy. They were also convinced that tolerating marriage for priests would completely undermine the radical reform of the clergy which was necessary if they were to become exemplary ministers of Christ.

34 Cf. Philip Hughes, *The Reformation in England*, II, London, 1954, p.115.   35 Cf. ibid., p.131.

Despite powerful political pressures Rome refused to legislate for a compromise solution, although it did show tolerance in particular mitigating circumstances. A dispensation could be given to priests, who wanted to keep their wives, to have their marriages validated (*sanatio in radice*), but they would have to give up their benefices and renounce the exercise of their ministry for the future. On the other hand, priests who desired to be readmitted to the ministry could do so only on condition that they separated from their concubines and showed an authentic spirit of repentance. These were the dispositions which were offered to Germany. Through Cardinal Pole, Rome made a similar arrangement with England during the period of the Catholic restoration under Mary (1553–8) to facilitate those priests who wanted to return to orthodoxy.

COUNCIL OF TRENT

From the time the Council of Trent first met in 1547, the question of priestly celibacy formed part of the agenda. However, because of interruptions, the council Fathers did not get round to addressing the issue until the third and last session in 1563. Clerical celibacy was studied by a commission of theologians in light of the Protestant affirmations that:

- marriage as a state in life was superior to celibacy, and
- that Western priests could marry licitly, ecclesiastical laws and vows notwithstanding; that to say otherwise is to disparage matrimony; and that all those who are not aware of having received the gift of chastity are free to marry.

Discussion of these two propositions opened in March 1563 in Trent and continued for thirteen sessions. It was the second issue which elicited a historical consideration of celibacy.

The commission studied the question under two headings (i) celibates who became priests, and (ii) married men who were accepted for ordination. In relation to the former it was discovered that at no time in the history of the Church had there been any exception to the prohibition on marriage for celibate priests. The majority of the commission considered this discipline to be of apostolic origin and the Council refused to define it as a discipline of merely ecclesiastical origin.[36] As regards married men

---

36 Cf. Session XIV of 11 December 1563, under the heading *De Sacramento matrimonii*; and

accepted for orders, some argued that the obligation to perfect continence was of apostolic origin, whilst others considered it as resulting from ecclesiastical discipline. In relation to the Apostles who were married before being called by Christ, all the theologians affirmed unhesitatingly that afterwards they gave up conjugal life with their wives in line with their own declaration: 'We have left everything and followed you ... ' (Mt 19:27).

The discussions of the theological commission led to the approval of the following canon by the Fathers of Trent on 11 November 1563: 'If anyone says that clerics constituted in sacred orders or regulars who have made solemn profession of chastity can contract marriage, and that the one contracted is valid notwithstanding the ecclesiastical law or the vow, and that the contrary is nothing else than a condemnation of marriage, and that all who feel they have not the gift of chastity, even though they have made such a vow, can contract marriage, let him be anathema, since God does not refuse that gift to those who ask for it rightly, neither does *he suffer us to be tempted above that which we are able* (1 Cor 10:13).'[37]

Two other decisions were taken at Trent which were of much greater significance for the future of celibacy in the Church. The first was the decision to set up seminaries for the formation of candidates for the priesthood from their adolescence. This was perhaps the single most important measure both for the restoration of the traditional discipline and the elimination of immoral situations.[38]

The fact that as a consequence an increasing number of candidates were celibate at ordination meant that it eventually became unnecessary to ordain married men. The formation programme in the seminary would allow, firstly, a judicious selection and screening procedure to ensure that only candidates with the necessary aptitudes were ordained. Secondly, seminarians would be given the necessary formation at the theological, moral and ascetical levels to ensure that they would have the maturity required to live up to the demands of consecrated celibacy in a dedicated priestly life.

Session XXV of 3 December 1563, under *Caput 14 : De reformatione generali*. This latter decree dealt with the question of discipline for clerics guilty of incontinence. Clerics should not cohabit with women of doubtful reputation nor associate with them. Those who were recalcitrant would be deprived of their benefices, and if they persisted they would be dismissed from the ministry. **37** *Canons and Decrees of the Council of Trent*, trans. H.J. Schroeder, Rockford, Ill., 1978, can. no. 9, p. 182. **38** The education of the clergy up to this time was haphazard and lacked structure. In the West from the seventh to the twelfth centuries the predominant focus for the formation of priests was the monastic or episcopal school. Subsequently the rise of the universities played a part, though only a small proportion of ordinands would have graduated from these centres of learning. Even so, as regards the seminaries, it would take time before the Tridentine decree would be enacted universally.

The second important consequence for celibacy was the decision by Trent to bring about a renewal of the priesthood and the episcopal ministry. Bishops were required to give first priority to their priests in the exercise of their pastoral concern, and to provide them with every help and encouragement to persevere in their vocation. They were encouraged to be real fathers to their priests, to be aware of their needs, anxieties, and difficulties and to support them in every way. It was precisely the lack of this paternal care and attention which was, for many priests, one of the main causes of infidelity to celibacy in the past.

The dispositions laid down by Trent for bishops and priests effectively constituted a new image and definition of priesthood.[39] Their duties were no longer to be restricted to the celebration of the liturgy and the administration of the sacraments; priests were also to be the pastoral leaders of the people in their care. The different decrees manifest how strongly Trent insisted on the prophetic office attached to the apostolic ministry. There is a remarkable new emphasis on the importance of preaching to instruct people in the teaching of Christ and the demands of the Christian life. Parish priests are required to preach daily during Lent and Advent, and also during the administration of the sacraments.[40]

The demands of this mission provided the priest with a new impetus to develop his moral and spiritual life, and consequently gave his priesthood a more supernatural grounding. In this way the Council provided the necessary theological and ascetical structure to prevent priests falling back into the bad habits of a worldly outlook and over-concern for material interests.[41]

Even so, the system of revenues accruing from benefices was not entirely broken, a situation which explains why the new dispositions laid down by Trent failed to have an immediate effect in relation to the renewal of the clergy and the practice of celibacy. Nevertheless, the Council

---

39 Cf. Aidan Nichols, *Holy Order: Apostolic Priesthood from the New Testament to the Second Vatican Council*, Dublin, 1990, pp 87–107.   40 To facilitate priests in the fulfilment of this responsibility, the Council commissioned a Catechism which was to be translated into the vernacular. Perhaps the main contribution of the *Roman Catechism* to the Tridentine reform from the point of view of the priest was its stress on the necessary spiritual qualities of the candidate for orders –holiness of life, faith, prudence, and a deep knowledge of the truths of divine revelation were demanded.   41 Writing on priestly spirituality became a topic of widespread interest as a result of the Council of Trent in the works of such as Anthony of Molina, Albert Michel and François de la Rochefoucauld. In addition men like Blessed John of Avila (1499–1569), St Philip Neri (1515–95), and St Charles Borromeo (1480–1547) demonstrated very practical concern for the spiritual formation of priests and gave real penetration to the work of the Counter-Reformation in this area.

was a landmark in the history of the Church in relation to celibacy, the benefits of which have lasted down to our own day.

In summary it can be said that all through the Middle Ages and into modern times, despite the pressures which were often brought to bear at its very centre, the Church never questioned the basis and the application of the law of celibacy in its essentials – candidates in major orders were never allowed to marry; any marriage so attempted was declared void. Those who were already married were forbidden to exercise their conjugal rights and were asked to make a commitment to perfect continence for the future. The ordination of married men gradually became the less favoured option, because over time the conviction grew that such ordinations created a certain ambiguity with regard to the appreciation of the celibate vocation and, as Stickler points out, called into question the close affinity between vocation to the priesthood and that to virginity.

The frequent reports of infraction of the discipline of priestly celibacy during this period suggests that in many places it was more honoured in the breach than in the observance. This led some commentators to the conclusion that celibacy *per se* was a commitment beyond the capacity of the normal run of clerics, and a charism which was only granted to a special few. Still, the evidence demonstrates that there was a high correlation between failure in celibacy and the decline in spiritual life of the clergy. As Stickler incisively comments, 'This demanding commitment, which involves a life of constant sacrifice, can only be lived out if it is nourished by a living faith, since human weakness is a constant reminder of its practical implications. It is only through a faith that is constantly and consciously sustained that the supernatural reasons underlying the commitment can be truly understood. When this faith grows weak, the determination to persevere fades; when faith dies, so does continence.'[42]

It is also true that at that time there was little rigour in the criteria of selecting candidates for orders. Their ascetical and doctrinal formation was seriously inadequate, making it almost inevitable that future priests would lack the necessary theological and spiritual habits of mind to understand the deeper meaning of celibacy and their priesthood.

---

42 *The Case for Clerical Celibacy*, pp 50–1. He goes on to point out that 'a constant proof of this truth is to be found in the various heretical and schismatic movements that have arisen in the Church. One of the first institutions to be attacked is clerical continence. Therefore we should not be surprised that one of the first things that was rejected by the heretical movements that broke away from the unity of the Catholic Church in the sixteenth century –Lutherans, Calvinists, Zwinglians, Anglicans – was in fact clerical celibacy' (ibid., p. 51). It is also significant that the Old Catholics, when they seceded after Vatican I, abolished celibacy and reverted to a married clergy.

In spite of all the difficulties and failures the Church never allowed herself to be invaded with a defeatist attitude about celibacy. The fact that, generation after generation, she got down to the work of reform, and was always ready to swim against the current of compromise, confirms her supernatural character as an institution. The fortitude to require her priests to observe this difficult discipline she drew from the conviction that this was a way of life that derived from apostolic tradition. As a result, she never doubted that, in spite of human weakness and all the vicissitudes to which such a commitment was prone, the grace of God would never be lacking to those who wanted to be faithful.

FROM TRENT TO THE PRESENT

Later, in the difficult times spawned by the French Revolution, the Church maintained its tradition of celibacy. However, the currents of thought generated by the Enlightenment paved the way for a brutal attack on celibacy, with inevitable losses, although thousands of priests were ready to choose martyrdom during the Reign of Terror. The Church's attitude was the praxis adopted at the time of the Reformation: priests who married during the Revolution had to decide either to renounce their invalidly contracted civil marriages, or to seek the sanation of the invalidity in the Church. In the first case they could be readmitted as ministers of the altar; in the second they remained permanently excluded from the sacred ministry, a solution which was long since established in the first written law on this topic, that is, by the Council of Elvira (305).

In the early nineteenth century an association was formed in Germany to advocate a change in the law, but Gregory XIV rejected this move in his encyclical *Mirari vos* (1834). Fourteen years later Pius IX defended the discipline in his *Qui pluribus*. At the beginning of the twentieth century, Modernism provoked a new attack on the law of celibacy, but its effects were limited, due largely to the decisive measures taken by St Pius X.[43]

After World War I, when a group of Czech priests tried to bring about a change in the law of celibacy by suggesting that Rome was ready to relax this discipline, Benedict XV's unequivocal response left no room for doubt:

---

43 In his apostolic exhortation on the priesthood, *Haerent animo*, published in 1908 to mark the Golden Jubilee of his ordination, he refers to celibacy as 'the fairest jewel of our priesthood'.

'We once more affirm, solemnly and formally, that this Apostolic See will never in any way lighten or mitigate the obligation of this holy and salutary law of clerical celibacy, not to speak of abolishing it.'[44]

Pius XI, in his detailed encyclical on the priesthood, *Ad catholici sacerdotii*, reaffirmed the appropriateness of the discipline of celibacy,[45] as did Pius XII[46] and John XXIII.[47]

Since Vatican II there have been a number of efforts to change the discipline on celibacy. One was the attempt to have married men (*viri probati*) ordained, but without requiring the renunciation of conjugal life; another was the proposal to allow priests to marry.

ORIENTAL CHURCH LEGISLATION

The criticism has often been made against the Church that, from a more liberal position at the beginning, its present discipline on celibacy expresses a more severe and hard-line approach. As proof of this point reference is made to the praxis of the Oriental Church where, we are told, the primitive discipline is preserved. Consequently it is suggested that the Latin Church should return to its original praxis of a married clergy because of the heavy burden which celibacy constitutes for the pastoral situation of the Church today.

The truth of the matter is, however, somewhat different. Authoritative witnesses of priestly celibacy in the fourth century Church of the East testify to a discipline parallel to what we have seen in the West. An important first witness is Bishop Epiphanius of Constantia in Cyprus (317–403). He was well known as an expert defender of orthodoxy and Church tradition. In his best known work, *Panarion*, he says that the charism of the new priesthood is shown through men who have renounced the use of their marriage contracted before ordination, or through those who have always lived as virgins. In his *Expositio fidei* he claims that most clerics come from young men who have chosen virginity or from monks. If these candidates are not sufficient for the Church's needs, future priests are recruited from married men, but only from those who are freed from conjugal duties either by widowhood or by a free profession of conti-

44 Allocution, 16 December 1920, in *The Catholic Priesthood: Papal Documents from Pius X to Pius XII*, Book I, Dublin, 1962, p. 145.   **45** Published 20 December 1935, where he refers to celibacy as 'the most precious treasure of the Catholic priesthood'.   **46** Apostolic Exhortation, *Menti nostrae*, on the Priestly Life, 23 September 1950.   **47** Encyclical, *Sacerdotii nostri primordia*, on Priestly Perfection, 1 August 1959.

nence. Men who have contracted a second marriage can never be accepted to the episcopate, the priesthood, or the diaconate. He does not
deny that in various places priests and deacons have fathered children after
ordination, but he makes the point that this does not conform to the norm
but is rather a consequence of human weakness.[48]

The Council of Nicea (325), the first ecumenical council, legislated
against bishops, priests and deacons having women in their houses which
could give rise to any possible scandal against their chastity. The only
exceptions permitted were the mother, sister, or aunt of the cleric or those
clearly above suspicion.[49] It was at this council that Paphnutius, a bishop
from Egypt, is supposed to have intervened to prevent the imposition of
the discipline of total continence on clerics in major orders. Nevertheless,
the arguments for the spuriousness of this intervention would seem to be
unanswerable.[50]

As already reported, St Jerome, because of his many travels in Egypt,
Syria and Palestine, was very familiar with the praxis of celibacy in the
Eastern Church. In his defence of celibacy against Vigilantius he gives
witness to a praxis in the East and in Egypt similar to that adopted by the
Apostolic See, which, he affirms, only accepted virgin clerics for ordination and, if they were married, only those who had renounced conjugal
relations.[51]

On the other hand, it is not surprising that, humanly speaking, such a
serious commitment as celibacy would, down through the centuries, pay
the price of human weakness. Fulfilment did not always correspond to
precept, but the Church persistently intervened by means of encouragement, sanction and legislation to restore the traditional praxis in spite of
difficulties and, at times, opposition from the clergy themselves. Nevertheless, it would seem that this attention and concern for the constant
renewal of celibacy was lacking to some extent in the Eastern Church,
partly because it was less well organised than the Churches of the Latin
rite, and also because the negative consequences of the Christological heresies had a more deleterious effect on the general discipline of the East.
Although East and West reached conciliar agreement in matters of dogma,
they were never able to achieve a common legislation on issues of discipline. The particular churches of the East were more independent and, as
a consequence, it was more difficult to achieve systematic agreement on
matters of general discipline, including that of clerical celibacy; each Church

48 Cf. Cochini, op. cit., pp 226–33.   49 Cf. ibid., pp 185–95.   50 Cf. Stickler, ibid.,
pp.62–5 for a detailed refutation of this supposed incident. See also note no. 3 above.   51 *Adversus
Vigilantium*, 2. PL 23: 340–1; cf. Cochini, ibid., p. 299.

tended to have its own individual approach in this area. The divergence from the Western tradition was also accelerated by the development over the years of certain tensions between the Byzantine and Latin Churches.[52]

During the seventh century the Byzantine empire of the East suffered in much the same way at the hands of invading infidels as did the West in the fourth and fifth centuries. Moslem, Bulgarian and Slavic incursions had a devastating effect on the Eastern Church such that of the four patriarchates which comprised it, only Constantinople remained; Antioch, Alexandria and Jerusalem were no more. These invasions had not only a profound effect on the ethnic structure of Byzantium, but had serious consequences for administration, and for religious and social development as well. The effects of these upheavals were to bring about a serious intellectual and moral decline. These internal disorders were to create lasting difficulties in the relationships between Byzantium and Rome, which were further exacerbated by the disputes surrounding the Monophysite and Monothelite heresies, disputes which the Council of Constantinople in 681 only partially resolved.

Given the general situation in the Eastern Church, it is not difficult to explain the lack of effective action against the ever-present temptation to give way in matters of celibacy, specifically in relation to the *lex continentiae*. The Eastern Church, however, maintained the ancient tradition of complete continence for bishops, even for those married before ordination. Nevertheless, for the reasons outlined above, Byzantium gradually came to the conclusion that, because it was increasingly abused, it was impossible to prohibit conjugal life to priests, deacons, and subdeacons. As a result they gave way to a *de facto* situation which had developed over the years.

IMPERIAL LAWS

While the councils of the Western Church were defending the Carthaginian and Roman discipline, and recovering ground lost as a result of the barbarian invasions, during the sixth century the Byzantine East was enacting a body of civil and ecclesiastical law which has come to be known as the *Corpus juris civilis*. This was an initiative of the emperor Justinian I (527–65) and related not only to civil law but covered every aspect of ecclesiastical discipline as well.

---

52 Cf. Stickler, *The Case for Clerical Celibacy*, pp 66–9. In his comprehensive study, *Rome and the Eastern Churches* (Edinburgh, 1992, pp 105–50), Aidan Nichols has identified the main causes of this cleavage.

The first laws sanctioning conjugal life for priests were in fact imperial laws which were primarily concerned with the civil situation of married clerics. The Justinian Code of 534, while still prohibiting clerics to marry after ordination, allowed for the use of marriage by priests, deacons, and subdeacons.[53] Other prescriptions of the Justinian legislation relate to the ordination of priests and deacons. The bishop is responsible for the selection of suitable candidates and must do a thorough investigation of their background to ensure that they fulfil the requirements of 'the laws and holy canons', that is, have lived up to then in perfect chastity if they were single, or have been married only once and to a virgin.

The sanctions for infraction of these regulations were severe.[54] All clerics who are single or widowers are forbidden to live with women who are not close members of their family circle, the reason, as usual, being to avoid the risk of suspicion that the presence of such a woman living under the same roof could bring on them. The Justinian law was even stricter in relation to bishops. No woman, not even mother or sisters, is permitted to live with him. The transgressor risked serious sanction, no less than the loss of his see.

COUNCIL OF TRULLO (691)

The Council of Trullo was convoked by the emperor Justinian II (685–711) with the express purpose of promulgating disciplinary decrees to complete the work of the previous ecumenical Council of Constantinople (681). Although a group of bishops from Rome was present, it was essentially a council of the Byzantine empire. The one hundred and two can-

---

53 Cf. Stickler, ibid., p. 69.   54 'As to the priests, the deacons, and the subdeacons, and all those who not having wives were enrolled into the clergy in conformity with the divine canons, we also forbid them, on the authority of the holy canons, to bring into their own homes any woman whatever, with the exception, however, of a mother, a daughter, a sister, or other female persons above all suspicion. Should anyone stray from this regulation and keep in his house a woman able to bring suspicion upon him, and after a first and second warning from his bishop or clerics requesting him not to live with such a woman, should he refuse to send her away or if somebody comes to accuse him and provides a proof that he lives in a dishonest way with that woman, his bishop will then have to demote him from the clergy, according to ecclesiastical canons, and surrender him to the council of the town where he was a cleric. As to the bishop, in no way do we permit him to have a wife or to live with her. If it is proven that he does not observe this regulation, let him be rejected from the episcopate; he himself shows that he is unworthy of the priesthood' (Imperial ordinance, dated 546; cf. Cochini, ibid., p. 365).

ons promulgated had as their primary objective the correction of abuses and the re-establishment of discipline.

There is no doubt that, as a consequence of the influences already referred to, the legislation was hostile in spirit to the Roman Church.[55] Because of the canons which were contrary to the Roman dispositions, the Pope refused to sign the acts of the Council, the first time in history that Rome formally disavowed the discipline of the Oriental Church. Yet Trullo was to determine the future of Byzantine legislation for centuries and to leave its mark on the Eastern church right down to the present day. Hence its most important decrees deserve to be considered in some detail.

Canon 3: Conditions for a married clergy   Not since Chalcedon (451) had a council faced up to disciplinary problems. In the meantime the church had tolerated many irregular marriage situations among the clergy. The purpose of Canon 3 was to restore the traditional discipline, specifically the following points:

a) the *unius uxoris vir* requirements of St Paul: this injunction excluded from orders any man who had taken a second wife after the decease of his first spouse;[56]

b) no man who had married a widow, a servant, or an actress could be accepted as a candidate for orders;[57]

c) a cleric's wife who was left a widow could not remarry.[58]

---

55 Cf. Cholij, ibid., p. 5; Stickler, ibid., p. 75.   **56** In the early Church, although second marriages were licit, they were regarded as the effect of incontinence. The Fathers of the Eastern Church took St Paul literally: 'To the unmarried and widows I say that it is well for them to remain single as I do. But if they cannot exercise self-control, they should marry. For it is better to marry than to be aflame with passion' (1 Cor 7:8–9). If therefore second marriages for lay people in the Eastern Church were tolerated rather than approved of, it is not surprising that the Church would disapprove of digamists (those who had remarried after the death of the first wife) as candidates for orders.   **57** This reflected the Levitical precept that a priest of the Old Covenant could only marry a virgin. The wife of the future priest had therefore to be a chaste virgin when entering marriage. This was the discipline of the early Church, which was a guarantee for the future chastity of their husbands who, once ordained, would have to live with their wives as brother and sister.   **58** In the Eastern and Western Churches ordination had always been considered an impediment to marriage and remarriage for the ordinand. The same was the case for a cleric's wife who was left a widow. The reason for this impediment was the fact of the wife's promise or vow of perfect chastity which was made at the time of giving her consent for the husband to be ordained.

Canon 6: Ordination an impediment to marriage   This canon forbade priests and deacons, who were ordained as single men, to marry after ordination. In addition, all clerics were forbidden to marry a second time should their first spouse die. These disciplinary norms, which still define the particular law of the Eastern Churches, bear witness to a deep concern for fidelity to the apostolic tradition. In addition, with the exception of canon 13 (which will be dealt with below), they paralleled exactly the legislation of the Latin Church.

The text of canon 6 runs as follows: 'Since it is declared in the Apostolic canons that of those who are advanced to the clergy unmarried, only lectors and cantors are able to marry, we too maintaining this determine that henceforth it is in nowise lawful for any subdeacon, deacon or presbyter after his ordination to contract matrimony, but if he shall have dared to do so, let him be deposed. And if any of those who enter the clergy wishes to be joined to a wife in lawful marriage, let it be done before he is ordained subdeacon, deacon or presbyter.'[59] This was a confirmation of the discipline affirmed at Chalcedon (451). The prohibition of marriage after the reception of orders was, in Cholij's opinion, a direct consequence of the law of continence: priests were forbidden to marry because the marriage could not be consummated.[60]

In addition to those already outlined, Cholij advances several compelling arguments to show that the prohibition on clerics marrying after ordination was due to the law of absolute continence, which leads him to the conclusion that there was a universal law of celibacy (in the broad sense) in the early Church: 'The logic of the legislation prohibiting mar-

---

59 Cholij, op. cit., p. 35.   **60** 'In the Western Church the first documents which legislate on celibacy contain no explicit prohibition of marriage after the reception of orders ... In the first pontifical documents, likewise, there is no special mention of the law prohibiting virgin clerics from contracting marriage. The reason for the omission is, however, quite obvious, given that if clerics were to be perpetually continent, once ordained, then *a fortiori* marriage could not be contracted because it could not be consummated. Given the strong preference that the early Church always had for strict (virgin) celibates [cf. *Canones ecclesiastici SS. Apostolorum*; St Jerome, *Adversus Vigilantium*, 2: PL 23, 340b–341a; St Gregory Nazianzen, *Discourse* 40: PG 36, 396b, among others], this omission would indeed otherwise appear inexplicable. The fact that writers have often confused these distinct prohibitions demonstrates how very closely they are related. It is our contention that in the Eastern Church, as much as in the Western Church, the prohibition of marriage after the reception of orders was but the direct consequence of the law of continence' (ibid., pp. 36–7). In the Justinian civil code of 535, related to the Eastern Church, priests and deacons are forbidden to marry. What is of particular interest in this document is the way a clear causal relationship between the discipline of continence and the prohibition of marriage is suggested (cf ibid., p. 38).

riage after the reception of orders indicates that, at least in the first centuries, a cleric by the fact of his ordination was "consecrated" to God with the full implications of such consecration – total continence. Ordination would be conferred if the wife agreed to this life of celibacy which she also freely chose to take upon herself.'[61] This, he claims, is the only satisfactory explanation for the impediment to clerical marriage.

Canon 12: Episcopal continence   This canon finds the Western praxis of bishops living with their wives reprehensible because of the scandal to which it could give rise. Bishops should not only be living perfect continence, but should also be seen to do so. This being so, once a man is ordained a bishop, Trullo legislated that his wife should enter a convent situated at a distance from the bishop's residence. At this time in the West the bishop's house had in fact in many places acquired a structure akin to a monastic institution, and in this way the scandal perceived by Trullo was largely theoretical. However, as a result of canon 12, the East was the first to impose the strict discipline of total physical separation of the bishop from his wife.[62]

While the Trullan legislation was to lead to a strictly celibate episcopate, it did not require that candidates for the episcopacy be monks. Yet by the second millennium this was practically the norm for all Eastern Churches. This situation arose because after Trullo the custom developed, which by the eleventh century had the force of law, that all secular clergy married before receiving orders. Those who wanted to remain celibate had to enter a monastery if they wished to be ordained.

Canon 13: Marriage of Clerics   It was however the content of canon 13,

---

61 Ibid, p.53.   **62** As we have already seen, the ground had been prepared for this innovation by the Justinian legislation of the previous century which had forbidden such cohabitation. To avoid the alienation of Church property, Justinian had prohibited the elevation of any man who was the father of a family to the episcopate. The combined effect of ecclesiastical and civil legislation was to foster the tendency to promote to the episcopal office only strict celibates.

In the West a parallel development was taking place. By the sixth century, it was considered improper for a married man with children to be ordained a bishop. This was also not unconnected with the question of possible misuse of ecclesiastical goods in relation to the bishop's family.

With time this same consideration became a determining influence in causing ecclesiastical authorities to withhold positions of responsibility, including church administration, from all married clergy, but especially those who still cohabited with their wives. The logical consequence was that strict celibacy gradually became normative for clerics in the Roman Church (cf Cholij, op. cit., pp 106–15).

limiting chastity for married men ordained as deacons or priests to a simple temporary continence, which introduced the main cleavage between the traditions of Byzantium and Rome on priestly celibacy.[63]

It is explicitly hostile to Roman custom and protests that no married cleric should be required to make a profession of continence. Cohabitation with one's wife and the use of marriage are not only strongly defended, but any alternative approach is severely punished by sanctions. Contrary to what the Trullan canon says, Rome did not view marriage as a prohibition to entering the priestly ministry. Nor did she try to dissolve the marriage bond as suggested by Trullo; rather by prescribing total continence to married clerics it raised their married life to a new level which it considered appropriate to what was required for service at the altar.

The Fathers of Trullo based their claim for temporary continence for deacons and priests 'on the ancient rule of strict observation and the apostolic discipline', as well as the Council of Carthage and the sixth Apostolic Canon. The inconsistency of their approach is underlined by the fact that they used the same tradition to deny to a bishop what they now offered to a priest.

63 The text of canon 13 is as follows: 'As we have learned that in the Church of Rome the rule was established that candidates, before receiving ordination as deacon or priest, make a public promise not to have relations anymore with their wives; we, conforming ourselves to the ancient rule of strict observation and apostolic discipline, want the legitimate marriages of consecrated men to remain in effect even in the future, without dissolving the bond uniting these men to their wives, nor depriving them of mutual relations at the appropriate times. In such a way, if someone is deemed worthy to be ordained subdeacon, deacon or priest, let him not be prevented from growing in this dignity because he has a legitimate wife, and neither should it be demanded that he promise, at the time of his ordination, to abstain from legitimate relations with his own wife; for otherwise we would insult marriage, which was instituted by God and blessed by his presence, while the voice of the Gospel calls to us: "let no man put asunder those whom God has united", and the Apostle teaches: "Let marriage be respected by all and the conjugal bed be without stain", and again: "Are you tied to a wife by the bonds of marriage? Then do not seek to break them".

'On the other hand, we know that the Fathers gathered at Carthage, as a precautionary measure because of the seriousness of the morals of the ministers of the altar, decided that "the subdeacons, who touch the sacred mysteries, the deacons and the priests too, should abstain from their wives during the periods that are specifically assigned to them, ... thus we also will keep what was taught by the apostles and observed since antiquity, knowing that there is a time for everything, especially for fasting and prayer; it is indeed necessary that those who approach the altar, when they touch holy things, be continent in every respect so that they can obtain in all simplicity what they are asking from God". If, therefore, anyone, acting against the apostolic canons, dares deprive a cleric in sacred Orders - i.e. a priest, a deacon, or a subdeacon - from conjugal relations and the society of his wife, let him be deposed; in the same way, "if a priest or deacon sends away his wife with the excuse of piety, let him be excommunicated, and if he persists, deposed"' (cf. Cochini, ibid., p. 405).

What is also surprising is the reference to the Council of Carthage. While the decrees of the African Councils are used by the Byzantine Fathers as an anchor point with antiquity, a comparison of the parallel passages in the Trullan and Carthaginian canons shows that: a) while Carthage legislates for *total* continence for married clerics, Trullo inexplicably makes it read *temporary* continence; b) the decrees of Carthage are applied to bishops, priests and deacons, yet in the Trullan canon the reference to bishops has disappeared.[64]

Cholij is of the opinion that the redactors of canon 13 of Trullo were aware they were citing the Carthaginian canons in a partial and selective sense which changed their meaning.[65] What in fact the Trullan Fathers proposed for priests was the discipline of periodic marital continence practised by all lay married Christians in the early Church, in line with the Pauline admonition in 1 Corinthians 7:5.

Although the Trullan legislation introduced a major difference between Byzantium and Rome on the issue of priestly celibacy, it is noteworthy that both agree on the apostolic origin of the duty of continence (temporary or perpetual) imposed on the ministers of the altar. To be worthy ministers of the divine mysteries and effective mediators for the people through prayer, they are bound to abstain from sexual relations. It also merits attention that both East and West did not consider it possible to justify the difficult discipline of priestly chastity except in relation to a mandate from the apostles themselves.

---

64 Cholij points to an anomaly in relation to canons 12 and 13 of Trullo. Although the Fathers of Trullo gave separate consideration to bishops in the matter of celibacy as compared with priests and deacons, in the writings of the Church Fathers and the documents of the early councils they are all considered together in this context. While it is true that bishops have the fullness of the priesthood and were considered under special obligation to live the virtues to the full, especially as regards chastity, yet in terms of strict sacerdotal functions of celebrating the Eucharistic sacrifice and acting as mediators between God and men, the bishop's dignity was no greater than that of the ordinary priest. Hence Cholij concludes to the doctrinal inconsistency between canons 12 and 13 of Trullo as expressed by the different disciplines. The Pauline exhortation (1 Cor 7:33) was the classic text used in the Church to defend and promote virginity and priestly celibacy. Greek commentators also used it to explain the celibacy of bishops but, in the light of Trullo 13, could not apply it to other clerics (cf. Cholij, op. cit., pp 110–11). **65** Cf. ibid., p. 121. Stickler reaches the same conclusion – cf. op. cit., pp 75– 6. At the same time he considers that the attitude and approach of the Trullan Fathers to the question of celibacy constitute a not unimportant argument that the tradition of the Western Catholic Church remains the authentic one. This tradition, he affirms categorically 'can be traced back to the apostles and is founded on the living consciousness of the entire early Church' (ibid., p. 77).

CONSEQUENCE OF TRULLO FOR WESTERN CANON LAW

Since the prohibition of clerical marriage was due to the obligation to live in total continence, whether the cleric was married or not, the discipline introduced by canon 13 of Trullo, which permitted priests to have conjugal life, created for the first time in legislative form a rupture between the prohibition on clerical marriage and its cause. This had serious consequences for later canonical theory when a reason was sought to justify the fact of orders being an impediment to marriage. Gratian, the famous twelfth century canonist, uncritically accepted canon 13 of Trullo as ecumenical and, as a consequence, not only accepted but legitimised the Oriental praxis regarding celibacy and established it as being of apostolic origin. The effect of Gratian's presentation of the Eastern discipline of celibacy was to make it impossible to establish a cause and effect relationship between the law of continence and the *impedimentum ordinis*. Decretists recognised the difference in disciplines between East and West and tried to accommodate it in a canonical theory which would explain the law of celibacy in the Latin Church. This inevitably led to the conclusion that the law forbidding marriage, and still more the law imposing continence on married clerics, had been introduced in the West at a fairly late date.[66]

Because they accepted uncritically the Greek texts presented by Gratian, the canonists of the twelfth century failed to see the immediate (and necessary) relationship between continence and the impediment to marriage. Canonical theory during the period developed an explanation of the impediment to marriage constituted by orders deriving mainly from the theory of the *votum*, or the *votum adnexum*, the vow of chastity attached to orders.[67] Nevertheless, this theory ran into difficulties because of its inability to explain the impediment from the point of view of the Greeks whose priests were not bound by any vow of continence.

This anomaly gave rise to another canonical theory towards the end of the twelfth century, which grounded the obligation to continence on ecclesiastical law. In the thirteenth century St Thomas synthesises the view of the different canonists as follows:

> But what impedes matrimony is the law of the Church. However, it binds the Latins in a different way from the Greeks; for among the Greeks the impediment to contracting marriage comes solely from

---

66 Cf. Cholij, ibid., p. 64. See also Stickler, ibid., pp 45–8   **67** Cf. ibid, p. 65.

the force of orders (*vi ordinis*) whereas among the Latins the impediment is both from the force of orders and from the vow of continence which is attached to sacred orders; so that if someone verbally does not take the vow, by the very fact of his receiving the order according to the rite of the Western Church it is understood that he has taken it. And again, among the Greeks and other Orientals holy orders impedes the contracting of marriage but not the use of previously contracted marriage, for they can use this marriage even though they cannot contract marriage again.[68]

From the time of the Second Lateran Council (1139) sacred orders, as well as the *votum*, were considered to be an invalidating impediment to marriage. Cholij's conclusion is that if the canonists and theologians of the twelfth and thirteenth centuries had not been presented with the difficulty of the Greek discipline, legitimised by Gratian, it is quite conceivable they would have had little difficulty in attributing the law of continence to the Apostles and of relating the impediment to marriage to this law alone. Any promise or vow of continence would then have been understood to be an external expression and guarantee of a commitment freely taken, but demanded by the very nature of the priestly vocation at the time of the reception of orders.[69]

In his elucidation of this conclusion Cholij poses the question: How can one sacrament render another invalid on the basis of a purely ecclesiastical law? His response is that unless a consecrating pact between the cleric and God is effected at the time of the reception of orders, then the law prohibiting marriage can only be regarded as a 'vestigial positive discipline expressing that simpler ancient discipline which harmonised the natural relation which exists between the priesthood and celibacy'. And so he concludes that the impediment to marriage in the Oriental canonical discipline, detached from its theological grounding, appears little more than juridical formalism.[70]

THE COMPULSORY MARRIAGE OF PRIESTS

While Trullo did not in fact forbid celibacy in the strict sense for priests, the tone of the canons was such that priests were expected to be married and to live conjugal life like the rest of the lay faithful. By the eleventh and

---

68 *Summa Theologiae, Suppl.*, 53, 3.   **69** Cf. Cholij, ibid., p. 67.   **70** Cf. ibid., p. 68.

twelfth centuries this counsel had in fact become a precept, and celibacy as known in the Latin rite for priests and deacons was definitively rejected.

This was at a time in the Western church when immorality among the clergy was such that it precipitated the Gregorian reform. Although both Greek and Latin traditions identified the need to eradicate the corruption of sexual morals among the clergy, the means used to do so in each case were very different. Rome did not consider celibacy itself to be the source of the problem. On the contrary, it confirmed the traditional discipline, but in addition it introduced new measures to protect the dignity of the clerical state and the chastity expected of ministers of the altar. The solutions applied were ascetical and disciplinary. Incontinence and infraction of this discipline were severely punished.[71]

Because of abuses in the Greek church in the ninth century, the Byzantine emperor Leo VI legislated to suspend the custom, which had developed since Trullo, of those in major orders reserving to themselves the right to marry within two years of ordination, reaffirming the prohibition on marriage after the conferring of orders. Clerics were either to remain celibate or, if they wished to marry, they had to do so before ordination.

Still, because of illegal marriages after ordination, by the eleventh century the Eastern church prohibited men being ordained to the secular clergy if they were unmarried. It was, as Cholij points out, from the perspective of the *remedium concupiscentiae* that marriage was considered a suitable state for the priesthood. Celibates who wished to be ordained had to enter a monastery. In this way all priests who lived in village parishes were required to be married, and their sons were expected to follow them into the priestly state. This practice was reinforced in some countries by the state providing special schools for sons of priests.[72] One of the consequences of this is the lack of emphasis on the supernatural aspect of the priestly vocation. Another is that all the higher positions in the Eastern Church are reserved for celibate monks who are generally better trained, as well as being free from family ties. It is not surprising, then, that a system which effectively accommodated two priestly castes gave rise to its own particular problems.[73]

The logic of a situation which effectively imposed marriage on its clerics inevitably had implications for widower priests and deacons. By the fourteenth century a discipline had become well established by which

71 Cf. Stickler, 'The Evolution and Discipline of Celibacy', pp 544ff.   **72** In Greece since 1923 civil law prohibits celibates from being appointed as parochial clergy; cf. Cholij, op. cit., p. 137.   **73** Cf. ibid.

they were forced to abandon their ministry. If they wished to continue as priests they had to enter a monastery. One of the consequences of this legislation was that it led to the overcrowding of monasteries by clerics who were there involuntarily or had no monastic vocation. This often resulted in serious problems of discipline and a decline in the vitality of monastic life.[74] However, a Moscow synod in the seventeenth century abrogated the decrees forbidding widowers to practise their ministry, and subsequently went on to allow them to marry a second time.

When the Ukrainian Orthodox church reunited with Rome in 1595, the law which prohibited celibates from being ordained, and which dismissed priest and deacon widowers from their pastoral ministry, were abrogated as these were considered grave abuses which were in complete opposition to the discipline of the Catholic Church. In synods of the Oriental Catholic Churches, especially during the eighteenth and nineteenth centuries, strict celibacy was promoted and encouraged as the preferred state for candidates for the secular priesthood.

CONSEQUENCES OF TRULLO FOR THE THEOLOGY OF THE PRIESTHOOD

The Trullan legislation had significant consequences from the point of view of the availability of a frequent liturgical service for the faithful. Canon 13 of Trullo prescribed continence for times of prayer and fasting, and liturgical service. The general norm was one day's abstinence during times of liturgical service, apart from the times of prayer and fasting to which all married people were bound. By the seventeenth century three days abstinence was expected. Hence daily Mass could not be celebrated as it was always assumed that priests used their conjugal rights.[75]

In the Carthaginian canons, and in general in the legislation of the

---

74 Cf. ibid., p. 141. **75** There are, however, no norms predating Trullo on temporary continence for clerics. On the other hand the Church during the first centuries was concerned to give prescriptions for temporary continence for married lay people. Cholij argues that the apparent deliberate legislative silence before Trullo as regards clerics, who were of more immediate concern to the Church, leads to the conclusion that there was in fact a very distinct discipline for them, that is total continence.

In the early centuries there are several indications that the practice in the Eastern Churches was frequent, if not a daily, celebration of the Eucharist. Still, this frequency was later reduced to celebrations at weekends and on feastdays. While there may have been other influences at work in bringing about this change, the discipline of temporary continence certainly disfavoured more frequent celebrations and made daily celebration, as a regular feature, impossible (cf Cholij, ibid., p.157).

Western Church, priests were bound to continence because of their consecration. This consecration was essentially related to their role as mediator, expressed above all in the administration of the sacraments, but also in any other act which could be understood as an exercise of the consecrated ministry. As a result, continence in the Latin rite was not simply a function of the Eucharistic ministry, but was rather a cogent expression of the special nature of the priest's total ministry of mediatorship. As early as the fourth century, theology and legislation in the Western Church understood the priesthood as a continuous and uninterrupted ministry, which provided an argument for perpetual continence. It is because the priesthood of the New testament has surpassed that of the Old Covenant that continence has to be perpetual rather than temporary.[76]

On the other hand, the Trullan legislation seems to imply that the priestly ministry is exercised only in the Eucharistic liturgy to which the discipline of continence is related. This suggests an understanding of the priesthood in functional rather than in ontological terms, and therefore a change of emphasis in the theology of the priesthood. It is in a certain sense a return to the Levitical concept of priesthood.

TEMPORARY CONTINENCE AND THE INTRODUCTION OF CELIBACY

From the perspective of celibacy it is instructive to consider the cases of different Oriental Churches who returned to unity with Rome over the past few hundred years. In the sixteenth century when the Albanians of the Greek rite sought unity, and again in the case of the Maronites in the eighteenth century, Rome respected the existing customs of temporary continence. The same applied to the Armenians, the Chaldeans and the Ukrainians, even though their laws precluded the possibility of the daily celebration of the Eucharist. Nevertheless, in these Oriental churches there were often requests from the faithful for a daily liturgy, especially in the larger towns. To facilitate this, Rome would not relax the norms of temporary continence, and so the only solution was to increase the number of celibates ordained in these churches. Thus the conflict between the discipline of temporary continence and frequent liturgical celebration was a very important factor in the movement to introduce strict celibacy in the Catholic Eastern Churches.

---

76 Cf. Decretals of Pope Siricius in 385 and 386; Synod of Rome Decree (*c*.400) and other sources quoted by Cochini, ibid., pp 6–17.

Local synods of these churches favoured celibates for important ecclesiastical appointments, because it was recognised that the responsibilities
of the married priest were such that they could not give the full dedication
required by these appointments. Although slow to set up their own seminaries to provide for the formation of a celibate clergy, some of these
churches began to send seminarians to the Urbanianum University in Rome
in the seventeenth and eighteenth centuries. There were still sociological
prejudices against a celibate clergy in these churches, but in general the
Oriental hierarchies pressed ahead with this task.

The question of celibacy in the Oriental Catholic Churches was discussed at Vatican I. The preparatory study document for the Council
indicated that the Oriental bishops in general were in favour of celibacy
for their own priests. In one of the Council debates (February 1870) an
Armenian archbishop said that the absence of a law of celibacy in the
Eastern churches was a real 'wound', because experience had shown the
grave ills that resulted in the life of the church as a consequence. Therefore he requested that the problems due to a lack of a celibate clergy be
openly discussed so that the wounds could be healed more quickly.[77]

Even so, it was decided by a commission of the Council that the Oriental churches were not yet sufficiently 'mature' to accept a complete law
of celibacy. Nevertheless an instruction was published which affirmed the
prohibition of marriage on those already ordained, and which recalled the
pre-Trullan discipline of perpetual clerical continence in those churches
where effective episcopal authority had been maintained.

Subsequent to Vatican I, various synods of the Oriental Catholic
churches used this instruction as a basis for legislating on clerical celibacy.
In fact by the end of the nineteenth century, the discipline of clerical
continence in the Eastern Uniate Churches had reverted to the praxis of
the early centuries in the Western church. Experience of the Trullan and
post-Trullan law of temporary clerical continence had taught the Oriental
churches that this discipline led to an unresolvable conflict where the
priesthood was considered as a daily ministry and one requiring a total
dedication to the church. As we have already seen, the Latin church had
its own problems with a married clergy, which were only satisfactorily
resolved when strict celibacy became the norm after the Gregorian reform
and the legislation of the Council of Trent. From the seventeenth century
the Eastern churches in union with Rome began to follow the same evo-
lutionary path along the road to strict celibacy.

77 Cf. Cholij, ibid., p.175.

2

Scriptural Foundations for Celibacy

In its teaching on divine revelation, Vatican II reminds us that there is a constant growth and development in our understanding of Sacred Scripture. This comes about in different ways – through the study and contemplation of the sacred text by believers, from the working of grace in the souls of Christians, and by the preaching of those who possess the sure charism of truth as successors of the apostles.[1] Paul VI, in his encyclical on priestly celibacy, referring to this very teaching of the Council, affirms that a consideration of these principles is necessary to allow us understand more profoundly the various reasons offered for celibacy, in different situations and by different mentalities.[2] Biblical exegesis, guided by the Magisterium, has helped to disclose the deeper implications of particular texts, and has demonstrated the mutual coherence between different passages of Scripture which refer to celibacy. This is to be expected since one of the basic principles of biblical hermeneutics is the unity of the message of Scripture as a whole.[3]

While there are a number of biblical texts which describe the spiritual and theological value of virginity or celibacy *in genere*, at first sight there does not appear to be any specific text which directly links celibacy with the ministers of the Church. Indeed the contrary might seem to be the case from a superficial reading of the Pastoral letters, in which St Paul deals with the qualities required in those appointed as bishops, priests or deacons. A candidate for a position of ministry in the Church should, he stipulates, be 'the husband of one wife' (cf. 1 Tim 3:2; Tit 1:6; 1 Tim 3:12). On closer examination, however, we will see that these texts establish an immediate connection between perpetual continence and the ministerial priesthood.[4]

At the same time, the scriptural validation of priestly celibacy derives more from the convergence of meaning of a number of different texts,

---

1 Cf. dogmatic constitution, *Dei verbum*, 8. See also the Pontifical Biblical Commission document, *The Interpretation of the Bible in the Church*, Section III: Characteristics of Catholic Interpretation, 15 April 1993.   2 Cf. *Sacerdotalis caelibatus*, 18, referring to *Dei verbum*, 8.
3 Cf. *Dei verbum*, 12.   4 Cf. Ignace de la Potterie, 'The Biblical Foundation of Priestly Celibacy' in *For Love Alone: Reflections on Priestly Celibacy*, Maynooth, 1993, p. 14.

and the cumulative thrust of their signification, rather than from the pro-bative value of individual texts. The different insights drawn from various scriptural passages, as understood by Tradition and proposed by the Magisterium, constitute the biblical case for priestly celibacy.[5] The Church has never claimed that this case is a definitive one, but it consistently refers to particular texts as an affirmation of the intimate congruence between the charism of celibacy and the exercise of the priestly ministry *in persona Christi* (in the person of Christ). In this chapter we will examine the more important of these texts.[6]

Because of the unity of Scripture as a whole, and bearing in mind that the New Testament is the fulfilment of the Old,[7] to arrive at a deeper appreciation of the full biblical meaning of celibacy, it will be instructive to review references and institutions in the Old Testament which prefig-ure in some way the celibacy of the new dispensation. Some arguments for celibacy see the temporary continence of the Levitical priesthood as a prefiguring of the total continence which would be required of Christ's priests. Consequently, a consideration of the Temple priesthood as a bib-lical institution will provide a background against which to review the cultic argument for celibacy.

History confirms that, in the early centuries of Christianity, there was a strong supernatural motivation, among men and women, to commit themselves totally to God through virginity or celibacy. It is clear from the teachings of Popes and the writings of the Fathers that this ascetical devel-opment had a positive influence in defining the continence of priests in the nascent Church. We will therefore examine the biblical grounding for consecrated virginity with a view to throwing more light on the commit-ment to priestly continence. Nevertheless, while there may be common elements in the theological justification for virginity and priestly celibacy, it has to be remembered that these two separate vocational currents in the

---

5 Cf. *Dei verbum*, 9 on the relationship between Scripture, the living Tradition of the Church, and the Magisterium. See also *Instruction on the Ecclesial Vocation of the Theologian*, nos. 13–24, published by the Congregation for the Doctrine of the Faith, 24 May 1990.   6 A review of the significant documents of the Magisterium on priestly celibacy since the beginning of the century shows that the following texts are consistently referred to: Lev 8:33–35; Mt 19:10–12; Mt 22:30; 1 Cor 7:7; 1 Cor 7:25–33; 2 Cor 11:2; Eph 5:25–32. Thus, for example, we find in Vatican II (*Lumen gentium*, 42; *Presbyterorum ordinis*, 16) the following references: Lk 20:35–36; Mt 19:11–12; 1 Cor 7:7; 1 Cor 7:32–34; 2 Cor 11:2; in *Sacerdotalis caelibatus*: Mt 19:11; Mt 22:30; 1 Cor 7:29–31; 1 Cor 7:32–33; Eph 5: 25–27; in *Pastores dabo vobis*: Mt 19:11; 1 Cor 7:7; 1 Cor 7:32–34; in the *Catechism of the Catholic Church*: Mt 19:12; 1 Cor 7:32.   7 This principle is best summed up by St Augustine's well known dictum: 'The New Testament lies hidden in the Old, and the Old becomes clear in the New' (cf. *Quaest. in Hept.*, 2, 73: CSEL 28, III, 3, p. 141).

Church had their origins in different ascetical traditions – one was inspired by the evangelical counsels, while the other derives from the function of mediation exercised by the priest *in persona Christi*.[8] We will study the main texts of the New Testament on virginity and celibacy and see how Christ, followed by St Paul, opened up a whole new horizon with their teaching in this area by comparison with the traditions of the Old Testament.

In addition, there are two groups of texts in the Pauline corpus which have a fundamental significance for priestly celibacy. The first is the 'husband of one wife' (*unius uxoris vir*) stipulation in the Pastoral letters as a condition for ordination, a text to which we have already referred. The second group constitutes those texts which illustrate the covenantal aspect of priestly celibacy (cf. 2 Cor 11:2; Eph 5:25–27). This will also involve a consideration of the relationship between marriage and virginity as seen in both the Old and the New Testaments.

Nevertheless, above and beyond the textual support for priestly celibacy, there is the Gospel witness to the celibacy of Jesus himself, God become a priest in the humanity of Christ. This is the most powerful of all scriptural statements in favour of priestly celibacy, the significance of which we will review here from a biblical perspective, and, in subsequent chapters, from the theological and ascetical points of view.

OLD TESTAMENT ATTITUDES

When Christ raised the question of celibacy (cf. Mt 19:3–12), he was speaking to men steeped in the Old Testament tradition where no ideal of celibacy had been handed on. Marriage was not only the common state of life but, through the promise made to Abraham, it had acquired a consecrated significance. Marriage as a source of fruitfulness and descendants was *'a religiously privileged state:* and privileged by revelation itself'.[9] Thus

---

8 A feature of the early Church was that many ordinary lay people lived a life of commitment to God in this way. It wasn't until the third or fourth century that the beginnings of religious life, as reflected in public consecration to virginity and the development of separate communities, took shape. Cf. K. Bihlmeyer and H. Tüchle, *Church History*, I, Westminster, 1968, pp 138–9, 360–2; H. Daniel-Rops, *The Church of the Apostles and Martyrs*, London, 1963, pp 232–3; Philip Hughes, *History of the Church*, I, London, 1947, pp 138–43.
9 John Paul II, Address, 17 March 1982, no. 3 (italics in original). In September 1979 John Paul II began a series of addresses on human sexuality. A number of these are devoted to the topic of priestly celibacy, and we will make reference to some of them in this chapter.

we find little of the tradition of celibacy as we know it today in the Old Testament. Nevertheless, since what was disclosed in Christ completed and perfected what was revealed to Israel, it is only natural that this charism would be prefigured in some way in the Old Testament. Some of the arguments for clerical continence, especially in the early Church, were clearly influenced by Jewish cultic and other traditions. Let us review the relevant aspects of this background.

In the Old Testament, where special emphasis was laid on the holiness of God, the contrast between 'clean' and 'unclean' was sharply drawn. The phenomena connected with sex were considered to bring about cultic uncleanness (cf. Lev 12:5; 1 Sam 21:5; 2 Sam 11:4) which excluded the subject from communion with Yahweh. Hence the priest who had incurred sexual uncleanness was thereby disqualified from normal priestly activities (cf. Lev 21:1–15). Certain purificatory rites were required to get rid of the particular defilement. This led to a type of exterior moral formalism which the prophets inveighed against, urging interior purity of mind and heart (cf. Hos 6:6; Amos 4:1–5; Is 6:5; Jer 13:27).

In the New Testament the idea of ritual cleanness was replaced by Christ's preaching on inner purity of heart (cf. Mk 7:1–23; Mt 15:1–20). It is what comes out of the heart of man that defiles him (cf. Mk 7:21–23). So the clean of heart are those who are blessed (cf. Mt 5:8), and purification is obtained through sacramental liberation from sin.

The notion that the sexual relationship in marriage might cause uncleanness in the *moral* sense (that is, include an element of sinfulness) is, in fact, foreign to the Bible. Such ideas, however, did circulate in early Christianity and were the result of a certain intermingling of the two distinct biblical concepts of *cultic* and *moral* uncleanness, coupled with the influence of Jewish ceremonial law on the theology of the young Church. In the development of the concept of celibacy in the Church we can detect elements of this influence (cf. Lev 15:18; 22:4; Ex 19:15).[10]

They have all been published in the English language edition of *Osservatore Romano*, and are also available from St Paul Editions (Boston): *The Theology of Marriage and Celibacy*, 1986.   10 Johannes Bauer, ed., *Encyclopaedia of Biblical Theology*, I, London, 1970, pp 118–20.

JEREMIAH'S CELIBACY

In the Old Testament context God used not only the words of the prophets but also events in their lives to transmit his revelation (cf. Hos 1–3; Ezek 24:15–27). Thus Jeremiah's celibacy conveyed a special message to the Jews, who considered a large family as a divine blessing (cf. Gen 22:17; Ps 127:3–4), and sterility a great misfortune (cf. Gen 30:1; 1 Sam 1:6–8). He lived at the most tragic period of Israel's history when Jerusalem was destroyed by Nebuchadnezzar and the inhabitants carried off into captivity.

Jeremiah remained celibate, not on the basis of personal preference, but because of a command he received from God (cf. Jer 16:3–4). In the context of the time it symbolised Yahweh's withdrawal of the covenantal blessing: peace, love, and all the virtues of an ideal married life which Jeremiah was forbidden to experience.[11] God commanded Jeremiah to be celibate not because it was better than marriage, but because in the days of starvation and destruction which would accompany the siege and fall of Jerusalem, he would be spared the anguish of witnessing the suffering of a wife and children. His celibacy was, consequently, a symbolic act declaring the imminence of Israel's chastisement, in which women and children would be slaughtered (cf. Jer 16:3, 10–13).

Jeremiah, under the influence of his predecessor Hosea, had a deep appreciation of the covenantal bonding between Yahweh and his people, a love symbolised by that which unites a man and woman in marriage. From his own words we know that he was a peace-loving man sent by God, against his inclinations, to rebuke kings, accuse his fellow Jews of infidelity to the covenant, and draw on himself scorn, contempt and the hatred of his enemies. He predicted God's judgement on his people; he tried to make them see that God loved them even when he chastised them. Yet, when he realised that Israel was not responding to God, that destruction was inevitable and that the old covenant was finished, he held out the promise of a new covenant (cf. Jer 31:31–34).

Apart from the example of Jeremiah, it is known that in the circle of the Essenes there was a tradition of celibacy, as ancient authors like Josephus, Philo, and Pliny testify. How extensive was this practice among them? There was a select group who were admitted after a period of three years to test their continence, but there were others who were married. Qumran was a celibate community of the Essenes, as the discovery of male skel-

---

11 Cf. *The New Jerome Biblical Commentary*, London, 1989, p. 280.

etons only, in the main Qumran burial ground, attest. It would seem that their commitment to celibacy was not uninfluenced by Gnostic dualism.

Philo also mentions the Theraputae, a celibate community of men and women living outside of Alexandria. Their piety and communal practices resembled that of celibate Essenes, with whom there may have been some connection.[12]

VIRGINITY A MISFORTUNE

In the Old Testament the value of virginity related to the idea that young girls should remain inviolate until they married (cf. Gen 24:16; 34:7; Judg 19:24). It also had a value from the point of view of cultic purity. Loss of virginity entailed loss of honour (cf. 2 Sam 13:2–18; Lam 5:11; Sir 42:9–11). All priests were required to marry a virgin (cf. Lev 21:13f, Ezek 44:22).

Virginity as a life-long state was unknown. Far from being a desirable condition, not to marry was regarded as the greatest misfortune (cf. Judg 11:37f). In later Judaism, however, there are some indications that the unmarried state was regarded in a more positive light (cf. Jud 16:22). At the dawn of the new dispensation we see that Anna refuses marriage in order to adhere more closely to God (cf. Lk 2:37).

Nevertheless, the real preparation for Christian virginity is to be found in the context of the promises and the covenant. By the mysterious economy of sterile women whom he makes fertile, as in the case of Sarah (cf. Gen 21), Rachel (cf. Gen 30) and Hannah (cf. 1 Sam 1–2), God wished to point out that the bearers of the promises have not been raised up by the normal procedure of fruitfulness, but by his infinitely powerful intervention. The gratuitousness of his choice is revealed in this discreet preference accorded to the sterile.[13]

THE NUPTIAL MYSTERY

By comparison with the Old Testament, the eschatological witness of virginity was a marked characteristic of the New Covenant, a testimony to the future, definitive state of man in eternity. But marriage was also transformed by the nuptial mystery of Christ and his Church. From the

---

12 Cf. ibid., p. 1075. See also *The Oxford Companion to the Bible*, Oxford, 1993, pp 393–4.
13 Cf. Xavier Léon-Dufour, SJ, *Dictionary of Biblical Theology*, London, 1970, pp 557–9.

time of Christ, the virgin Israel is called the Church. Believers who wish to remain virgins share in the virginity of the Church. Virginity is an essentially eschatological reality and assumes its full meaning only in the final fulfilment of the Messianic nuptials. As in the Old Testament, the motive of virginity, paradoxically enough, goes back to the idea of espousal; for the union of Christ and the Church is a virginal union though symbolised by marriage: 'Christ loved the Church and delivered himself for her' (Eph 5:25). The Church of Corinth was engaged to Christ, so Paul wants to present her to him as an immaculately pure virgin (cf. 2 Cor 11:2, Eph 5:27).

The virginity of the Church crystallises at the point of fusion between the two covenants, that is, in Mary the virgin mother of Christ. Through Joseph, his legal father, Jesus inherits the promises made throughout the Old Testament. Mary, on the other hand, is the beginning of the New Testament through a motherhood bestowed through the action of the Holy Spirit.[14]

Jesus' life of celibacy revealed the true meaning and the supernatural character of virginity. It is not a command (cf. 1 Cor 7:25) but a personal call from God (cf. Mt 19:12; 1 Cor 7:25). Only in relation to the kingdom of heaven can virginity or celibacy be justified, and only those who have been given this charism can identify with it (cf. Mt 19:11).

Christ's explanation of celibacy ('for the sake of the kingdom of heaven') reveals its essentially eschatological character. The married state is intimately related to the present time (cf. 1 Cor 7:31). As a permanent manifestation of the Church's virginity, the lives of celibates and virgins testify that we do not have here a lasting city. Celibacy became a major life-style choice for men and women in the early Church and, by the third and fourth centuries, segregated communities of men and women celibates had developed.[15]

FRIEND OF THE BRIDEGROOM

The ministry of John the Baptist, the last of the prophets, straddles the period of the Old and the New Covenant and is thus unique in biblical terms. John's mission was inextricably linked with that of Christ, a point which is underscored by Luke's account of the parallelism between the

14 Cf. Archbishop Desmond Connell, 'The Fruitful Virginity of Mary', *Position Papers*, no. 173, Dublin, May 1988, pp 149–58. 15 Cf. note 8.

infancy of both and the events which surrounded them. Although he was not a priest of the New Law, his whole life was given over to being the voice of Christ,[16] preparing souls for conversion and the grace of the Saviour. He also had the privilege of pointing out Christ to his own disciples, and was therefore instrumental in bringing about the apostolic vocations of Andrew and John and Peter (cf. Jn 1:35–42).

The Church has always seen a particular appropriateness about John's celibacy, for it was he who described himself as 'the friend of the bridegroom' (Jn 3:29), using that very nuptial symbolism which is a fundamental dimension of the theology of celibacy. The Precursor is therefore seen as the inheritor of the prophetic tradition of the nuptials between Yahweh and his people, which was really a preparation for Christian virginity. By the manner of his dying (cf. Mk 6:14–29), he also gave witness to what John Paul II has often emphasised – how celibacy throws light on the sanctity of the marriage bond.[17]

The English bishop, St John Fisher, made the same point in his defence of the validity of Queen Catherine's marriage to Henry VIII at the onset of the Reformation. The Baptist's martyrdom had long been a familiar subject of contemplation for Fisher. 'One consideration,' he writes, 'that greatly affects me to believe in the sacrament of marriage is the martyrdom of St John the Baptist, who suffered death for his reproof of the violation of marriage. There were many crimes in appearance more grievous for rebuking which he might have suffered, but there was none more fitting than the crime of adultery to be the cause of the blood-shedding of the Friend of the Bridegroom, since the violation of marriage is no little insult to Him who is called the Bridegroom.'[18] History was to repeat itself in the case of the intrepid bishop of Rochester, who suffered judicial murder at Henry's instigation rather than condone the king's adulterous marriage with Anne Boleyn.

CHRIST PREACHES ON CELIBACY

When Christ called his first apostles to make them 'fishers of men' (Mt 4:19; Mk 1:17), they 'left everything and followed him' (Lk 5:11; cf. Mt 4:20, 22; Mk 1:18, 20). It was Peter who recalled this aspect of the apostolic vocation when one day, with characteristic frankness, he said to Jesus

---

16 Cf. St Augustine, *Senno* 293, 1–3; PL 38, 1327ff.   **17** Cf. Apostolic Exhortation, *Familiaris consortio*, 22 November 1981, no. 16.   **18** T.E. Bridgett, *Life of Blessed John Fisher*, London, 1890, p. 175 (translation of extract from Fisher's *Defensio Regiae Assertionis*).

'we have left everything and followed you' (Mt 19:27) and asked what the rewards would be. The Master in his reply opened up unexpected horizons of self-giving. His call envisaged that his disciples would leave behind home, property, and loved ones – family, wife, children – 'for my name's sake' (Mt 19:29; cf. Lk 18:29–30). Indeed, on another occasion he makes the same point in even more demanding language: 'Whoever loves father or mother more than me is not worthy of me' (Mt 10:37), all pointing to the fact that practical renunciation is an essential element of the apostolic vocation. This clear scriptural doctrine, John Paul II has pointed out, provides the context for Christ's teaching on celibacy.[19]

From St Matthew we see that Christ recommends celibacy in the same setting in which he affirms the indissolubility of marriage (cf. 19:10–12). The disciples had reacted strongly to Christ's forbidding a man to put away his wife: 'If such is the case of a man with his wife', then, they concluded, 'it is not expedient to marry' (19:10). Christ's reply was challenging:

> Not all men can receive this precept, but only those to whom it is given. For there are eunuchs who have been so from birth, and there are eunuchs who have been made eunuchs by men, and there are eunuchs who have made themselves eunuchs for the sake of the kingdom of heaven. He who is able to receive this, let him receive it. (19:11–12)

As Jean Galot points out, this text has a marked Semitic structure, similar to other *logia* of Jesus in the Sermon on the Mount. Yet, in the context of the contemporary Jewish mentality, the idea is a complete innovation.[20] The eunuch, born thus or made so, was an outcast, denied by Jewish law the right to bring offerings to the Temple (cf. Lev 21:17–20), and excluded from the assembly of Yahweh (cf. Deut 23:2), because it seemed improper that a person deprived of the power of transmitting life would associate with the God of life.[21] There are, however, words of praise for

19 Cf. Address, 17 July 1993. 20 'This saying is traceable to words spoken by Jesus himself. Its form exhibits a marked Semitic colouring, and its structure discloses an ascending rhythm in three steps found elsewhere, as in markedly Semitic *logia* embodied in the Sermon on the Mount (cf. Mt 5:22; 5:39–41). There is also an opening admonition and a matching warning at the end. In vocabulary and style, we note expressions similar to those current among the Jews. Yet, compared to the Jewish mentality of the day, the idea is new, and the way of expressing it is paradoxical, which is an index of authenticity. In a genuinely Semitic idiom, a revolutionary thought is being expressed' (*Theology of the Priesthood*, San Francisco, 1986, p. 232). 21 Some Israelites were castrated for working with the harem of Israelite or foreign kings (cf. 2 Kings 9:32; Esther 2:3; 4:4–5).

the eunuch who does no evil and who is faithful to the covenant (cf. Wis 3:14; Is 56:3).

But Christ goes further than merely show benevolence. He dares to portray eunuchry as a freely chosen state, something unthinkable for Jews, who look on marriage and the procreation of children as a religious obligation, and who considered lack of descendants as one of the greatest misfortunes. In trying to explain why Jesus would use the pejorative word 'eunuch', some exegetes suggest that this was probably because Jesus' enemies had used it about him and his disciples to chide them on their renunciation of marriage. Jewish tradition regarded a celibate as somebody less than a man.[22]

CELIBACY A TURNING POINT IN SALVATION HISTORY

Consequently, from the perspective of the Old Testament, Christ's affirmation of celibacy for a supernatural motive marks a decisive turning point in salvation history. It points, as John Paul II reminds us, to 'the eschatological "virginity" of the risen man, in whom will be revealed the absolute and eternal nuptial meaning of the glorified body in union with God himself'.[23] Hence, earthly continence for the sake of the Kingdom is a testimony to the truth that the end of the body is not the grave, but glorification, and in this sense it anticipates a future resurrection (cf. Rom 8:22–23).

Ultimately celibacy derives from the will of Christ as manifested in the Gospel. The link between celibacy and priesthood was first established in him, which shows that, in its most perfect realisation, the priesthood involves the renunciation of marriage.

Christ's celibacy was appropriate to his universal love and his spiritual engendering of a new humanity. It did not distance him from people – on the contrary it enabled him to draw close to every human being. Through his humanity he was able to reveal the infinite love of the Father for all mankind, expressed in so many different ways in the Gospel narrative – his compassion on the crowds who followed him, his sharing of the successes and disappointments of his disciples, his grief at the death of his friend Lazarus, his affection for children, his experience of all human limitations except sin.

---

22 Cf. Galot, ibid., p. 235.   **23** Address, 24 March 1982, no. 1.

By freeing himself from the claims of family, Christ was totally available to do his Father's will (cf. Lk 2:49; Jn 4:34), to constitute the new and universal family of the children of God. Thus 'his celibacy was not a defensive reaction against anything, but an enhancement conferred upon his life, a greater closeness to his people, a yearning to give himself unreservedly to the world'.[24]

This new vision implicit in Christ's celibacy had already been set in train by Mary's virginal motherhood and by Joseph's sharing in the same virginal mystery.[25] While the mystery of the conception and birth of Christ was hidden from his contemporaries, it was a totally new departure in relation to the Old Testament tradition which, because of its exclusive favouring of marriage, rendered continence incomprehensible. Mary and Joseph were therefore the first and intimate witnesses to a 'fruitfulness different from that of the flesh, that is, of a fruitfulness of the spirit', realised in the gift of the incarnation of the Eternal Word.[26] This mystery was only gradually revealed to the eyes of the Church on the basis of the witness of the infancy narratives in the gospels of Matthew and Luke. The divine maternity of the Virgin Mary helps us to understand more fully, on the one hand, the sanctity of marriage, and on the other, the mystery of continence for the sake of the Kingdom of Heaven.[27] Here again we see two correlative aspects of the one baptismal vocation to holiness.

CHRIST CALLS TO CELIBACY

When Christ first opened the horizon of celibacy to the disciples, the example of his own life would have given them a clear reference point for this supernatural life-style, which they would associate directly with the kingdom which Christ was preaching. From Christ's words it is clear that a special grace is necessary to understand the meaning of celibacy and to respond to it. 'He who is able to receive it', he tells his disciples, 'let him receive it' (Mt 19:12). Celibacy is therefore a response to the experience of God's kingdom as made present in the example and teaching of the Master. It is not, and can never be, a human initiative alone, nor is there ever a question of obligation to it. It must be appropriated as an expression of personal freedom in response to a particular grace. It is not merely a question of understanding the vocation to celibacy; there is also associated

---

24 Galot, ibid., p. 232. **25** Cf. John Paul II, Address, 24 March 1982, no. 2. **26** Cf. ibid.
27 Cf. ibid., no. 4.

with it a motivation in the will to follow this way, drawn by the example and the mystery of Christ.

We see this attitude clearly reflected in the response of the disciples to Christ's call. Several decades later, the apostle John would vividly remember every detail of his first encounter with the Master, when he came to write his Gospel (cf. Jn 1:35–42). The impact of Jesus on the beloved disciple is indelibly engraved on John's consciousness: 'That which we have heard, which we have seen with our eyes, which we have looked upon and touched with our hands ... that which we have seen and heard we proclaim also to you, so that you may have fellowship with us; and our fellowship is with the Father and with his son Jesus Christ' (1 Jn 1:1–3).

CELIBACY AND SELF-GIVING

Response to a celibate vocation is a decision based on faith. Nevertheless, the calling does not eliminate the sacrifice involved in giving up the attraction to conjugal love in this life, a renunciation which is implied in Christ's teaching in Matthew 19:10–12. Yet, acceptance of it is based on the conviction that by following this life-style one can make a particular contribution to the realisation of the Kingdom of God in its earthly dimension, with the prospect of a higher and definitive level of self-fulfilment in the next life.

Implicit in the response to God's call is the readiness to share in the sacrifice involved in Christ's redeeming work. It is therefore a decision based on love, but as John Paul II reminds us, 'it is natural for the human heart to accept demands, even difficult ones, in the name of love for an ideal, and above all in the name of love for a person'.[28]

A commitment to celibacy is in no way a rejection of the value of human sexuality; rather it respects the 'duality' inherent in man's being made to the image and likeness of God.[29] Indeed, it is precisely the person who understands the full potential for self-giving that marriage offers who can best make a mature offering of himself in celibacy.[30]

---

28 Address, 28 April 1982, no. 1.   **29** Address, 7 April 1982, no. 2.   **30** Cf. Address, 5 May 1982, no. 2. As John Paul II points out (cf. ibid., no. 3), this renunciation is, paradoxically, at the same time an affirmation of the value from which the person abstains. Thus he reminds us that the vocation to celibacy is, in a certain sense, indispensable so that the nuptial meaning of the body may be more easily recognised in conjugal and family life. And this is because the key to understanding the sacramentality of marriage is the spousal love of Christ for his Church, so eloquently described by St Paul in his letter to the Ephesians (cf. Eph 5:22–33).

By choosing continence for the sake of the Kingdom of Heaven, a man fulfils himself 'differently' and, in a certain sense, more fully than through marriage.[31] This is the implication of Christ's response to Peter's very honest question about the rewards to be expected by those who had left everything to follow the Master (cf. Mk 10:29–30).

PAULINE TEACHING

In reply to questions about virginity and celibacy from the primitive Christian communities, St Paul, in his first Letter to the Corinthians, gives a magisterial and, at the same time, a pastoral interpretation of the doctrine of Christ. The uniqueness of Paul's teaching is that, while transmitting the truth proclaimed by the Master, he gives it his own personal stamp based on the experience of his missionary activity. In the Apostle's doctrine we encounter the question of the mutual relationship between marriage and celibacy or virginity, a topic which created difficulties among the first generation of converts from paganism at Corinth.

He emphasises with great clarity that virginity, or voluntary continence, derives exclusively from a counsel and not from a command: 'With regard to virgins, I have no command from the Lord, but I give my opinion' (1 Cor 7:25). But it is an opinion of 'one who by the Lord's mercy is trustworthy' (ibid.). At the same time he gives his advice to those already married, to those who have still to make a decision in this regard, and to those who have been widowed (cf. 1 Cor 7, _passim_). In his explanations Paul tries to give reasons why those who marry do 'well', and why those who decide on a life of continence or virginity do 'better' (cf. 1 Cor 7:38).[32]

From the perspective of apostolic zeal, celibacy allows a man to be concerned about 'the affairs of the Lord', and thus be able 'to please the Lord with all his heart' (cf. 1 Cor 7:32). By contrast, St Paul points out that the married man doesn't have the same availability to devote himself to the things of God (cf. 1 Cor 7:33). He was celibate himself (cf. 1 Cor 7:7), and recommends celibacy as a way of having the freedom to love God totally and unconditionally.

The perishability of human existence ['I tell you this, brothers: the time is already short ...'(1 Cor 7:29)], and the transience of the temporal

---

31 Cf. Address, 7 April 1982, no. 2.   32 Cf. Address, 23 June 1982.

world ['the form of this world is passing away' (1 Cor 7:31)] should, he tells the Corinthians, cause 'those who have wives to live as though they had none' (1 Cor 7:29). In this way Paul prepares the ground for his teaching on continence.[33]

Christ's doctrine on celibacy 'for the sake of the kingdom of Heaven' (cf. Mt 19:12) finds a direct echo in the Apostle's teaching that 'the unmarried man is anxious about the affairs of the Lord, how to please the Lord' (1 Cor 7:32). This concern of Paul's to serve the Lord finds similar expression in his 'anxiety for all the Churches' (2 Cor 11:28) and his desire to serve all the members of the Body of Christ (cf. Phil 2:20-21; 1 Cor 12:25). The unmarried person is anxious about all this, and this is why Paul can be, in the full sense of the term, an 'apostle of Jesus Christ' (1 Cor 1:1) and minister of the Gospel (cf. Col 1:23), and would wish that others would be like him (cf. 1 Cor 7:7).

At the same time, apostolic zeal and pastoral activity ('anxiety for the affairs of the Lord') do not exhaust the content of the Pauline motivation for continence. The root and source of this commitment is to be found in the concern 'how to please the Lord' (1 Cor 7:32). This is a desire to live a life of deep friendship with Christ, expressing at the same time the spousal dimension of the vocation to celibacy.[34]

St Paul observes that the man who is bound by marriage 'is divided' (1 Cor 7:34) by reason of his family obligations, implying that the commitment 'to please the Lord' presupposes abstention from marriage. This state of being unmarried allows virgins to be 'anxious about the affairs of the Lord, to be holy in body and spirit' (1 Cor 7:34). In biblical terms, especially in the Old Testament setting, holiness implies separation from what is 'profane', of this world, in order to belong exclusively to God.[35]

In his affirmation of the value of virginity or celibacy, some of the phrases used by St Paul in reference to marriage, if taken out of context, could suggest that he sees marriage primarily as a remedy for concupiscence.[36] Nevertheless, we have to understand Paul's observations on marriage in light of what he says: 'I wish that all were as I myself am. But each has his own special gift from God, one of one kind, one of another' (1 Cor 7:7). Consequently the vocation to marriage is a gift of

---

33 Cf. Address, 30 June 1982, nos. 1–5. 34 Cf. ibid., nos. 6–10. 35 Cf. Address, 7 July 1982, nos. 1–5. 36 'To the unmarried and the widows I say that it is well for them to remain single as I do. But if they cannot exercise self-control, they should marry. For it is better to marry than to be aflame with passion' (1 Cor 7:8–9); 'Because of the temptation to immorality, each man should have his own wife and each woman her own husband' (1 Cor 7:2).

God, a grace proper to this way of living. In light of the situation in pagan Corinth, Paul, as regards marriage, adverts to the reality of the concupiscence of the flesh, but at the same time he stresses its sacramental character.[37] He will develop this teaching more completely in Ephesians 5, where he removes any doubts about understanding marriage as a residual vocation.[38]

PRIESTHOOD, CELIBACY AND SERVICE

There are further texts of St Paul which, taken in conjunction with other passages of the New Testament, fill out our appreciation of the relationship between priesthood, celibacy, and service.

Priesthood has to be considered in light of the fact that God himself became a priest in the sacred humanity of Christ and instituted a new priesthood in the temple of his body (cf. Jn 2:21). He offered himself to God (cf. Heb 9:11), 'and wished to perpetuate his sacrifice to the end of time (cf. Lk 22:19; 1 Cor 11:24) through the action of other men whom he made and makes sharers in his supreme and eternal priesthood (cf. Heb 5: 1–10; 9:11–28)'.[39]

So rich is the bonding with Christ which comes as a result of sacramental ordination that the priest can make his own the words of St Paul, 'For to me to live is Christ' (Phil 1:21), 'it is no longer I who live but Christ who lives in me' (Gal 2:20).[40] Consequently, as the priest grows in his understanding of the content and meaning of his vocation, he sees how appropriate his celibacy is in the light of the Gospel. He finds the deepest meaning of his life not only in the example of Christ, but also in the Master's reply to Peter: 'Truly, I say to you, there is no man who has left house or wife or brothers or parents or children for the sake of the kingdom of God, who will not receive manifold more in this time, and in the age to come eternal life' (Lk 18:29–30). Matthew (cf. 19:29) and Mark (cf. 10:28–30) report a similar response from Christ in different contexts. Clearly, the question of celibacy was so counter-cultural that it came up several times in our Lord's discussions with his disciples.

The Christian priesthood is intimately bound up with the ministry, life and growth of the Church, the Virginal Spouse of Christ (cf. Rev 19:7; 21:2; 22:17; 2 Cor 11:2). Because of the nature of his service to the Church, 'the priest is father, brother and servant of all; his person and his life be-

---

37 Cf. Address, 7 July 1982. **38** Cf. Address, 14 July 1982, nos. 2–6. **39** Alvaro del Portillo, *On Priesthood*, Chicago, 1974, p. 44. **40** Cf. *Presbyterorum ordinis*, 16.

long to others, they are the property of the Church who loves him with nuptial love; and her relationship with, and rights against, the priest are such as no one else may share in ... For this very reason one can understand the suitability of celibacy (which better guards the unity of the human heart: cf. 1 Cor 7:33) for protecting, filling and enriching the bonds of nuptial love which unite the Christian priesthood with the spouse of Christ.'[41] This is the complementary aspect of celibacy: just as Christ, and his priests, have a spousal relationship with the Church, so the Church as virginal spouse of Christ has in a very real sense exclusive nuptial rights over the priest as icon of Christ.

As he exercises his ministry, the priest discovers the greatness of his vocation: 'his capacity for affection and love is filled by the pastoral and paternal task of engendering the people of God in faith, training them and bringing them "as a chaste virgin" to the fullness of life in Christ'.[42] Looking at the priesthood from this perspective, we understand more deeply the affection that fills Paul's heart for his beloved Corinthians, and why he asks them to overlook his seeming foolishness in his expression of affection for them. 'I feel a divine jealousy for you', he tells them, 'for I betrothed you to Christ to present you as a pure bride to her one husband' (2 Cor 11: 2). His celibacy allows Paul, as it does the priest, to receive and exercise in a special way his paternity in Christ. It elevates and extends, the better to fulfil his ministry of regeneration, 'the need the priest, like every man, has of exercising his capacity for generation and leading to maturity those children who are the fruit of his love'.[43]

LEVITICAL PRIESTHOOD AND CONTINENCE

We have seen that in some places in the early Church, to justify the exercise of conjugal rights after ordination, appeal was made to the style of the priesthood of the Old Testament. During their period of service in the Temple the Levitical priests practised continence, but afterwards they returned to normal conjugal life in their homes.[44]

Generally we find a twofold response to this objection. Firstly, that the Temple priesthood was entrusted to a particular tribe – only the descend-

---

41 del Portillo, ibid., p. 48. **42** Ibid. **43** Ibid. **44** The responsibilities of the Levitical priesthood included maintaining faith in God among the Israelites, interpreting the Law, and teaching the people (cf. Deut 17:9). But the Temple priests' main function was the offering of sacrifice, which was the highest expression of the religion of the Old Testament.

ants of Aaron had a right to this office – and thus the Levites had an obligation to marry and beget children to perpetuate the priesthood of the Chosen People. On the other hand it was pointed out that the priesthood of the New Testament was not based on family descent. At another level, the theological argument explained that the priesthood instituted by Christ brought to perfection the priesthood of the Old Law. This was reflected in the fact that, while the ministry of the Levites was limited to their time of service in the Temple, the priests of the New Testament were engaged in a continuous and uninterrupted ministry of prayer, service at the altar, and administration of the sacraments. Since Scripture teaches them to be completely pure in the exercise of the ministry, the praxis of temporary continence of the Temple priests became an obligation of permanent continence for the priests of Jesus Christ.

Pope Siricius, in his *Directa* decretal to the Spanish Bishop Himerius (385), clarifies these distinctions. He goes on to point out that Christ, who formally affirmed that he had not come to abolish the law but to bring it to perfection, wanted his priests of the New Law to be permanently continent. If the ministers of the Temple had to abstain periodically so as to make their offerings to God worthy of acceptance, the conclusion, as far as Siricius was concerned, is that the ministers of Christ who offer sacrifice daily, and also a sacrifice infinitely superior to that of the Old Covenant, should be permanently continent in order to make themselves pleasing to God. The principle of ritual purity required that there would be no intercourse the day before the celebration at the altar, and since Mass was said every day, clerics would be bound to total continence. This was the cultic argument for celibacy advanced in the early Church by Popes and the Fathers.[45]

CULTIC ARGUMENT FOR CELIBACY

Such an approach, it is claimed, is based on a negative view of human sexuality and marriage, and an exaggerated perception of the cultic aspect of priestly duties. While Pope Siricius does draw on the argument from ritual purity for clerical continence, he does so only in a peripheral sense.[46]

45 PL 13, 1138a–39a, as quoted in Cochini, op. cit., p. 9.   46 There is mention of the cultic argument for celibacy in Pius XI's *Ad catholici sacerdotii* (1935) and in Pius XII's encyclical *Sacra virginitas* (1954). Nevertheless, in both cases it has only a marginal status in the overall case for priestly celibacy. In documents of the Magisterium referring to priestly celibacy subsequent to Vatican II, this argument has disappeared.

On the other hand, in his *Dominus inter* decretal to the bishops of Gaul, he gives particular emphasis to deriving the reason for clerical continence from the conviction that virginity or continence is characteristic of the New Testament, and therefore required of clerics in major orders. Because virginity was held in high esteem and recommended by the Church, it was felt appropriate that clerics should reflect in their own lives what they encouraged others to do.[47] Above all, as we shall see later, he draws on reasons from Scripture and apostolic tradition, and concludes that absolute clerical continence is a demand of the sanctity of the priestly office.

MARRIAGE, CONTINENCE, AND CULT

While we can find expressions in the Fathers which seem to disparage human sexuality and marriage in order to justify continence and celibacy, the essential validation of this charism is grounded on deeper reasons – total self-giving to God, spiritual fatherhood, and imitation of the celibacy of Christ for the sake of the kingdom of heaven. At the same time, the writings of the Fathers do not reflect any reservations about the use of marriage by the laity, nor is there any suspicion of a Gnostic dualism in their affirmation of continence for married priests.[48]

Hence, for St Jerome, while marriage was privileged in the Old Testament, virginity is singularly characteristic of the new dispensation ushered in with the Incarnation, where Mary's virginity was central to that transition. When he refers to the absolute continence of clerics in major orders, the main justification he gives is the imitation of the higher state of virginity.[49] Both he and St Ambrose rejected the idea that by emphasising the ascetical superiority of virginity they were debasing marriage – how could the institution which produced virgins be evil in any way? Marriage is good but virginity is better. The ideal of virginity has its origin in Christ, it was validated by the teaching of St Paul (cf. 1 Cor 7), and realised especially in Mary and the Church.[50]

It has also to be remembered in this context that, in the early Church, Christian couples practised periodic marital continence in line with St Paul's counsel: 'Do not refuse one another except perhaps by agreement for a season, that you may devote yourselves to prayer' (1 Cor 7:5). It was

---

47 PL 13, 1184a–86a, as quoted in Cochini, op. cit., pp 14–15. 48 Cf. Daniel Callam, 'Clerical Continence in the Fourth Century: Three Papal Decretals', *Theological Studies*, 41, no. 1 (1980), pp 3–50. 49 Cf. *Ep.* 49,2 (CESL 54, 352) and *Ep.* 49, 21 (CESL 54, 387). 50 Cf. St Ambrose, *Ep* 63,10 and 33: PL 16, 1191–2, 1198. See Callam, ibid., pp 14–15.

expected that they would do so especially when it was time to celebrate the memorial of the Lord's Passion and Death.[51] Conjugal abstinence was also recommended during the period of Lent.[52] Popes and Fathers of both the East and West attest to the fact that periodic continence was regarded as normal practice for Christian couples.[53] Therefore it can be said that, in the early Church, the theological thinking was that marital continence for lay people was regarded as a better way to prepare for the celebration of the Eucharist. In this sense one can detect a certain resonance between the cultic argument for celibacy of the early centuries and the theology of marriage in vogue at that time.

In retrospect, from the vantage point of subsequent developments in the theology of celibacy, we can see the limitations of the cultic argument. At the same time, in justification of the early Church writers, it is not surprising that the Fathers, for whom Sacred Scripture was the basic source of theology, would see the temporary continence of the Levitical priesthood as a type or prefiguration of the celibacy of the priests offering the unique sacrifice of the New Covenant. The use of the ritual argument was a practical answer with some force, even though theologically it was an inadequate one. Ultimately, however, the conviction of the early Church about this charism derived from something deeper – the example of Christ's own choice of celibacy, his teaching about it, and the tradition which was handed down from the Apostles.

It was not perhaps until relatively recently that the Western Church, guided by the Holy Spirit and drawing on the results of historical research, articulated more clearly in *theological* terms what she always *believed* about celibacy. Both the theology of marriage and the theology of celibacy have advanced significantly since the early centuries, and the complementarity of both vocations is now perceived much more clearly. This is the result of several new insights, but of two in particular: the vision of marriage as a divine vocation to holiness which was affirmed by Vatican II, and the spousal theology of celibacy expounded so cogently by John Paul II. We will be returning to these themes later.

51 Cf. St Cyril of Jerusalem, *Catechetical Lectures* 4,25: PG 33, 488a-b; St Jerome, *Ep* 18, no. 15: PL 22, 506.   52 Cf. Cholij, op. cit., pp 143f.   53 Cf. Pope Siricius: *Cum in unum*: PL 13, 1160a–61a; Gregory the Great in his *Letter to Augustine of Canterbury* II 56, 8: MGH, Epist. 22, 340, 19-341; St Ambrose: PL 17, 217; St Augustine: PL 38, 1052; St Gregory Nazianzen, *Oration on Holy Baptism* 18; St John Chrysostom: *Homily on 1 Cor 19*; etc. Both Gregory Nazianzen (PG 36, 381b-384a) and John Chrysostom (PG 61, 152d-154c) seem to regard temporary continence, when motivated by charity, as a practice that predisposed one in a particular way to prayer, guaranteeing at the same time the real dignity and supernatural worth of marriage.

MAN OF ONE WIFE: *UNIUS UXORIS VIR*

Apart from the texts reviewed above, there is another Pauline stipulation for the appointment of bishops, priests and deacons which is uniquely important for establishing a specific connection between celibacy and priesthood.

As we have already seen, to understand the history of celibacy it is necessary to distinguish between celibacy and continence. In the ancient Church many priests were married, but a condition for ordination was the commitment to perpetual and total continence subsequent to taking Orders. St Paul laid down a norm stipulating that bishops (1 Tim 3:2), priests (Tit 1:6) and deacons (1 Tim 3:12) be *unius uxoris vir* (the husband of one wife), as a special requirement for exercising the ministerial priesthood.[54] At first sight this condition for ordination would seem to be puzzling i.e., that the candidate should not have married after the death of his first wife. However, it is only in the light of tradition and exegetical research that the full significance of the formula becomes clear.

To elucidate the meaning of this Pauline passage, one has to draw on both the patristic and pontifical tradition which, as Stickler points out, is either neglected or ignored in modern biblical exegesis. This was a tradition which gave to the Pauline text the signification of a biblical argument in favour of celibacy as having been inspired by the Apostles. The Pauline norm was interpreted as having the meaning of 'a guarantee ensuring the effective practice of continence by married ministers before they were ordained'.[55]

In the year 386, Pope Siricius sent a letter, the *Cum in unum* decretal, to different ecclesiastical provinces, communicating the decisions of a synod of bishops held in Rome earlier that year. Among these decisions were stipulations about the observance of clerical continence and sanctions enacted against the guilty parties. It is clear from the decretal that some had claimed that the expression *unius uxoris vir* (1 Tim 3:2) specifically guaranteed the bishop the right to use marriage after ordination. In Chapter 1 we have already referred to the witness of Pope Siricius in this regard. However, his authoritative interpretation of the Pauline text (*unius uxoris vir*) deserves fuller attention:

---

54 'Now a bishop must be above reproach, the husband of one wife' (1 Tim 3:2); 'A priest must be blameless, the husband of one wife' (Tit 1:6); 'Let deacons be the husband of one wife' (1 Tim 3:12). **55** Cf. Foreword by Alfons M. Stickler to Christian Cochini, op. cit., p xiii.

Perhaps does one believe that this [begetting children] is permitted because it is written: 'He must not have been married more than once' (1 Tim 3:2). But Paul was not talking about a man persisting in his desire to beget; he spoke about the continence one should observe [*propter continentiam futuram*]. He did not accept those who were not beyond reproach in this matter, and he said: 'I should like everyone to be like me' (1 Cor 7:7). And he stated even more clearly: 'People who are interested only in unspiritual things can never be pleasing to God. Your interests, however, are not in the unspiritual, but in the spiritual' (Rom 8:8–9).[56]

Siricius claims that his is the only interpretation faithful to St Paul's mind on the requirements for ordination. A man who remarried after the death of his first wife could not be a candidate for Orders, because it would be a contra-indication to his being able to practise the perfect continence that would be required after ordination. By means of this exegesis Siricius and the Roman Synod established continuity with apostolic tradition. To make it clear that this decretal is not introducing a new discipline, the document states that it is not a question of 'ordering new precepts', but rather one of dealing with 'matters that have been established by an apostolic constitution and by a constitution of the Fathers'.[57]

This same interpretation is found in a number of patristic writers. Thus St Ambrose: 'The apostle is a master of virtue; he teaches how to convince the contradictors patiently; he orders that the bishop be the husband of only one wife, not in order to exclude in such a way one who would not have been married (this is indeed above the law), but so that, through conjugal chastity, he keeps the grace of his baptism; on the other hand the apostolic authority is not an invitation to beget children during his priesthood; the apostle spoke about a man who already had children, but not about one who is begetting them or who contracts a new marriage.'[58]

St Epiphanius of Salamis is even clearer: 'Since the Incarnation of Christ, the holy Word of God doesn't admit to the priesthood monogamists who, after the death of their wives, have remarried; this is so because of the exceptional honour of the priesthood. This is observed with great exactitude, without failing, by the holy Church of God. But the man who goes on living with his wife and begetting children is not admitted by the Church as deacon, priest or bishop, and subdeacon, even if he married

---

56 PL 13, 1160a-61a, as quoted in Cochini, ibid., p. 11.   57 Cf. Cochini, ibid., p. 13.   58 *Ep.*, 63:62; PL 16, 1205, as quoted in Cochini, ibid., note 18 on p. 12.

only once, but only the one who, being monogamous, observes continence or is a widower; above all in those places where the ecclesiastical canons are very precise.'[59]

The Pauline norm, as authoritatively interpreted by Pope Siricius, was that the Apostle was not speaking of a man who might persist in the desire to beget children, but rather 'about continence which they had to observe in future (*propter continentiam futuram*)'. In other words, a man who had married a second time after his first wife died could not be considered as a prospect for ordination, as the fact of his remarriage would be regarded as a clear indication that he would not be able to observe the perfect continence which was required afterwards. It is important to remember that Paul uses this formula *unius uxoris vir* only in relation to ministers of the Church, and never to lay Christians, a fact which has been too little noted.[60]

This authoritative interpretation made by Pope Siricius, and afterwards by Pope Innocent I,[61] was a reference datum during the subsequent centuries. The *Glossa Ordinaria* to the *Decretum* of Gratian explains that remarriage by a man whose first wife died would be regarded as a sign of incontinence, and he would thus not qualify as a candidate for ordination.[62] As recently as 1935 Pius XI, in his encyclical *Ad catholici sacerdotii* on the priesthood, interprets *unius uxoris vir* as an argument in favour of priestly celibacy.[63]

Eusebius of Caesaria, the historian of the early Church, gives testimony to the fact that this was also the interpretation of *unius uxoris vir* which was accepted in the East. He was present at the Council of Nicea (325) and sympathetic to the Arians, and, as Stickler points out, one would have expected him to come to the defence of the use of marriage by priests already married. Nevertheless, he specifically affirms that, in comparing the Temple priests with those of the New Testament, one is comparing corporal with spiritual generation, and 'that the sense of *unius uxoris vir* consists in this ... that those who have been consecrated and dedicated to the service of the divine cult must therefore properly abstain from sexual relations with their wives'.[64]

---

59 *Panarion (Adversus Haereses) Haer.* 79,4. CGS 31, 367 as quoted in Cochini, p. 12. **60** Cf. de la Potterie, op. cit., p. 21. **61** Cf. Stickler, *The Case for Clerical Celibacy*, op. cit., pp 32–3. **62** Cf. ibid., pp 91–2. **63** Published 20 December 1935. He quotes the passage from St Epiphanius given above, and in footnote 89 adds a reference to the relevant texts in St Paul's letters – 1 Tim 3:2; Tit 1:6; 1 Tim 3:12. But in addition he refers to 1 Tim 5:9, the correlative text about widows being *unius viri uxor*, the significance of which is explained later in this chapter under the heading 'Covenantal Dimension of Celibacy'. **64** Ibid., p. 92, referring to *Demonstratio evangelica* 1:9, PG 22, 88. Stickler adds the following

The Pauline prohibition on the admission to Orders of a man who had remarried after the death of his first wife was strictly preserved throughout the centuries, and was still to be found among the irregularities for Orders in the 1917 Code of Canon Law (can. 984, §4).[65]

A WOMAN COMPANION

Stickler[66] draws attention to another Pauline reference which throws further light on the *unius uxoris vir* text. In 1 Corinthians 9:5 St Paul affirms that he also could have claimed the right to have had the company of a woman on his missionary journeys 'as did the other apostles and the brethren of the Lord and Cephas'. Paradoxically the same text is used today as an argument against the continence of the Apostles themselves. Many interpret this 'woman' as a 'wife' of the apostles, which in the case of Peter would have been true. But Paul does not speak simply of the word '*gunē*', which can well mean a wife. Rather he adds, not unintentionally, the word 'adelphé', or 'sister', to exclude any possibility of misunderstanding.[67]

This fact has added significance when we consider that subsequently all the important evidence related to the continence of sacred ministers continually points out that, when speaking of the wife of such ministers in the context of consequent sexual continence, the word '*soror*', sister, is always used. The relationship after ordination of the husband is that of brother and sister. Thus St Gregory the Great: 'The priest from the moment of his ordination will love his wife as a sister.'[68] The Council of

interesting observation 'It is also worth noting that the celibacy legislation of Trullo, canon 3, maintains this prohibition for priests, deacons and subdeacons, namely, that the candidates to these orders cannot have been married to a widow or with someone who had already been married once. On this point the Fathers of Trullo only wanted to mitigate the severity of the Church of Rome by conceding to those who had sinned against the prohibition of digamy the possibility of conversion and of penance. If within the time limit set by the Synod they had renounced this marriage, they could have remained in the ministry. The illogical nature of canon 3 in comparison with canon 13, which permits to priests and deacons the use of marriage contracted before ordination, is explained only by the fact that this apostolic prohibition was also profoundly anchored in the Eastern tradition, but without taking into account its true original meaning. We have here another tacit proof and guarantee for the authentic original meaning of complete continence after ordination as it remained alive in the Western Church and whose observance was always faithfully accepted by the Church of Rome' (ibid., pp 93–94). For a detailed analysis of canon 3 of the Council of Trullo, cf. Cholij, op. cit., pp 9–34. **65** Cf. Stickler, op. cit., p. 92. **66** Cf. ibid., pp 94–5. **67** The Latin text of 1 Cor 9:5 gives *mulierem sororem*. **68** *Dialoghi*, Bk. 4, c. II; PL 77, 336.

Gerona (517) stipulated that 'if those who were previously married have been ordained, they must not live together as if they were spouses, for she who was a spouse has become a sister'.[69] Similarly the Second Council of Auvergne (535) decided: 'If a priest or a deacon has received the orders of divine service, the husband immediately becomes a brother to his former wife.'[70] This particular use of the word *soror* is found in many patristic and conciliar texts.

COVENANT AND SCRIPTURE

The formula *unius uxoris vir* is in fact a covenantal stipulation, reflecting the spousal love of Christ for his Church. To appreciate the full theological implications of such a covenantal formula for celibacy, it will be useful to review the rich scriptural significance of this institution.

The idea of the covenant dominates all the religious thought of the Old Testament and we see it deepening with the passage of time. At Sinai the Chosen People entered a covenant with Yahweh.[71] God had chosen Israel without merit on her part (cf. Deut 9:4) because he loved her and wanted to keep an oath he made to her fathers (cf. Deut 7:6) – the foundation of the covenant lies in this freely bestowed divine love. Having separated her from pagan nations he reserved her exclusively for himself. Israel would be his own people, she would serve him with her worship, and she would become his kingdom. In return Yahweh assures her of his aid and protection – he will fill her with blessings and endow her with life and peace (cf. Ex 23:20–31). While giving his covenant to Israel, Yahweh also imposes conditions which Israel will have to observe as constituted by the Law. Through the covenant of Sinai, God wishes to bring men to himself by making them a community of worship dedicated to his service, ruled by his Law.

The message of the prophets refers constantly to the covenant. If they consistently denounce the infidelity of Israel towards God, if they preach misfortunes which threaten a sinful people, it is because of the covenant of Sinai to which she agreed.

Turning their eyes towards the future, the prophets promised the new

69 Can.6: *Canones Apostolorum et Conciliorum saec. IV-VII*, 2 (Berlin, 1839), 19, as referenced in Stickler, ibid., p. 95. **70** C. 13: *Corpus Christianorum*, Series Latina 148 A (Turnhout, 1974): 108 (cf. Stickler, ibid.). **71** 'If you will obey my voice and keep my covenant, you will be my own possession among all peoples; for all the earth is mine, and you shall be to me a kingdom of priests and a holy nation' (Ex 19:5).

covenant. Hosea speaks about a new betrothal which would bring to the bride love, justice, fidelity, and knowledge of God, and which would re-establish peace with the rest of creation. Jeremiah promises that with the advent of the new dispensation the human heart will be changed (cf. Jer 31:33; 32:37–41).

In the New Testament the covenant acquires all its fullness because henceforth it has as its content the total mystery of Christ. At the Last Supper, with the institution of the Eucharist, the new covenant is sealed in Christ's blood: 'This is my blood of the covenant, which is poured out for many' (Mk 14:24). And Matthew adds 'for the forgiveness of sins' (26:28). Christ is the mediator of the new covenant. The covenant theme is the background to the Letter to the Hebrews, where the superiority of the new over the old is clear.

MARRIAGE AS COVENANT

Marriage is also described as a covenant in the Old Testament (cf. Prov 2:17 and Mal 2:14). Because marriage was 'God's Covenant', the prophets loved to depict the relationship between Yahweh and Israel in terms of marriage (cf. Os 1:2; Is 50:1; 54:5; Jer 2:2; Song 16:4).

The communion of love between God and his people, which was so central to the faith of Israel, also finds meaningful expression in the marriage covenant between a man and a woman. The faithful conjugal love of the couple is the image and the symbol of the covenant which unites God with mankind. The definitive covenant finds its fulfilment in Christ, the Bridegroom who loves humanity as its Saviour, uniting it to himself as a body. When Christ offers himself in sacrifice on the Cross for his Bride, the Church, the greatness of God's plan for conjugal love is disclosed in that the marriage of two baptised persons becomes a real symbol of the new and eternal covenant sanctioned in the blood of Christ. By virtue of the merits of the Cross, man and woman are rendered capable of loving one another as Christ has loved us (cf. Eph 5:32-33).[72]

John Paul II reminds us that 'Marriage and virginity or celibacy are two ways of expressing and living the one mystery of the covenant of God with his people.'[73] The two vocations are so mutually supportive that where marriage is not esteemed, celibacy cannot exist. And when human

---

72 Cf. *Familiaris consortio*, op. cit., nos. 12–13.   **73** Ibid., 16.

sexuality is not respected as a great good, renunciation of it for the same of the Kingdom of heaven loses its meaning.[74]

As a consequence of the New Covenant, the celibate priest awaits, also in a bodily way, 'the eschatological marriage of Christ with his Church', giving himself completely to the Church, in the hope that Christ will give eternal life to his Bride the Church. By virtue of this witness, celibacy keeps alive in the Church a consciousness of the mystery of marriage and defends it from any impoverishment or reductive approach.[75]

COVENANTAL DIMENSION OF CELIBACY

Having reviewed the deep biblical implications of the covenant, let us now return to consider how the formula *unius uxoris vir* is not only a text grounding the celibacy of priests, but is also a covenantal formula which enriches the theology of celibacy.[76] This becomes clear when the parallelism between the formula in the Pastoral letters (*unius uxoris vir*) and the passages in 2 Corinthians 11:2 and Ephesians 5:22–23 are considered.

In the first (2 Cor 11:2), Paul describes the Church of Corinth as a woman, as a bride, whom he has presented to Christ as a chaste virgin: 'I feel a divine jealousy for you, for I betrothed you to Christ to present you as a pure bride to her one husband (*uni viro*)' (2 Cor 11:2). The context of this passage is very clear if it is read in conjunction with 1 Timothy 5:9: 'Let a widow be enrolled if she is not less than sixty years of age, having been the wife of one husband (*unius viri uxor*)'. Hence the same formula, *unus vir,* is used of the relations whether of the *Church* with *Christ* or of the *widow* who had only one *husband*.[77]

In 2 Corinthians 11:2, Christ's bride is the Church herself. The jealousy of which Paul speaks is a sharing of God's jealousy over his people. It is an expression of his zeal that his Corinthian converts may remain faithful to the covenant made with Christ who is their true and only Bridegroom. This interpretation is confirmed by reference to the Old Testa-

74 Cf. ibid.   **75** Cf. ibid.   **76** This analysis is based primarily on de la Potterie, op. cit., pp 13–30.   **77** In this context Cholij comments: 'It is not without some interest to us that St Paul also, in the same letter to Timothy, speaks of the qualities required for women to be listed as widows, indicating that they are to have been "married but once"(1 Tim 5:9); this is stipulated within a context that strongly suggests that this was a precaution against future incontinence (1 Tim 5:11–12). The parallelism between Paul's injunction for widows and that for clerics in 1 Tim 3:2 can be proffered as evidence to further the thesis that the Pauline injunction was a guarantee for future chastity by clerics who, once ordained, were to live as if they had no wife or as brother and sister' (op. cit., p. 19).

ment: the Church-Bride is presented to Christ the Bridegroom as a 'pure virgin', which is a reference to the Daughter of Sion (cf. Is 10:32: Jer 6:2), sometimes called the 'virgin Sion' (cf. Is 37:22; Lam 2:13) or 'virgin Israel' (cf. Jer 18:13, 31:4; Amos 5:2) by the prophets,[78] especially when she is invited after past infidelities to be faithful once more to the covenant, to her marriage relationship with her only Bridegroom.

The second text is the classical passage in Ephesians 5:22–23 where it describes how husband and wife united in marriage are the image of Christ's union with his Church: 'Wives be subject to your husbands, as to the Lord. For the husband is the head of the wife as Christ is the head of the Church, his body, and is himself its Saviour'. St Paul develops the analogy by telling us that Christ the Bridegroom sacrifices himself for the Church, so that she may become his holy and spotless Bride (cf. vv. 25–27). But, as de la Potterie points out, the fact that the expression *unius uxoris vir* is not used here in Ephesians to refer to all Christians, but is reserved to describe the married *minister* in the Pastoral Letters, shows that the formula refers directly to the priestly ministry and the Christ-Church relationship: the minister must be like Christ the Bridegroom.

Another important consequence of the connection between the *unius uxoris vir* of the Pastoral Letters and the passage in 2 Corinthians 11:2 is that the Church-Bride is called a 'pure virgin' (*virginem castam*). Consequently the spousal love between Christ the Bridegroom and his Church-Bride is always a *virginal* love. For the Church of Corinth, where most Christians would have been married, the reference (*virginem castam*) is to what St Augustine calls the virginity of the faith (*virginitas fidei*) or virginity of the heart (*virginitas cordis*), that is unblemished faith. Yet for the married ministers of the Pastoral Letters, in this spiritual view of their ministry, the radical call to a virginity of the heart (*virginitas cordis*) is also a vocation to virginity of the flesh (*virginitas carnis*) as regards their wives, that is a call to continence.[79]

From this covenantal interpretation of priestly celibacy it is clear that we are no longer dealing with an external, canonical prescription but with 'an inner perception of the fact that ordination makes the priestly minister a representation of Christ the Bridegroom in relation to the Church, bride and virgin, and hence he cannot live with another wife'.[80]

---

78 Cf. Ignace de la Potterie, *Mary in the Mystery of the Covenant*, New York, 1992, pp xxiii–xxv, xxxv–xxxvii.   **79** Cf. R. Hesbert, *Saint Augustin et la virginité de la foi, in Augustinus Magister*, Congrès international augustinien II, Paris, 1954, pp 645–55. It is also well described by St Leo the Great: *Discat Sponsa Verbi non alium virum nosse quam Christum* (*Epistolae*, 12, 3: PL 54, 648b).   **80** de la Potterie, 'The Biblical Foundation of Priestly Celibacy', p. 24.

This sacramental and spiritual argument of the *unius uxoris vir,* based on the theology of the covenant, emerges in the Western tradition with Tertullian, is developed by St Augustine and St Leo the Great, and summed up by St Thomas in his commentary on 1 Timothy 3:2 (*Oportet ergo episcopum ... esse unius uxoris virum*): 'This is so, not merely to avoid incontinence, but to represent the sacrament, since the Church's bridegroom is Christ and the Church is one: *Una est columba mea* (Song of Songs 6:4).'[81]

Nevertheless, as de la Potterie points out, 'St Thomas does not as yet make the connection with the text in 2 Corinthians 11:2, which speaks of the bride-virgin; and therefore he does not add that the representational role of the monogamous priesthood also entails the call to *continence* for the married minister, and consequently, for the unmarried ones, the call to celibacy.'[82] This may have been due to the reasons I have already adverted to in Chapter 1. Because Gratian uncritically accepted canon 13 of Trullo as ecumenical, this legitimised the Oriental praxis of temporary continence for priests and established it as being of apostolic origin. The permanent continence in the Western Church was thus seen by St Thomas to be grounded in ecclesiastical law.[83]

The covenantal formula introduced the married minister into the marriage relationship between Christ and his Church. However, the connection between the minister and Christ as a result of ordination today no longer requires as human support for the symbolism a real marriage on the part of the minister, but the formula is still valid for priests of the Church, although they are not married, because the symbolic and spiritual meaning of *unius uxoris vir* remains the same. Nevertheless, since it contains a direct reference to the marriage relationship between Christ and his Church, it suggests that a greater importance than in the past be attached to the fact that the minister of the Church represents Christ the Bridegroom to the Church his Bride. In this sense 'the priest must be "the husband of one wife"; but that one wife, his bride, is the Church, who, like Mary, is the bride of Christ'.[84]

The covenantal aspect of celibacy is an idea which finds fuller expression in John Paul II's *Pastores dabo vobis*. Among other passages which illustrate this point there is the following, which is a commentary on Ephesians 5:25–27:

---

81 *In I ad Tim., c.III, lect. 1* (ed. Marietti, Turin, 1953, no. 96). ('My dove, my perfect one, is only one'). See also de la Potterie, ibid., pp 24–5. **82** Ibid., p. 25. **83** Cf. St Thomas' doctrine on celibacy in quote referred to in note 68 of Chapter 1. **84** Cf. de la Potterie, ibid., p 26.

The Church is indeed the body in which Christ the Head is present and active, but she is also the Bride who proceeds like a new Eve from the open side of the Redeemer on the Cross. Here Christ stands 'before' the Church, and 'nourishes her and cherishes her' (Eph 5:29), giving his life for her. The priest is called to be the living image of Jesus Christ, the Spouse of the Church ... In virtue of his configuration to Christ the Head and Shepherd, the priest stands in this spousal relationship with regard to the community ... In his spiritual life, therefore, he is called to live out Christ's spousal love towards the Church, his Bride. Therefore, the priest's life ought to radiate this spousal character, which demands that he be a witness to Christ's spousal love, and thus be capable of loving people with a heart which is new, generous and pure, with genuine self-detachment, with full, constant and faithful dedication and at the same time with a kind of 'divine jealousy' (cf. 2 Cor 11: 2), and even with a kind of maternal tenderness, capable of bearing the 'pangs of birth' until 'Christ be formed' in the faithful (cf. Gal 4:19).[85]

The Pauline image of marriage in Ephesians brings together the redemptive and the spousal dimensions of love. Christ has become the Spouse of the Church, his Bride, because 'he has given himself up for her' (Eph 5:25). This same image of spousal love is also the fullest incarnation of the ideal of 'celibacy for the kingdom of Heaven' (Mt 19:12). In this case too the spousal and redemptive aspects of love are reciprocally united, though differently from marriage. Following the example of Christ, priestly celibacy confirms the hope of redemption not only for spouses, but for the whole of mankind.[86]

In Chapter 3 we will be returning to the spousal dimension of celibacy, which is central to a theological consideration of this charism.

85 No. 22; cf. also nos. 12, and 29.   **86** Cf. John Paul II, Address, 15 December 1982, nos. 5–7.

3

Theology of Celibacy

More than a quarter of a century has elapsed since the publication of Pope Paul VI's encyclical *Sacerdotalis caelibatus* on priestly celibacy.[1] At the time the document was published, just two years after the Council, theological confusion and defections among the clergy had begun to accelerate. The Pope's clear articulation of the meaning and value of clerical celibacy, at a time of doubt and hesitation, was a great light and support to priests; three decades later its teaching and pastoral encouragement are as relevant as ever.

The encyclical takes up the doctrine on celibacy of the Vatican II decree on the ministry and life of priests[2] and develops it. John Paul II has returned to this theme several times during his pontificate, particularly in his first Holy Thursday letter to priests in 1979, and more recently in his apostolic exhortation *Pastores dabo vobis* on the formation of priests. It shouldn't come as a surprise that Popes have felt it necessary frequently to reaffirm the value of the charism of celibacy. On the one hand the wisdom of the world has always been hostile to the Christian virtue of chastity, and to priestly celibacy in particular, and so the priest needs to be reminded of the purpose of this gift and its essentially supernatural meaning. On the other hand, precisely because celibacy is a commitment which goes to the very root of the priest's being, he needs to reflect regularly on the fact that celibacy 'for the sake of the Kingdom' is a wellspring of spiritual energy that enables him, with the help of God's grace, to have a truly fruitful priesthood and to overcome all the difficulties that can arise in being faithful to this commitment.

The moral environment in which priests have to live out their celibacy has, doubtless, become more difficult over the past twenty-five years. While the increasing thrust in modern society towards hedonism and sexual permissiveness aggravates the situation, a more humanistic approach to priesthood has tended to undermine theological convictions about celibacy, and to see it as an unnecessary burden. In a culture which promotes a short theological memory and an over-concern with the existential present, it is

---

1 24 June 1967; published in English as *Priestly Celibacy*, London, 1967. 2 *Presbyterorum ordinis*, 16.

important that the accumulated wisdom of Christian tradition about celibacy be restated and reaffirmed to enable priests give an intelligible explanation for the hope they cherish.

Celibacy cannot be assessed at the human level alone. It involves not only the sexual nature of man but is, above all, a work of grace, a response to a divine initiative. In a secularised society people easily lose sight of the transcendent and, thus, of the ontological connection between the sacrament of Order and priesthood. Hence it is necessary to recall the theological reasons which underpin the practice of celibacy in the Western Church.

In this chapter we will review the Christological, the ecclesial, and the eschatological dimensions of celibacy. In particular, as a development of the covenantal dimension of celibacy considered in the last chapter, we will examine the spousal implications of this charism as seen in the light of St Paul's teaching, and the related aspect of the spiritual paternity of the priest. We will discuss how an authentic theology of celibacy leads to a deeper appreciation of the vocation to marriage, and conclude with a summary of John Paul II's theology of the priest's pastoral relationships with women.

CHRISTOLOGICAL SIGNIFICANCE

The priesthood, Paul VI tells us in his encyclical *Sacerdotalis caelibatus*,[3] can be understood only in the light of the newness of Christ, who instituted it as a real ontological participation in his own priestly being. Christ is therefore the model and prototype of the Catholic priesthood. By means of the paschal mystery he gave birth to a new creation (cf. 2 Cor 5:17; Gal 6:15); man was reborn to the life of grace, which transformed the earthly condition of human nature (cf. Gal 3:28).

Christ, as mediator between heaven and earth, remained celibate throughout his life, signifying his total dedication to God and man. This deep connection between celibacy and the priesthood of Christ is reflected in the life of the man-priest; the freer he is from the bonds of flesh and blood, the more perfect is his participation in the dignity and mission of Christ.[4]

By remaining celibate Jesus went against the socio-cultural and religious climate of his time, since in the Jewish environment no condition

3 Cf. no. 19.   4 Cf. *Presbyterorum ordinis*, 16.

was so much deprecated as that of a man who had no descendants. Yet Christ freely willed to combine the virginal state with his mission as eternal priest and mediator between heaven and earth.

By sacramental ordination every priest is configured to Jesus and shares in his priesthood in such an intimate way that he acts *in persona Christi* (in the person of Christ). From this identification with the Master, it follows that the man who wishes to imitate Christ in his priesthood assents to becoming his witness and to adhering strictly to the ontological connotations of that priesthood. It is on the strength of this 'essential, ontological and existential assimilation to Christ' that the congruity and relevance of priestly celibacy can and should be judged. The priest, in as much as he is an *alter Christus* (another Christ), finds his true identity in this intimate, personal relationship with Christ.[5] The ontological bond which unites the priesthood to Christ is the source of priestly identity.[6]

Because Christ is 'the same yesterday, today and forever' (Heb 13:58), at a fundamental level, sociological interpretations or changing fashions have little to tell us about the relevance of celibacy to the lifestyle of the priest. It is primarily by reflection on the mystery of Christ, his life and his work, and the experience of celibacy as lived in the Church through the centuries under the guidance of the Holy Spirit, that we can come to valid conclusions in this regard. The call to priesthood, and the charism of celibacy offered with it, is a gift of God, a supernatural reality to which no individual has a right. To follow it calls for a committed, but not impossible, effort on the part of the priest. As John Paul II reminds us in *Pastores dabo vobis*, this charism brings with it the graces that are necessary for the recipient to be faithful to it throughout his life.[7]

Through sacramental ordination there is such an intimate assumption by God of the person of the priest that, while respecting fully his human nature, the priest becomes integrally bonded and consecrated to the love and service of Christ the Priest. Ordination imposes a character on his soul which configures him in a special way to Christ the Head and Shepherd, to enable him prolong through history the work of Redemption.[8] Priesthood after the manner of Christ is not just a function; it engages the whole of a man's existence. Theological reflection on this reality has led the Church to see the deep congruence of celibacy with the life of the priest, of which the virginity of Christ is the prototype and exemplar.

The priest has a very special task in the Mystical Body in that he has to

---

5 Crescenzio Sepe, 'The Relevance of Priestly celibacy Today', in *For Love Alone*, op. cit., pp 69–70. **6** Cf. *Pastores dabo vobis*, 12. **7** Cf. no. 50. **8** Cf. ibid., nos. 14–15.

make the priesthood of Christ the Head sacramentally visible in history. Hence the figure of the priest is eminently sacramental in that he is the instrument of the mediation of Christ, especially through the Eucharistic sacrifice. As we have already seen, the reason for celibacy is dedication to Christ to build up the kingdom of Heaven on earth in response to a divine vocation. By living it authentically, the priest manifests that Christ is sufficiently rich and great to fill the heart of man. In his own way the priest gives witness that Christ is the one to whom ultimately all love refers. By his celibacy he lets it be known that henceforth he expects everything from God, the Creator of all love, in whose hands he places his human completion and his human fruitfulness. Consequently celibacy makes a constant appeal to the priest to live in intimacy with Christ.

ECCLESIAL CONSIDERATIONS

The consecrated celibacy of the priest is a sign and manifestation of the virginal love of Christ for his Spouse the Church. It is a visible reminder of the virginal and supernatural fruitfulness of this marriage by which the children of God are engendered.[9]

The priest is fundamentally a consecrated person, who by his very calling, as we are reminded in the letter to the Hebrews, is placed outside and above the common history of the rest of men (cf. Heb 5:1, 7:3). As a result of the Incarnation the priesthood of the Old Law was given a new configuration, a mysterious and sacramental transformation of the man-priest into the very person of Christ himself, in such a way that he could act in his name, and communicate the life of grace to men down through the centuries.[10]

If the Incarnate Word left himself free of all human attachments, no matter how noble they might have been, so as to facilitate his total availability for his ministry, we can easily understand how appropriate it is that the man-priest would do the same, renouncing freely, through celibacy, something which is good and holy in itself, so that he might more easily unite himself to Christ (cf. Mt 19:12; 1 Cor 7:32–34), and, through him, dedicate himself with complete freedom to the service of God and of souls.

The priest devotes himself to the service of Christ and his Mystical

---

9 Cf. Vatican II constitution on the Church, *Lumen gentium*, 42; *Presbyterorum ordinis*, 16. 10 Cf. del Portillo, op. cit., p. 44.

Body with a total dedication; in his prayer and Eucharistic life he imitates the Eternal High Priest who stands in the presence of God constantly interceding for us. Acting *in persona Christi* he is most intimately united to Christ's sacrifice on Calvary as he makes the daily offering of the Mass. By his life and example he makes Christ present among the faithful. To the people of God he is a sign and a pledge of that new life to which they are called through Baptism. His total availability makes him accessible and approachable at all times.

The priesthood, with its associated charism of celibacy, is a gift bestowed by the Holy Spirit, not for the use of the person who receives it, but for the benefit of the whole Church. John Paul II explains the ecclesiological implications of the intimate relationship between celibacy and priesthood as follows:

> It is especially important that the priest understand the theological motivation of the Church's law on celibacy. In as much as it is a law, it expresses *the Church's will*, even before the will of the subject expressed by his readiness. The will of the Church finds its ultimate motivation in the *link between celibacy and sacred Ordination*, which configures the priest to Jesus Christ the Head and Spouse of the Church.[11]

The Holy Father subsequently developed this point in an address to an international symposium on *Pastores dabo vobis*. Perpetual and freely chosen celibacy can only be fully understood in a Christological context. And 'therefore the ultimate reasons for the discipline of celibacy are not to be sought in psychological, sociological, historical or legal areas, but in those which are essentially theological and pastoral, that is within the ministerial charism itself'.[12]

While vocation to the priesthood is a personal grace, it belongs to the Church to choose those whom she judges to be qualified. The Church will never try to impose a charism on anyone, but she does have the right to lay hands exclusively on those who have received the free gift of chastity in the celibate life from the Holy Spirit. The priestly vocation, therefore, is not simply a subjective self-giving on the part of the individual, but also requires clear signs of a calling which only the bishop is deputed to ascertain and confirm.

---

11 *Pastores dabo vobis*, 29 (italics in original).   **12** Address, 28 May 1993.

SPOUSAL LOVE

Since the time of Paul VI's encyclical (1967) there has been a greater emphasis on the spousal meaning of celibacy. Up to then it was explained primarily from a christological, ecclesial, and salvific perspective. However, celibacy as an icon of the nuptial relationship between Christ and his Church acquires much more significance in *Pastores dabo vobis*.[13]

Probably nobody has done more than John Paul II himself to penetrate the nuptial dimension of Christology.[14] He highlights how central to our understanding of the faith is the spousal aspect of the Redemption, and thus the spousal dimension of the priest as icon of Christ. This idea of spousal love is one which the Holy Father has explored in several of his writings, especially at the beginning of his pontificate in his detailed commentary on chapters 1–4 of Genesis related to 'the nuptial meaning of the body'.[15] He returned to the same theme in *Mulieris dignitatem* in 1988.[16] This is a letter which has special significance for our understanding the nuptial meaning of the Redemption wrought by Christ as the Bridegroom of the Church, and hence also for our understanding of priestly celibacy.

The loss of the feminine sense of the Church as Bride and Mother has obscured for many an appreciation of its intimate nature. As a result, dissident voices protest against *it* as an oppressive, impersonal organisation for which they exhibit little affection. By contrast the saints and those who understand the real meaning of *sentire cum Ecclesia* (thinking in tune with the Church) see the Church as Mother, as a *She* who protects and nourishes her children. They also know how to distinguish between the Church as an institution, which is holy and immaculate as given us by Christ, and the activity of individual Christians subject to all the inherent ambivalence of a defective nature.[17]

The priest is 'the living image of Jesus Christ, the Spouse of the Church', this Christ who is Spouse in a special way in the sacrifice of Calvary, because the Church as Bride 'proceeds like a new Eve from the open side of the Redeemer on the Cross'.[18] His supreme priestly act is a spousal one, as St Paul explains when he encourages husbands and wives to love each other 'as Christ loved the Church and gave himself up for her' (Eph 5:25).

13 Cf. nos. 22, 23, 29.   14 Cf. John Saward, *Christ is the Answer: The Christ-Centred Teaching of Pope John Paul II*, Edinburgh, 1995, pp 65–7; 125–8.   15 Cf. John Paul II, *Original Unity of Man and Woman: Catechesis on the Book of Genesis*, Boston, 1981. This is a series of twenty three addresses given at the Wednesday audiences, between 5 September 1979 and 2 April 1980.   16 Apostolic letter on the dignity of women, 15 August 1988.   17 Cf. Saward, ibid., p. 67. See also Matthias J. Scheeben, *The Mysteries of Christianity*, London, 1961, pp 545–57.   18 *Pastores dabo vobis*, 22.

This is why 'Christ stands "before" the Church, and "nourishes and cherishes her" (Eph 5:29), giving his life for her'.[19] For this reason John Paul II invites us all to look at Christ with the bridal attitude of the Church: 'All human beings – both women and men – are called, through the Church, to be the "Bride" of Christ, the Redeemer of the world.'[20] Drawing on the rich analogy in St Paul's letter to the Ephesians he tells us that the gift generated by Christ's spousal love for man exceeded all human expectations: 'He loved them to the end' (Jn 13:1). He is husband of all the redeemed, and this is why Christ, who became the son of Mary, true man, is male, and why his maleness is an essential aspect of revelation.[21]

The Holy Mass, the sacrament of our Redemption, is also the 'Sacrament of the Bridegroom and the Bride', making present and realising anew in a sacramental manner 'the redemptive act of Christ the Bridegroom towards the Church the Bride. This is clear and unambiguous when the sacramental ministry of the Eucharist, in which the priest acts *in persona Christi*, is performed by a man'.[22] In this affirmation we see the basic reason why only men can be admitted to the priesthood. The priest, in the lambent phrase of Léon Bloy, is a generator of the infinite, and this is especially so on the altar.

Hence, 'in virtue of his configuration to Christ, the Head and Shepherd, the priest stands in a spousal relationship with regard to the community'.[23] The priest is an image of the nuptial love of Christ for his Church. Consequently, 'in his spiritual life he is called to live out Christ's spousal love towards the Church, his Bride. Therefore the priest's life ought to radiate this spousal character which demands that he be a witness to Christ's spousal love, and thus be capable of loving people with a heart which is new, generous, and pure, with genuine self-detachment, with full, constant and faithful dedication and at the same time with a kind of "divine jealousy" (cf. 2 Cor 11:2), and even with a kind of maternal tenderness, capable of bearing "the pangs of birth" until "Christ be formed" in the faithful (cf Gal 4:19).'[24]

Here we have the fundamental theological reason for priestly celibacy. The priest's total self-giving to the Church finds its justification in the fact that she is the Body and the Bride of Christ.[25] Following Christ, the Church as Bride is the only woman the priest can be wedded to, the only Body

19 Ibid. **20** *Mulieris dignitatem*, 25. **21** Cf. ibid. See also Manfred Hauke, *Women in the Priesthood? A Systematic Analysis in the Light of the Order of Creation and Redemption*, San Francisco, 1988, pp 249–67. **22** Cf. *Mulieris dignitatem*, 26. **23** *Pastores dabo vobis*, 22. **24** Ibid. **25** Cf. ibid., no. 23. See also Hauke, op. cit., pp 297–325.

over which he can have nuptial rights. He has to love her with an exclusive, sacrificial love which results in all the fruitfulness of spiritual paternity. For the priest, Christ is the source, the measure, and the impetus of his love for the Spouse and service of the Body.[26]

And so John Paul II can affirm: 'the Church, as the spouse of Jesus Christ, wishes to be loved by the priest in the total and exclusive manner in which Jesus Christ her Head and Spouse loved her. Priestly celibacy, then, is the gift of self *in* and *with* Christ *to* his Church and expresses the priest's service to the Church in and with the Lord'.[27] The demands of such a love clearly suggest the incompatibility of any other nuptial commitment on the part of the priest.

In the same way that the sacrificial love of Christ for his Spouse is consummated on Calvary, so in the Eucharist, the sacrifice of the Mass, the priest *in persona Christi* represents and makes present once more his love for the Church, and from it derive the grace and obligation of the priest to give to his whole life a 'sacrificial' dimension.[28] Hence we read in the recently published *Directory on the Ministry and Life of Priests*:

> The letter to the Ephesians (cf. Eph 5:25–27) shows a strict rapport between the priestly oblation of Christ (cf. 5:25) and the sanctification of the Church (cf. 5:26), loved with a spousal love. Sacramentally inserted into this priesthood of exclusive love of Christ for the Church, his faithful Spouse, the priest expresses this love with his obligation of celibacy, which also becomes a fruitful source of pastoral effectiveness.[29]

Because bishops are ordained with the fullness of the priesthood, they image Christ the Bridegroom in a paramount way. This is why they wear a wedding ring[30] and are always celibate in both East and West. In Church

---

26 Cf. *Pastores dabo vobis*, 23. At the same time it has to be admitted that the introduction of the permanent married diaconate with conjugal rights after Vatican II does create difficulties for the development of a coherent theology of celibacy; cf. Alfons M. Stickler, 'La continenza dei Diaconi specialmente nel primo millennio della Chiesa', in *Salesianum* 26 (1964) 275–302; George W. Rutler, 'A Consistent Theology of Clerical Celibacy' in *Homiletic and Pastoral Review*, February 1989, pp 13–14; Roman Cholij, 'Observaciones críticas acerca de los canones que tratan sobre el celibato en el Código de Derecho Canónico de 1983' in *Ius Canonicum*, 31 (1991) 295–305.   **27** *Pastores dabo vobis*, 29 (italics in original).   **28** Cf. ibid., no. 23   **29** Op. cit., no. 58.   **30** In the Middle Ages the *vinculum matrimonale*, or conjugal relationship of the bishop with his church, was symbolised by the handing over of the ring at his consecration with the formula: *Accipe anulum, fidei scilicet signaculum: quatenus sponsam Dei, sanctam videlicet ecclesiam, intemerata fide ornatus, illibate custodias* (cf. Josef Sellmair, *The Priest in the World*, London, 1954, p. 27).

history there is no precedent for a bishop obtaining a dispensation to marry on being laicised, as Talleyrand discovered to his chagrin, when in 1801 he tried to get the Vatican to ratify his civil marriage.

Since one can only go a certain distance in deriving a theology of celibacy by means of a logic of propositions, there is frequent recourse to symbolism in *Pastores dabo vobis* to describe the relationship between the priest and Christ. Here he is considered under the more suggestive titles of representative, image, and icon of the Lord Jesus. Because the gift of celibacy is such an integral part of the mystery of Christ, its understanding requires not only intellectual reflection but, above all, contemplation in prayer and adoration to achieve that deeper disclosure of its fuller meaning which only comes through the light of the Holy Spirit, the ultimate source of this charism.

MARY AND JOSEPH

The priest can also learn much about the nature of spousal love by reflecting on the love Joseph had for Mary, his virgin wife. Joseph's total and irrevocable gift of himself to our Lady, and the mystery of her life centred on the Incarnate word, is rich in meaning for the priest. Just as his life was a full commitment to God in the service of Mary and Jesus, so the priest's vocation is a total gift of himself to Christ for the service of the Church.

In his Apostolic Exhortation, *Redemptoris custos*, John Paul II describes the significance of the spousal love of St Joseph as follows: 'Analysing the nature of marriage, both St Augustine and St Thomas always identify it with an "indivisible union of souls", a "union of hearts", with "consent". These elements are found in an exemplary manner in the marriage of Mary and Joseph. At the culmination of the history of salvation, when God reveals his love for humanity through the gift of the Word, it is precisely the marriage of Mary and Joseph that brings to realisation in full "freedom" the "spousal gift of self " in receiving and expressing such a love.'[31]

The contemporary mentality finds it difficult to come to terms with this idea. By and large it is only familiar with the concept of love as possession, or the indulgence of sensation and emotion. Love as gratuitous self-giving is incomprehensible to a culture in which an essentially hedonistic and utilitarian ethic prevails.

---

31 Apostolic Exhortation on *The Person and Mission of St Joseph in the Life of Christ and of the Church*, 15 August 1989, no. 7.

One of the ideas frequently affirmed by John Paul II is that of 'the person as gift' as the only basis for authentic human, spousal love, or indeed for the response of any individual to the love of Christ. This approach enables us to raise up the concept of love to something that goes far beyond the domains of sensation or mere possession. On this higher plane love incorporates the ideas of admiration, gratitude for the gift received, and self-giving for the sake of the beloved.

This pattern of love is not something which comes naturally; it has to be learned through a process of formation and self-education, a struggle against selfish and sensual tendencies, and has to be based on specific models. For the priest, Christ is the exemplar *par excellence* of the spousal love which by vocation he has to aspire to and to imitate. As we have already said, he will also learn much about the nature of this commitment by reflecting on the relationship between Joseph and Mary: 'A man who, showing his full trust in God and a faith marked by an incredible strength and humility, and free from suspicion, accepted a difficult gift. By somehow overcoming his own human dimension, Joseph was able to understand what seemed incomprehensible.'[32] As Paul VI reminds us, his fatherhood is expressed concretely 'in his having made his life a service, a sacrifice to the mystery of the Incarnation and to the redemptive mission connected with it; in having used the legal authority which was his over the Holy Family in order to make a total gift of self, of his life and work; in having turned his human vocation to domestic love into a superhuman oblation of self, an oblation of his heart and all his abilities into love placed at the service of the Messiah growing up in his house'.[33]

SPIRITUAL PATERNITY

Celibacy, then, is not just an external constraint imposed on the priestly ministry, nor can it be considered as a merely human institution established by law. Rather 'this bond, freely assumed, has theological and moral characteristics which are prior to the juridical characteristics, and is a sign of that spousal reality present in sacramental Ordination'.[34] Another consequence, directly related to this, is that the priest acquires a 'true and real spiritual paternity which has universal dimensions'.[35]

32 Wanda Poltawska, 'Roots of Spousal Love', in *Osservatore Romano*, 28 September 1994.
33 Paul VI, Address, 19 March 1966.   34 *Directory on the Ministry and Life of Priests*, op. cit., no. 58.   35 Ibid.

Celibacy has a deep inner affinity with the calling to be a priest and, consequently, it is misleading to speak of the 'burden of celibacy', as if priesthood and celibacy were in some sense irreconcilable. The priest who lives for Christ, and from Christ, usually has no insurmountable difficulties in living out his celibacy. He is not immune to the normal temptations of the flesh but, as a result of his ascetical training, the daily cultivation of his spiritual life, and the prudent distancing of himself from anything which could constitute a danger to his chastity, he will encounter great joy in his vocation and experience a deep spiritual paternity in bringing supernatural life to souls.

As Fr Stanley Jaki comments, 'A priest has compensations for celibacy which a married man (or woman), who in St Paul's divinely inspired observation is always divided between earthly and heavenly concerns, can but vaguely suspect. That compensation is the spiritual fatherhood which a priest may experience on not a few occasions. He may do so above all when he celebrates Mass with the extraordinary faith that thereby he enters into the closest imaginable symbiosis with the crucified Christ. If his faith makes him see in that symbiosis the highest life-giving role available to man, he will have the only truly positive perspective in which priestly celibacy can be seen. It will become for him the implantation of St Paul's experience of being "crucified with Christ". It takes no degree in New Testament Greek to perceive that experience as the deepest living truth available to priests. Margaret Bosco, a desperately poor, largely uneducated, and incredibly hard-working peasant woman, saw far deeper than most recent authors on Mass and priesthood when she walked the long miles home with her son, the future saint, after his first Mass. Suddenly she said to him: "So now you are a priest, John, my son, and will say Mass every day. You must remember this: beginning to say Mass means beginning to suffer. At first you won't notice it, but in time, one day, you will see your mother is right ... Henceforth think of nothing but the saving of souls and don't worry about me". Such was the inner logic of spiritual fatherhood, a logic accurately perceived by a simple Christian widow.'[36]

Thanks to this total self-giving which the priest freely embraces, and the renunciation of a paternity according to the flesh, he receives in return a notable enrichment of 'paternity according to the spirit'. This renunciation is rooted in a spousal love for Christ and his Church, a love which

---

36 Stanley L. Jaki, 'Man of One Wife or Celibacy', in *Homiletic and Pastoral Review*, January 1986, pp 20–21.

develops in its care and concern for people, and which makes possible a better pastoral service:

> The Church is virgin because 'she guards whole and pure the faith given to the Spouse'. Christ, according to the teaching contained in the Letter to the Ephesians (cf. Eph 5:32), is the Spouse of the Church. The nuptial meaning of the Redemption impels each of us to guard our fidelity to this vocation, by means of which we are made sharers in the saving mission of Christ, priest, prophet and king. The analogy between the Church and the Virgin Mother has a special eloquence for us, who link our priestly vocation to celibacy, that is, to 'making ourselves eunuchs for the sake of the kingdom of heaven'. We freely renounce marriage and establishing our own family in order to be better able to serve God and neighbour. It can be said that we renounce fatherhood 'according to the flesh' in order that there may grow and develop in us a fatherhood 'according to the Spirit' (cf. Jn 1:13) which, as has already been said, possesses at the same time maternal characteristics.[37]

In virtue of this renunciation for the kingdom of heaven, the priest, 'consecrated to God', realises existentially that which he already is ontologically through the grace of the sacrament: he becomes 'a man for others': 'Our celibacy manifests on its part that we are entirely consecrated to the work to which the Lord has called us. The priest, seized by Christ, becomes "the man for others", completely available for the kingdom, his heart undivided, capable of accepting fatherhood in Christ.'[38] This is a reality which he makes visible and operative in the total dedication of his person to the good of the community of the faithful entrusted to him: 'The celibacy of the priest does not have only an eschatological significance, as a witness to the future Kingdom. It also expresses the profound connection which unites him to the faithful, in so far as the community of faith is born from his charism and is intended to sum up all the capacity for love which the priest bears within himself.'[39]

That priestly charity, which flowers in the heart thanks to celibacy, knows no barriers of time or place, nor does it make any exception of persons. It ought to be a universal charity, a reflection of the charity of Christ the priest for all men and for each one: 'The priest who, in the

---

37 Holy Thursday Letter to Priests, 1988, no. 5.   38 Address, Paris, 30 May 1980, no. 8.
39 Homily, 4 November 1980.

choice of celibacy, renounces human love in order to be open completely to love of God, becomes free to give himself to men through a gift that does not exclude anyone, but embraces them all in the flow of charity, which comes from God (cf. Rom 5:5) and leads to God.'[40] This is a charity which is expressed in pastoral care for the salvation of each person with whom the priest comes in contact. No one can be excluded from an authentically priestly heart.

Observing celibacy for the sake of the kingdom of heaven does not mean being any less a man. As a consequence the heart is free to love Christ and to love others in an inclusive way. There is the joy of the apostolate, of the care of souls, of leading others to Christ and to an awareness of their Christian vocation: 'By freely choosing priestly celibacy the priest renounces earthly fatherhood and gains a share in the Fatherhood of God. Instead of becoming father to one or more children on earth, he is now able to love everybody in Christ. Yes, Jesus calls his priest to carry his Father's tender love for each and every person. For this reason, people call him "Father".'[41]

ESCHATOLOGICAL AND SALVIFIC MEANING

While celibacy is a sign of the kingdom of God on earth, it is above all a sign of future glory where, as Christ said, 'in the Resurrection they neither marry nor are given in marriage but are all like angels in heaven' (Mt 22:30). In this sense celibacy proclaims on earth the final stages of salvation (cf. 1 Cor 7:29–31), and acts as a reminder for all that we don't have here a lasting city, but are mere pilgrims on the way to our definitive homeland. This witness is essential at the present time when there is so much pressure to give absolute value to concerns of the present life at the expense of the only thing that matters in the long run – our eternal salvation.

The Synod Fathers in October 1990 emphasised that priestly celibacy was a prophetic sign for today's world, a sign of the kingdom which is to come where, as we have said, marriage will no longer be a feature.[42] The celibate priest is thus not only able to speak about the world to come, but bears witness to it by his life-style, giving hope to believer and nonbeliever alike in the resurrection to a future life of glory. Priestly celibacy

---

40 Address, Kinshasa, 4 May 1980, no. 4.   **41** Mother Teresa of Calcutta, 'Priestly Celibacy: Sign of the Charity of Christ' in *For Love Alone*, op. cit., p. 212.   **42** Cf. *Pastores dabo vobis*, 29.

is a witness to the conviction that man does not find the deepest meaning of his life within the apparent self-sufficiency of the present world. By his life-style the priest should bear testimony to the fact that death is not the end, but rather the beginning of a definitive future. His life should be a constant reminder to people that this life has real value only in so far as it an opportunity to realise one's baptismal vocation and establish one's Christian identity. The celibate priest points to the value of the one thing necessary (cf. Lk 10:42) – personal holiness which is achieved through the power of God's grace and our response to it.

The world, as the Holy Father has frequently affirmed, is in great need of re-evangelization, especially the countries of the Old World. If this new evangelization is to be effective it needs the radical gospel commitment which was always the basis of winning souls for Christ in the past. Historically one of the most important elements in this work of evangelization was the dynamic of priestly celibacy. It will continue to be so in the future.

Celibacy is not then just an extrinsic element of the priestly state, a 'superstructure' added to his priesthood as a result of influences derived from the monastic or religious life; rather it is something which is intimately connected to his participation in the priesthood of Christ. It is not merely an historical element in the priesthood, but is the result of the action of the Holy Spirit in the Church.[43]

CELIBACY AND MARRIAGE

In its deepest Christian sense celibacy, as we have seen, cannot be reduced to the mere fact of not getting married. It is a response to a particular vocation from God to devote oneself fully, body and soul, to his service. Although marriage is a 'great sacrament' (Eph 5:32), and is blessed by the Church as a way to holiness, the same Church clearly affirms that celibacy for the sake of the kingdom of heaven is *of itself* superior to marriage.[44] This doesn't imply in any way a disdain for human sexuality, or that those who are married are called to a lesser or second-rate holiness. To reason in this way would reveal a truncated understanding of the Incarnation and its implications. Certainly Vatican II has a very different perception of the case in that it recommends celibacy in the context of affirming marriage as

---

43 Cf. del Portillo, op. cit., p. 51.   44 Cf. Council of Trent, *De sacramento matrimonii*, can. 10, DS 1810. See also John Paul II, 1979 Holy Thursday Letter, no. 8.

a vocation and a way to holiness.[45] And so John Paul II can testify, 'Virginity and apostolic celibacy not only do not contradict the dignity of marriage but presuppose it and confirm it.' More specifically, 'Virginity keeps alive in the Church the awareness of the mystery of marriage and defends it against all attempts to impoverish it or reduce its importance.'[46]

Priests have a duty of fidelity to Christ, the Church, and especially to those who are married. In his first Holy Thursday Letter to Priests, John Paul II counselled: 'Our brothers and sisters joined by the marriage bond *have the right to expect from us*, Priests and Pastors, good example and the *witness of fidelity to one's vocation until death*, a fidelity to the vocation that we choose through the sacrament of Orders just as they choose it through the sacrament of Matrimony. Also in this sphere and in this sense we should understand our ministerial priesthood as "subordination" to the common priesthood of all the faithful, of the laity, especially of those who live in marriage and form a family.'[47]

He emphasised this point in his very first encyclical, *Redemptor hominis*, which was published around the same time, in the context of reminding us that fidelity to vocation in general was an expression of the 'kingly service' arising from our baptism:

> Married people must be distinguished for fidelity to their vocation, as is demanded by the indissoluble nature of the sacramental institution of marriage. Priests must be distinguished for a similar fidelity to their vocation, in view of the indelible character that the sacrament of Orders stamps on their souls. In receiving this sacrament, we in the Latin Church knowingly and freely commit ourselves to live celibacy, and each one of us must therefore do all he can, with God's grace, to be thankful for this gift and faithful to the bond that he has accepted forever. He must do so as married people must, for they must endeavour with all their strength to persevere in their matrimonial union, building up the family community through this witness of love and educating new generations of men and women, capable in their turn of dedicating the whole of their lives to their vocation, that is to say to the 'kingly service' of which Jesus Christ has offered us an example and the most beautiful model.[48]

---

45 Cf. *Lumen gentium*, 11 and 41; *Gaudium et spes*, 48 and 52. **46** *Familiaris consortio*, 16. **47** Holy Thursday Letter to Priests, 1979, no. 9 (italics in original). **48** Encyclical *Redemptor hominis*, 4 March 1979, no. 21.

Celibacy is then a commitment which is similar to the fidelity which spouses reciprocally offer each other in marriage.[49] It is a 'duty which demands of priests a fidelity to death'.[50]

The priest is not simply an ordained bachelor. Priestly celibacy is a renunciation of marriage for the sake of the kingdom of heaven; it is a unique form of self-giving to Christ, coupled with the desire to be totally available and to become *alter Christus* to all men. Human reasoning alone is insufficient to understand such a commitment; it is only in the light of faith that one can appreciate how a man would want to give his heart totally to Christ, as a response to the immense love which the Master has already shown him.

This self-giving to God 'does not emasculate or neutralise the celibate'.[51] There is a radical difference between sexual repression and a conscious, free self-donation to Christ which, informed by grace, enables the priest to forego the demands of the flesh and give himself, body and soul, to the Lord. In responding to his vocation to celibacy the future priest is not unaware of the difficulties which this commitment involves. He also becomes conscious, as he grows in his priesthood, of the danger that, surreptitiously, other sources of human fulfilment (over-involvement in sport, social activities, etc.) could begin to substitute themselves for the renunciation of marriage, which contradict and could even undermine the real reason for his celibacy.

When we hear talk of the so-called 'burden of celibacy', it should also be remembered that Christ promised a more abundant recompense, even in this life, to those who would leave home, family, wife and children for the sake of the kingdom of God (cf. Lk 18:29–30). In words which showed that human perception alone was insufficient to grasp the mystery involved, he recommended a more perfect consecration to the work of spreading the kingdom of heaven by means of celibacy, as a special gift (cf. Mt 19:11). It is perhaps the most radical sign of the new creation brought about by Christ

CELIBACY, FREEDOM AND FAITH

Apostolic celibacy gives the priest a total freedom to love the Lord with all his mind and soul. Consequently there is a need for a deep understanding

---

49 Cf. ibid.   **50** Cf. Holy Thursday Letter, 1979, no. 9.   **51** Cf. von Hildebrand, op. cit., p. 38.

of freedom from a human and supernatural point of view to really understand celibacy. It cannot be imposed by law; it is a gift freely offered by God, and freely accepted by the seminarian as a precondition to his ordination.[52]

The Holy Father reminds us that the widespread view that priestly celibacy in the Catholic Church is imposed by law is the result of misunderstanding, if not of downright bad faith. Commitment to celibacy is, in the first place, a consequence of a free decision after a number of years of preparation; it is a lifelong commitment accepted with full personal responsibility; it is, as John Paul II emphasises, 'a matter of keeping one's word to Christ and the Church'. This is a duty which is an expression of inner maturity. The dignity and maturity of the priest is shown when this conscious and free decision 'encounters difficulties, is put to the test, or is exposed to temptation', which, like any other Christian, the priest is not spared.[53]

Cardinal Joachim Meisner, archbishop of Cologne, made a number of very relevant points in this context. 'Celibacy,' he says, 'is plausible only if one believes in Jesus Christ. For a person who does not experience the existence of Jesus Christ, for a person who does not believe in him, the celibate is, in fact, a madman or somebody who is sick. Consequently some do not even conceive or tolerate that others can live it. It is not a problem related to canon law or to dogma, but to faith in God; a man can come so close to God that he prefers union with God to any other type of union. Celibacy cannot be explained by sociological, psychological or pedagogical reasons, but only by spiritual and theological ones. Without prayer, without dialogue with God, celibacy makes no sense. I repeat: if a person does not take God seriously, he will not be able to understand the essence of celibacy. At times I have the impression that criticism of celibacy is only

---

52 For a discussion of formation in freedom, see chapter 5.   53 Cf. Letter, Holy Thursday 1979, no. 9. The Holy Father developed this point the following year in an address to priests at Fulda in Germany. He reminded them that they had perceived the call of God from the depths of their own weakness, and that the constant awareness of this weakness should never be a reason for being unfaithful to that call. He continued: 'Christ has taught us that man has above all a right to his greatness, a right to that which really towers above him. For it is precisely here that his special dignity emerges: here is revealed the wonderful power of grace: our true greatness is a gift deriving from the Holy Spirit. In Christ man has a right to such greatness. And the Church, through the same Christ, has a right to the gift of man: to a gift by which man offers himself totally to God, in which he also opts for celibacy "for the Kingdom of Heaven" (Mt 19:12) in order to be the servant of all' (Address, 17 November 1980, in *Osservatore Romano*, 15 December 1980).

an alibi for those who want to dispense themselves from that radical change of lifestyle which the following of Christ demands.'[54]

Indeed the priesthood is so charged with potential for self-realisation that, through the grace of God, it can give to the man who has chosen this life a fullness which is often lacking in the lives of others. And so 'spiritual fatherhood, the power to bind and loose, the joy of bearing, with his own hands, the supreme gift of God himself to others: these place the priestly dignity on so high a plane in the hierarchy of human possibilities that it cannot be compared with anything else whatsoever and leaves no room for frustration.'[55]

FORMATION IN CELIBACY AND HOLINESS

We can perhaps best understand celibacy in the context of the fact that the priest has a very specific vocation to holiness,[56] and that 'the Holy Spirit, poured out in the sacrament of Holy Orders, is a source of holiness and a call to sanctification'.[57]

In his 1992 synodal document the Holy Father dwells on the fact that priests have the duty to become 'saints', and sees the Vatican II decree on

---

54 Cf. *Osservatore Romano*, 25 October 1992. The Cardinal went on to say: 'Celibacy is too sacred and too important an issue to be subjected to the judgement of public opinion which is fundamentally non-Christian.' He recalled the gospel scene of Jesus in Bethany when Mary anointed his feet with a very expensive perfume which provoked the criticism of Judas. But Jesus defended Mary's generosity, and Meisner comments : 'I ask those narrow-minded people – doesn't the Lord merit that men would give their lives totally to him? Isn't it also possible that if they didn't do this they could squander their lives? On the contrary, isn't it normal that the mean-spirited, the Judases ... distance themselves from him? People do not understand celibacy, but what really escapes them is not why so many answer yes, but rather why in fact God calls them. Love responds only to love'.

Meisner affirms that celibacy will continue to exist: 'God is always magnanimous and we cannot deceive him with our limited human conceptions of things. Celibacy is a gift of that loving God, a precious gift for his Church. This gift has enriched the Church down through the centuries, and to reject it would mean an impoverishment. The Church will continue to be faithful to its spouse Jesus Christ, and one particular form of that fidelity is to give oneself completely to Christ in celibacy, to say yes without reserve to that God who makes us capable of it and who offers it to us as a gift. There are other ways of giving oneself to God, in Christian marriage, for example, or by entering a monastery or responding to some other type of vocation. We know that God is not giving us a loan of something, but rather a present which is not just for today or tomorrow, but forever. For those who know this, celibacy presents no problem'.   **55** Wanda Poltawaska, 'Priestly Celibacy in the light of Medicine and Psychology' in *For Love Alone*, op. cit., p. 89.   **56** Cf. *Pastores dabo vobis*, 20.   **57** Cf. ibid., no. 27.

the ministry and life of priests as offering a particularly rich theological synthesis of this responsibility.[58] Basically what it says is that, if lay people are called and obliged to holiness, 'priests are bound in a special way to strive for this perfection, since they are consecrated to God in a new way by their ordination'.[59] This is the spiritual context in which the living out of celibacy makes most sense. It is in the light of this specific vocation to holiness that the gift and responsibility of celibacy acquire their fullest meaning. The quest for holiness allows the priest to grow in faith. Commitment to celibacy and supernatural faith are inextricably linked, because such faith will be a constant reminder to the priest of the incredible power that is in him as a result of the imposition of episcopal hands, a power which he exercises in a unique way on the altar. For believer and unbeliever alike, the celibate priest is a permanent intimation, and a powerful witness to the fact that man, in spite of all his propensity to sin, is called to a supernatural vocation, and that his life has real meaning only in so far as he tries to follow in the footsteps of Christ.

THEOLOGY OF RELATIONSHIPS WITH WOMEN

John Paul II has considered in some depth the question of the priest's relationship with women. As always when he writes about woman he considers her in relation to the Blessed Virgin. For a Christian, he tells us, a theological consideration of women is always linked to Mary, Mother and Virgin, because of her special relationship with the Incarnate Word and with the Church, his Mystical Body. But this, he reminds us, is also true at the historical, anthropological and cultural levels.[60]

In his many commentaries on human love, he emphasises that 'in God's eternal plan, woman is the one in whom the order of love in the created world of persons first takes root'.[61] This leads him to the conclusion that 'the dignity of woman is measured in the order of love', a love which she receives by the very fact of her femininity. By reference to the Pauline analogy between Christ's love for his Church as between Bridegroom and Bride, he draws attention to the way in which this shows how every human being – man and woman – is loved by God in Christ, and con-

---

58 Cf. *Presbyterorum ordinis*, 12. **59** Ibid., quoted in no. 20 of *Pastores dabo vobis*. **60** Cf. Holy Thursday Letter to Priests, 1995, no. 2. **61** *Mulieris dignitatem*, 29.

cludes that it is precisely the woman, the bride, who manifests this truth to everyone in a special way. This he refers to as the 'prophetic' character of women in their femininity, something which finds its highest expression in the Virgin Mother of God.[62] It is in this context that the Holy Father analyses the relationship between the priest and the role of woman as *sister*. This arises in the first place because the priest in his ontological identity with Christ 'shares in a special way in the relationship of brotherhood offered by Christ to all the redeemed'.[63]

Reflecting perhaps on his own youth, he tells us how every priest, from childhood on, has met girls, if not in his own family certainly in his neighbourhood or at school. In this setting, not only vocations to marriage but also vocations to the priesthood take root. What he is affirming is that these priestly vocations do not develop in isolation, and consequently every candidate for the priesthood, when he crosses the threshold of the seminary, has behind him the experience of having known many young people of his own age, men and women. When he tells us that, in order to live as a celibate in a mature and spontaneous way, the priest should develop deep within himself the image of women as sisters, there is little doubt that, apart from theological considerations, he is opening up to us a window on his personal experience.[64]

Because men and women are brothers and sisters in Christ independently of any family relationship, the priest can always exercise a ministry of authentic spiritual fatherhood to all on the basis of this universal bond.[65] John Paul II sees in the idea of 'woman as sister' a 'specific manifestation of the spiritual beauty of women', which is at the same time 'a revelation that they are in a certain sense "set apart"'. If the priest with the help of divine grace, and under the special protection of Mary, gradually develops such an attitude to women, he will see, the Holy Father assures him, that his ministry will be responded to with 'a sense of great trust' on the part of women as sisters and mothers in the great variety of life situations.[66]

The figure of woman as sister has a unique significance in Christian culture, in that through her generous self-giving she develops a particular spiritual motherhood.[67] Thus the priest should follow the advice given by

---

62 Cf. ibid.   **63** Cf. Holy Thursday Letter to Priests, 1995, no. 4.   **64** This impression is reinforced by the moving and detailed account of the life of the young Karol Wjotyla as schoolboy and university student in Tad Szulc's *Pope John Paul II: The Biography*, New York, 1995.   **65** Cf. Holy Thursday Letter to Priests, 1995, no. 4.   **66** Cf. ibid., no. 5.   **67** 'The figure of woman as sister has considerable importance in our Christian civilisation, in which countless women have become *sisters to everyone*, thanks to their exemplary attitude towards their neighbour, especially to those in need. A *"sister" is a guarantee*

Paul to Timothy: 'to treat older women like mothers, younger women like sisters, in all purity' (1 Tim 5:2). Because of his deliberate choice of celibacy for the sake of the kingdom of heaven, women for the priest have always to be sisters, and therefore the only adequate response of the priest to them is to consciously foster their dignity as sisters. If the priestly ministry is inspired by this Marian spirit, 'then our priesthood will be kept safe in her hands, indeed in her heart, and we shall be able to open it to everyone. In this way our priesthood, in all its dimensions, will be fruitful and salvific'.[68]

---

of selflessness: in the school, in the hospital, in the prison and in other areas of social service. When a woman remains single, in her "gift of self as sister" by means of apostolic commitment or generous dedication to neighbour, she develops a particular *spiritual motherhood*. The selfless gift of femininity "as sister" lights up human existence, evokes the best sentiments of which human beings are capable and always leaves behind gratitude for the good freely offered' (ibid., italics in original). In his articulation of this theology of women, it would seem that John Paul II has drawn on, among others, the insights of the German philosopher, Edith Stein, a Jewish convert who later, as a Carmelite nun, St Teresa Benedicta of the Cross, was martyred in Auschwitz in 1942. She was beatified by John Paul II in 1987 (cf. Laura Garcia, 'Edith Stein – Convert, Nun, Martyr', in *Crisis* magazine, June 1997, pp 18–23). **68** Holy Thursday Letter, 1995, no. 8.

4

Anthropological Considerations

DEVELOPMENT OF A CHRISTIAN ANTHROPOLOGY

The theology of the body as developed by John Paul II offers many insights which will help priests not only to understand celibacy at a deeper level, but also to preach with more conviction about chastity as a virtue to be lived by every Christian. In addition it offers a clear anthropological vision for dealing with the pastoral aspects of marriage.

The development of anthropology as an individual science or discipline is primarily a modern phenomenon. It was a consequence of the detachment of the study of man from the larger framework of theological and metaphysical inquiry. In addition, Descartes' particular vision of man gave scientific anthropology its definitive direction, which was developed either as a scientific investigation of the human body, or as a humanistic examination of man as a knowing and acting subject. However, 'with the differentiation of scientific methodology and the dissolution of the philosophy of history into a positivistic science of history, discourse about the essence of man increasingly lost its foundation. Besides, with the growing acceptance of the theory of evolution, the essential difference between man and animal became more and more fluid, so that the privileged position of man became ever more dubious.'[1]

In the first half of the twentieth century, in response to this reductionist approach, various attempts were made to re-establish a philosophical anthropology fuelled by the neo-Thomist revival. As a consequence there was a recovery of the need to postulate a unity of man's essence which embraced both his subjectivity and his objectivity, and the ethical consequences which derive from this position.

As Kasper points out, the fact that Vatican II was the first council of the Church to take up the question of anthropology as a subject in its own right has to be seen in this context. This it did in the constitution on the Church in the modern world, *Gaudium et spes*, articulating the essential relationship between Christology and an authentic anthropology, against a theological background which assumes the unity of the orders of creation and redemption in salvation history.

1 Walter Kasper, 'The Theological Anthropology of *Gaudium et spes*', *Communio* 23, Spring 1996, p. 130.

The Church discovers its doctrine on anthropology in the pages of Sacred Scripture. Beginning with the creation in Genesis, it considers man's essential nature, his capacity to know himself, and to recognise that he has a spiritual and immortal soul. It does not deny his ambivalent response to God's plan, his wounded condition after the fall, his propensity to sin. It also sees that his dignity derives from his capacity to grasp the truth and to be guided in his behaviour by moral conscience.[2]

It proclaims Jesus Christ as the origin and end of true humanity. Or as the conciliar text puts it: 'In reality it is only in the mystery of the Word made flesh that the mystery of man truly becomes clear ... Human nature, by the very fact that it was assumed, not absorbed, in him, has been raised in us also to a dignity beyond compare. For, by his incarnation, he, the son of God, has in a certain way united himself with each man. He worked with human hands, he thought with a human mind. He acted with a human will, and with a human heart he loved. Born of the Virgin Mary, he has truly been made one of us, like to us in all things except sin.'[3]

This statement of Vatican II is the core of the Church's anthropology, which identifies it not only in a general way as Christian but even more as a Christological anthropology. What binds anthropology and Christology together is the concept of man as *imago Dei*, image of God. This is because, 'as the image of God, man finds his ultimate and definitive fulfilment and completion only in that intimate communion with God which has appeared in a unique and unsurpassable way in Jesus Christ, the God-man'.[4]

But the Christology of the Incarnation finds its completion in the Christology of the Cross, so that we would be freed from the bondage of the devil, sin and death. By suffering for us, Christ gave us an example and showed us the way to follow 'so that life and death are made holy and acquire a new meaning'.[5] Consequently, the same conciliar document can summarise: 'Such is the nature and the greatness of the mystery of man as enlightened for the faithful by the Christian revelation. It is therefore through Christ, and in Christ, that light is thrown on the riddle of suffering and death which, apart from his Gospel, overwhelms us. Christ has risen again, destroying death by his death, and has given life abundantly to us so that, becoming sons in the Son, we may cry out in the Spirit: Abba Father!'[6] This is the fundamental truth about our being and existence: we

---

2 Cf. *Gaudium et spes*, 12–21.   3 Ibid., no. 22.   4 Kasper, op. cit., p. 137. Cf. *Gaudium et spes*, 12.   5 *Gaudium et spes*, 22.   6 Ibid.

have been created to become children of a God who loves us as a Father, following the way carved out by his Son, and moulded to that pattern by the work of the Spirit.[7]

It is this anthropology which John Paul II takes as his point of departure in his reflection on human sexuality and its purpose in God's plan of creation and redemption. Given that, as a Council Father, while still Archbishop of Krakow, he was one of the main drafters of the text of *Gaudium et spes*, it is not surprising that he frequently returns to this conciliar document to illustrate his considerations. His very first encyclical *Redemptor hominis*[8] was a restatement and a development of the Christian anthropology of Vatican II. There he tells us that in Christ 'has been revealed in a new and more wonderful way the fundamental truth concerning creation ... In Jesus Christ the visible world, which God created for man, recovers again its original link with the divine source of Wisdom and Love.'[9] Here he repeats the words of Vatican II: 'Christ the new Adam, in the very revelation of the mystery of the Father and of his love, *fully reveals man to himself* and brings to light his most high calling.'[10] In subsequent years, in his many documents and addresses, this truth and its implications was to become the central refrain of his pontificate. Only recently he emphasised again the idea that the answers to the deepest questions of the human heart can only be found in Jesus Christ who is 'the key, the centre and the purpose of the whole of man's history'.[11]

John Paul II insists that 'the special attention that must be paid to the human being and to his dignity must not let us forget that God is the goal of our journey. *"Ambula per hominem et pervenis ad Deum"*, St Augustine writes, in reference to the holy humanity of Christ, stressing how he is the "one mediator between God and men" (1 Tim 2:5) and how he mediates through man. St Teresa of Jesus, doctor of the Church, echoes him by recalling that, to go to God through Christ, we must pass through the Man whom the Son became, taking our humanity on himself (cf *Libro de la Vida*, chap.22).'[12]

---

7 Cf. St Thomas Aquinas, *Summa Theologiae*, III, 23, 2, ad 3.   8 Published 4 March 1979.   9 Ibid., no. 8.   10 *Gaudium et spes*, 22 (emphasis John Paul II).   11 Address, 8 November 1995, quoting *Gaudium et spes*, 10.   12 Message to the Pontifical Lateran University, Rome, 7 November 1996, no. 6. He goes on to remind the Lateran that 'it is called to reaffirm the primacy of God, entering into the debate about the *humanum*, which has marked a large part of the 20th century, and on which the Second Vatican Council reflected deeply, especially in the Pastoral Constitution *Gaudium et spes*. All this is possible through a continuous conversion to Christ, never separated from the careful study of theology and the sciences connected with it' (ibid.)

THE NUPTIAL MEANING OF THE BODY

It is not without significance that on the very occasion when Christ most powerfully enunciated his teaching on the indissolubility of marriage, he also affirmed the vocation to celibacy 'for the sake of the kingdom of heaven' (cf. Mt 19:3–12). In reply to his disciples' objection that Moses had allowed divorce, he directed their minds back to man's condition at 'the beginning' (cf. Gen 2:24), to his situation before the fall. Christ was making the point that it is only by reflection on man's identity in the state of original innocence that we can begin to understand the reasons for the indissoluble nature of the marriage bond. The same holds true if we are going to be able to establish an anthropological grounding for celibacy.

As we have already seen, John Paul II makes the challenging affirmation that it is precisely the person who understands the full potential for self-giving offered by marriage who can best make a mature offering of himself in celibacy. Indeed he goes so far as to assert that vocation to celibacy is, in a certain sense, indispensable so that 'the nuptial meaning of the body' may more easily be recognised in conjugal and family life. And this is because the key to the understanding of the sacramentality of marriage is the spousal love of Christ for his Church.[13]

After his election as Pope in 1978, John Paul II turned to the creation accounts in Genesis to establish from Revelation the elements of a Christian anthropology which would attempt to understand and interpret man in what is essentially human. Just as Christ referred his questioners about the indissolubility of marriage to 'the beginning' (cf. Mt 19:4), so the Holy Father returns to the same Old Testament source to draw out of that original human experience many deep insights into the notions of innocence, grace, lust, sin, etc. This 'beginning' is not merely something which refers to the historical past; it is also a sure guide to the knowledge of man in his present condition.

In preparation for the 1980 Synod of Bishops, convoked to study the topic of the Christian Family, he began a series of addresses in his Wednesday audiences on 'the nuptial meaning of the body', which was to run intermittently, in over a hundred sessions, from September 1979 to November 1984.[14] This is rightly regarded as a brilliant, magisterial restatement of

13 Cf. Address, 5 May 1982, nos. 3–7.   14 These addresses are available in the weekly English language edition of *Osservatore Romano*. They are also published in collected form by St Paul Editions, Boston: *Original Unity of Man and Woman: Catechesis on the Book of Genesis* (1981); *Blessed are the Pure of Heart: Catechesis on the Sermon on the Mount and Writings of St Paul* (1983); *Reflections on Humanae Vitae* (1984); *The Theology of Marriage and Celibacy* (1986).

Christian anthropology and its implications for sexual morality, related both to marriage and celibacy. In it he brings together a vast range of scriptural and philosophical insights, focused from the perspective of the human person as 'image of God'.

Cardinal Ratzinger, identifying a series of fundamental moral errors which afflict our times, observes that in the culture of the 'developed' world, where the indissoluble link between sexuality and marriage has been broken, followed by a rupture between sexuality and procreation, sex has remained without a *locus* and has lost its essential point of reference. In this context it follows logically that 'every form of sexuality is equivalent and, therefore, of equal worth', since no other objective justification can be found for it than the subjective one of the pleasure. The next stage is that all forms of sexual gratification are transformed into 'rights' of the individual and become an expression of human 'liberation'.[15]

This uprooting of the person from his nature leads to the trivialization of human sexuality by science and technology, because the natural and fundamental connections between sexuality and procreation are destroyed. The vision of man made to the image of God is lost sight of; he is no longer regarded as a person but as a thing. He becomes the object of technical categories and is redefined according to functional requirements, thus stripping him of his individuality and his dignity.[16]

It is precisely because of the crisis of moral values, and especially those related to sexual morality, that the Pope saw it was necessary to reaffirm the fundamental elements of an authentic anthropology if we are to understand the meaning of the Christian virtue of chastity. John Paul II, fully aware of the challenge involved, has over the past twenty years articulated more clearly than anybody else the framework of such an anthropology. Let us examine some of its core ideas.

OLD TESTAMENT TEACHING ON CHASTITY

In his analysis of the first three chapters of Genesis, he affirms that creation is an expression of God's gratuitous love, and hence man's existence is

---

15 *The Ratzinger Report*: Joseph Cardinal Ratzinger with Vittorio Messori, Leominister, 1985, pp 84–5. The separation of sexuality from procreation has led to the opposite extreme, the nightmare scenario of making procreation independent of sexuality through medico-technical experimentation.   **16** Cf. Alice Ramos, 'Man and Woman, the Image of God who is Love' in *The Church at the Service of the Family* (Proceedings of the Sixteenth Convention of the Fellowship of Catholic Scholars, 1993), Stubenville, Ohio, 1993, p. 27.

essentially a gift – he is created out of love and also for love. A particular characteristic of the gift of personal existence is that man realises he only exists 'for some one'; he is made for relationship with others in a relationship of mutual gift.[17]

Scripture reveals to us something of the dignity of man when it says that he was made to God's image and likeness. Created in the image of God, with intellect and will, man is capable of knowing and loving his Creator. While this refers primarily to his soul, the body also reflects the divine image. St Thomas tells us that the soul united with the body is more in the image of God than when separate, because in this way it realises its own essence more perfectly. The human soul is in every part of the body and, thus shaped by its spirituality, the body also participates in the imaging of God.[18] It is difficult to appreciate fully the goodness of the body in God's plan in that in our experience it is ultimately subject to death and corruption. However, in John Paul II's 'theology of the body' the human body is a 'sacrament of the person': 'The body in fact, and it alone, is capable of making visible what is invisible.'[19]

In the Genesis account of creation, man and woman are seen as a gift for each other, which brings about a communion of persons. Man is therefore 'image of God' not only in his humanity 'but also from the communion of persons which man and woman form right from the beginning'.[20] This communion of man and woman before the fall was meant to mirror God's very life, a communion of love ordered to the gift of life. 'The human body', John Paul II says, 'is not only a source of fruitfulness and procreation, as in the whole natural order, but includes right "from the beginning" the "nuptial" attribute, that is the capacity of expressing love: that love in which the man-person becomes a gift and – by means of this gift – fulfils the very meaning of his being and existence.'[21]

From the Genesis account we are given another fundamental insight into the nature of man in the state of original innocence. We are told that the man and woman 'were both naked, and were not ashamed', which is a statement of the interior freedom of the couple, a freedom which im-

---

17 Cf. Address, 9 January 1980, nos. 1 and 2. **18** Cf. *De Potentia 5, 10 ad 5*, quoted in Ramos, op. cit., p. 35. **19** Address, 20 February 1980, no. 4. In this way is revealed the sacramentality of creation and the world as image of God. The body alone 'is capable of making visible what is invisible: the spiritual and the divine. It was created to transfer into the visible reality of the world the mystery hidden since time immemorial in God, and thus be a sign of it' (idem). Against this background we understand more fully the words which constitute the sacrament of marriage, present in Genesis 2:24 ('A man leaves his father and his mother and cleaves to his wife, and they become one flesh'). **20** Address, 14 November 1979, no. 3. **21** Address, 16 January 1980, no. 1. See also *Familiaris consortio*, 11–16.

plies self-mastery. This freedom from sexual desire is the freedom necessary to be able to give oneself as a gift to the other. It is by means of this
gift that man discovers his true self – that he is the only creature God
willed for himself. Freedom from concupiscence lies at the basis of the
nuptial meaning of the body, a freedom understood as the self-control
essential if man is to be able to give himself, and in this way discover his
true self.[22] It is only by reference to this anthropology and theology of 'the
beginning' that one can fully understand the condition of historical man
after original sin.

CONSEQUENCES OF THE FALL

The state of original innocence, where the couple accept each other as
gift, is soon replaced by the condition whereby each experiences shame of
his body as a result of sin. The body as gift and the physical expression of
the person is replaced by a perception of the body as an object of appro-
priation or lust. This is the antithesis of true love and self-giving. Man
then loses the original conviction of the body being the image of God,
which, as a result, ceases to draw on the power of the spirit; the body in
fact becomes a centre of resistance to the spirit, so graphically described by
St Paul in his letter to the Romans.[23] This is in fact a state of privation,
where man's heart, in the words of the Holy Father, becomes 'a battlefield
between lust and love'.[24]

As a consequence of original sin Adam and Eve lost the gift of supernatural life, a sharing in the divine life through grace. Not only did they
lose grace, but they also damaged themselves as a result of the sin committed. No longer were their bodies easily subject to their wills – they had
lost the gift of integrity as a constitutive element of their being. Our first

---

22 Cf. *Gaudium et spes*, 24.   **23** 'We know that the law is spiritual; but I am carnal, sold
under sin. I do not understand my own actions. For I do not do what I want, but I do the
very thing I hate. Now if I do what I do not want, I agree that the law is good. So then it
is no longer I that do it, but sin which dwells within me. For I know that nothing good
dwells within me, that is, in my flesh. I can will what is right but I cannot do it. For I do
not do the good I want, but the evil I do not want is what I do. Now if I do what I do not
want, it is no longer I that do it, but sin which dwells within me. So I find it to be a law
that when I want to do right, evil lies close at hand. For I delight in the law of God, in my
inmost self, but I see in my members another law at war with the law of my mind and
making me captive to the law of sin which dwells in my members. Wretched man that I
am! Who will deliver me from this body of death?' (Rom 7:14–24).   **24** Address, 23 July
1980, no. 3.

parents were immediately conscious of their lack of integrity through a mutual awareness of their physical nakedness and the sense of shame which they experienced as a consequence of it. They were ashamed, as John Paul II explains, not so much of their bodies, but because of the lustful desires they experienced. Their feelings of sensuality and sentiment were no longer under the control of their wills.

Concupiscence, an after-effect of original sin, undermines the capacity for self-control, and consequently the freedom necessary for complete self-giving. Personal communion, or the communion of love appropriate to the state of innocence, is rendered unattainable.[25] Nevertheless, the redemption wrought by Christ was a redemption of soul and body, thus making it possible for man to recover the capacity to love with purity of heart once more.

Consequently, we can say that the primary purpose of chastity is to free love from a utilitarian attitude towards the person, by controlling sensuality and concupiscence.[26] In this way chastity enables love to be true, because it is the virtue which causes us to respect the other as a person made to the image and likeness of God, in soul and body. The essence of chastity is, then, to affirm the value of the person in everything that relates to the body and sexuality. It does not consist in blind self-control or sexual repression, but in a positive affirmation of the heart in response to God's grace. It is a virtue that draws its resources from a practised orientation of the appetites of the soul under the dynamism of the life of the Spirit.[27]

ADULTERY OF THE HEART

John Paul II devotes several addresses to drawing out the implications of Christ's teaching in the Sermon on the Mount: 'You have heard that it was said, "You shall not commit adultery". But I say to you that every man that looks at a woman lustfully has already committed adultery with her in his heart' (Mt 5:27–28).

This passage has a key meaning for the theology of the body, but one which must be seen in the context of the first three chapters of Genesis. It represents a fundamental revision of the way of understanding the Law of the Old Covenant, particularly as expressed in the sixth commandment, 'You shall not commit adultery'. Christ shifts the focus of the morality of adultery from the external act to the interior dispositions of the heart, and

25 Ibid, no. 4   **26** Cf. Karol Wojtyla, *Love and Responsibility*, London, 1981, p. 170.   **27** Cf. ibid., pp 144–6.

in this way brings to completion the Old Testament teaching.

The lust that man feels in his heart is a consequence of his breaking the original covenant with his Father God, leading to that sense of shame which accompanies all sin (cf. Gen 3:7). That shame is reflected in the need both man and woman felt to hide themselves, but it is something deeper than mere physical shame. It is the sense of nakedness which comes as a result of an awareness of being deprived of the gift of participating in the very life of God, a deprivation of the preternatural and supernatural gifts which were part of man's endowment before sin entered his life.

Man's first response to being aware of his nakedness is an eloquent expression of that interior shame which he feels as a result of lust. The birth of shame in the human heart is associated with the beginning of the threefold concupiscence, but especially the lust of the body. This shame, John Paul II affirms, has a double meaning: it indicates the threat to the intimacy of the body arising from lust, but it is at the same time a means to preserve this intimacy or purity of heart.[28]

CHASTITY IN THE TEACHING OF THE NEW TESTAMENT

The words of Christ in the Sermon on the Mount also specify the demands of purity of heart which should define the mutual relations between man and woman both inside and outside of marriage. For Christ the heart of man is the source of purity, but also of moral impurity in its most general sense. 'Out of the heart of man', he tells his disciples, 'come evil thoughts, murder, adultery, fornication, theft etc'(Mt 15:18–20; cf. Mk 7:20–23). Christ was here making use of the opportunity to clarify the implications of ritual purity in the Old Testament, which gave rise to a false understanding of moral purity, frequently understood in an exclusively exterior or material sense.[29] At the same time he makes clear that sins of unchastity have their source in the heart, in the will of man.

Based on the teaching of St Paul (cf. Gal 5:16–17), we can say that purity of heart is 'life according to the Spirit'. Paul sees a tension between the demands of the flesh and the demands of the Spirit in the heart of man; it is a struggle between the forces of good and evil at the very core of his being. This tension is developed more fully in his Letter to the Romans.[30]

28 Cf. Address, 28 May 1980, no. 6. **29** Cf. Address, 10 December 1980, nos. 2 and 3. **30** 'For those who live according to the flesh set their minds on the things of the flesh,

Paul contrasts the works of the flesh (fornication, impurity, licentious-ness, idolatry etc.: cf. Gal 5:19–21) with the fruits of the Spirit (charity, joy, self-control, modesty, continence, chastity, etc.: cf. Gal 5: 22–23). These latter are the graces made available by Christ as a consequence of the redemption of the body. But behind each of these realisations are individual acts of the will to choose the life of the Spirit and to reject the demands of the flesh. In the struggle between good and evil, thanks to the power of the Holy Spirit, man's desire to do good wins out.[31] For Pauline theology the freedom won by Christ has deeper implications than that perceived by contrasting it with the Old Law: true freedom is grounded on the law of charity brought by and articulated by Christ (cf. Gal 5:13). In this context we can say that purity (related to any state in life) is an affirmation of love; it is not 'suspension in nothingness'. It is a response to that appeal which Christ addresses to the heart of each person.[32]

CHASTITY AND THE CALL TO HOLINESS

In his first Letter to the Thessalonians St Paul speaks about purity in the context of the call to holiness (cf. 1 Thess 4:3–5). It is manifested in the fact that man knows 'how to control his body in holiness and honour, not in the passion of lust like the heathen who do not know God' (1 Thess 4:5). He considers purity not only as a capacity of man's subjective facul-ties, but at the same time as an essential virtue to achieve sanctity, 'for God has not called us for uncleanness, but in holiness' (1 Thess 4:7).[33] Com-menting on this text, Blessed Josemaría Escrivá affirms:

but those who live according to the Spirit set their minds on the things of the Spirit. To set the mind on the flesh is death, but to set the mind on the Spirit is life and peace. For the mind that is set on the flesh is hostile to God; it does not submit to God's law, indeed it cannot; and those who are in the flesh cannot please God. But you are not in the flesh, you are in the Spirit, if the Spirit of God really dwells in you. Anyone who does not have the Spirit of Christ does not belong to him. But if Christ is in you, although your bodies are dead because of sin, your spirits are alive because of righteousness' (Rom 8:5–10). At the same time Paul anticipates the final victory over sin and death as a consequence of Christ's resurrection: 'he who raised Christ Jesus from the dead will give life to your mortal bodies also through his Spirit who dwells in you' (Rom 8:11). **31** Cf. Address, 17 December 1980, nos. 4-6. **32** Cf. Address, 14 January 1981. **33** Cf. Address, 28 January 1981, nos. 2–4. Analysing this text (1 Thess 4:3–5; 7–8), John Paul II says that chastity is a practical capacity, a virtue, which makes man capable of acting in a given way, and at the same time of not acting in the opposite way. It is therefore an aptitude rooted in the will, or, as St Thomas specifies, in the *appetitus concupiscibilis*. Purity is then a particular form of the virtue of temperance which controls the impulses of sensitive desire. See *Love and Responsibility*, op. cit., pp 143–53.

We belong to God completely, soul and body, flesh and bones, all our senses and faculties. Ask him, confidently : Jesus, guard our hearts! Make them big and strong and tender, hearts that are affectionate and refined, overflowing with love for you and ready to serve all mankind. Our bodies are holy. They are *temples of God*, says St Paul. This cry of the Apostle brings to mind the universal call to holiness which Our Lord addresses to all men: 'You are to be perfect, as your heavenly Father is perfect' (Mt 5:48) ... He demands that each of us, in accordance with his particular state in life, should put into practice the virtues proper to the children of God ... If one has the spirit of God, chastity is not a troublesome and humiliating burden, but a joyful affirmation. Will-power, dominion, self-mastery do not come from the flesh or from instinct. They come from the will, especially if it is united to the will of God. In order to be chaste (and not merely continent or decent) we must subject our passions to reason, but for a noble motive, namely, the promptings of Love.[34]

In his first Letter to the Corinthians St Paul gives us some further insights into the virtue of holy purity. He is speaking about the Church as the Body of Christ and this gives him an opportunity to make some comments about the human body: 'the parts of the body which seem to be weaker are indispensable, and those parts of the body which we think less honourable we invest with the greater honour, and our unpresentable parts are treated with greater modesty, which our more presentable parts do not require' (1 Cor 12:22–24). This Pauline description corresponds to the spiritual attitude of respect for the human body due to it because of the 'holiness' which springs from the mysteries of creation and redemption (cf. 1 Thess 4:3–5, 7–8).[35]

MODESTY AND CHASTITY

In *Love and Responsibility* John Paul II had already analysed in depth the nature of the virtue of modesty in relation to chastity under the rubric of the 'metaphysics of shame'. The phenomenon of shame arises when something, which of its very nature or in view of its purpose ought to be kept private, somehow becomes public. Each person has a particular interiority which gives rise to a need to conceal, that is to retain internally certain

34 *Friends of God*, Dublin, 1981, no. 177.   35 Cf. Address, 4 February 1981, nos. 2–3.

experiences or values. Human nature shows a universal tendency to conceal those parts of the body, which determine its sex, from the gaze of others, especially from members of the opposite sex. An essential feature of this tendency is to conceal sexual values in so far as they are 'a potential object of enjoyment' for persons of the other sex, that is in so far as they provoke a sensual reaction in others. This is the origin of modesty, which is connected with the inviolability of the person, and protects the body from being seen as 'an object of use'. Sexual modesty is thus a defensive reflex that protects the value of the person.[36]

Consequently the sense of modesty which keeps the body 'in holiness and honour' is an essential part of the virtue of purity. It is precisely this modesty, which respects the 'weaker' or 'unpresentable' parts of the body (cf. 1 Cor 12:22–25), that restores the exterior harmony, but also the interior harmony of 'purity of heart', enabling man and woman to see each other again as made to the image and likeness of God.[37]

MARRIAGE AND EARTHLY LIFE

John Paul II devoted several addresses to applying the foregoing anthropological principles to the context of marriage.[38] In reply to the man who had posed the question about the marital status in the after-life of the woman who had successively married seven brothers (cf. Mt 22:15–22;

---

36 Cf. *Love and Responsibility*, op. cit., pp 174–80. In an age when modesty is regarded as an outdated virtue, the insight of a secular commentator is not without relevance: 'Modesty in the old dispensation was *the* female virtue, because it governed the powerful desire that related men to women, providing a gratification in harmony with the procreation and rearing of children ... Diminution or suppression of modesty certainly makes attaining the end of desire easier – which was the intention of the sexual revolution – but it also dismantles the structure of involvement and attachment, reducing sex to the thing-in-itself. This is where feminism enters. Female modesty extends sexual differentiation from the sexual act to the whole of life. It makes men and women always men and women. The consciousness of directedness towards one another, and its attractions and inhibitions, inform every common deed. As long as modesty operates, men and women together are never just lawyers or pilots together. They have something else, always potentially very important, in common –ultimate ends, or as they say, "life-goals"... Modesty is a constant reminder of their peculiar relatedness and its outer forms and inner sentiments, which impede the self's free creation or capitalism's technical division of labour. It is a voice constantly repeating that a man and a woman have a work to do together that is far different from that found in the marketplace, and of a far greater importance' (Allan Bloom, *The Closing of the American Mind*, London, 1987, pp 101–2)   **37** Cf. Address, 4 February 1981, nos.5–6.   **38** Cf. *The Theology of Marriage and Celibacy*, op. cit., for the Pope's addresses on this subject.

Mk 12:24–25), Christ told him he had misread the Scriptures: 'When they rise from the dead, they neither marry nor are given in marriage, but are like angels in heaven' (Mk 12:25). For John Paul II this text has a key meaning for the theology of the body.[39] The human body will then have reacquired the fullness of perfection characteristic of a creature made to the image and likeness of God.

Marriage, therefore, belongs to the earthly stage of man's existence because in eternity there will be a completely new state of life. The sense of being male and female will be understood in a different way: 'They are equal to the angels and are sons of God' (Lk 20:36). This implies a spiritualization of man in contrast to the present mode of existence, without at the same time his losing the essential human condition of a creature constituted by body and soul. It does not mean a 'disincarnation' or a dehumanisation of man, but rather a 'divinization' that comes from the definitive realisation of our vocation as children of God.

Man and woman in the beatific vision will enjoy a perfectly mature subjectivity, with no felt need for the completion that comes from conjugal life on earth. Man's gift of himself will be total. The virginal state of the body will then be manifested as the eschatological fulfilment of its 'nuptial' meaning, as the specific sign and authentic expression of all personal subjectivity.[40] This revelation has obviously deep implications for the theology of priestly celibacy. Consequently, a proper theological understanding of the body has two principal co-ordinates – what Christ has revealed to us about man's condition at 'the beginning', and what his definitive status will be in eternity as a child of God.

The words of Christ about the body in the after-life find a deep resonance in the doctrine of St Paul (cf. 1 Cor 15:42–46; Rom 8:19–20) which develops the teaching of Christ and completes it.[41] Risen man will be the completion of the earthly man, and will be endowed with some of the attributes of the risen Christ. Every man bears within himself the image of the first Adam, but he is also called to reflect the image of the new Adam, the Risen Christ. In eternity there will be a restoration of his integrity with the definitive reception of the Holy Spirit.[42]

---

39 Cf. Address, 2 December 1981, no. 2.   **40** Cf. Address, 16 December 1981, no.3.   **41** Cf. Address, 27 January 1982.   **42** Cf. Addresses, 3 and 10 February 1982.

MARRIAGE IN EPHESIANS

St Paul's text in Ephesians 5:22–33 [43] constitutes a crowning of the other texts from Scripture on marriage which we have considered. As we have already seen, it also has a particular significance for the theology of priestly celibacy.

In this passage the Apostle's words are centred on the body, both in its metaphorical meaning (the Body of Christ which is the Church), and in its concrete meaning – the human body in its masculinity and femininity. These two meanings converge in the Letter to the Ephesians to give us the classic text about the sacramentality of marriage. It is also very illustrative of the spousal dimension of the priestly vocation to celibacy.

Paul goes beyond the merely moral aspects of the marriage relationship to discover therein the very mystery of Christ's relationship with his Church-Bride (Eph 5:22–25), drawing an analogy between the love of husband and wife and that of Christ for his Church. [44] This means that marriage is a Christian vocation only when it reflects the love which Christ the Bridegroom has for his Bride the Church, and which the Church tries to return to Christ. 'This', John Paul II tells us, 'is a redeeming love, love as salvation, the love with which man from eternity has been loved by God in Christ.' [45] It is a love which is transformed into spousal love, Christ giving himself for his Church. Because marriage encloses some element of the mystery of Christ's love for his Church, St Paul can refer to it as a *sacramentum magnum* (cf. Eph 5:32), a great mystery.

Within the fundamental Pauline analogy – Christ and the Church on the one hand, man and woman as spouses on the other – there is another analogy, that of the head and the body. In marriage there is, as it were, one organic bond between husband and wife which does not at the same time

---

43 'Wives, be subject to your husbands, as to the Lord. For the husband is the head of the wife as Christ is the head of the church, his body, and is himself its Saviour. As the church is subject to Christ, so let wives also be subject in everything to their husbands. Husbands, love your wives, as Christ loved the church and gave himself up for her, that he might sanctify her, having cleansed her by the washing of water with the word, that he might present the church to himself in splendour, without spot or wrinkle or any such thing, that she might be holy and without blemish. Even so husbands should love their wives as their own bodies. He who loves his wife loves himself. For no man ever hates his own flesh, but nourishes and cherishes it, as Christ does the church, because we are members of his body."For this reason a man shall leave his father and mother and be joined to his wife, and the two shall become one flesh." This mystery is a profound one, and I am saying that it refers to Christ and the church; however, let each one of you love his wife as himself, and let the wife see that she respects her husband'. **44** Cf. Address, 11 August 1982. **45** Address, 18 August 1982, no. 2.

blur the individuality of the spouses, in the same way that Christ the head is united to his body the Church.

It is not without significance that the image of the Church in splendour is presented as a bride all beautiful in her body (cf. Eph 5:27). It is surely a metaphor, but a very eloquent one because it shows how deeply important is the body in the analogy of spousal love. Christ with his redemptive and spousal love ensures that the Church not only becomes sinless, but also that it remains 'without spot or wrinkle', that is, eternally young.

The analogy of the body has rich implications of a moral, spiritual and supernatural significance. The beauty of the body is the beauty of holiness. Love obliges the bridegroom-husband to be solicitous for the welfare of the bride-wife, but it also counsels him to appreciate her beauty and care for it, with a loving desire to find everything that is good and beautiful in her. Husbands have to love their wives as their own bodies, deferring to the moral unity achieved through love. They have to nourish and cherish them in a protective way as Christ does his Church (cf. 5:29). In general this idea helps us to understand the dignity of the body and the moral imperative to care for its well-being. It emphasises a sense of the sacredness of the body in the relationships of husband and wife, in particular for the wife as mother of their children.[46]

In Ephesians 5:37 St Paul recalls Genesis 2:24: 'For this reason a man shall leave his father and mother and be joined to his wife, and the two shall become one', the fundamental scriptural text on marriage. He uses this text to present the mystery of Christ's unity with his Church, from which he deduces the profound truth about the unity of spouses in marriage. In doing so he links the salvific plan of God with the most ancient revelation about marriage, and affirms with a sense of wonder, 'This is a great mystery, and I mean in reference to Christ and the Church' (5:32), a mystery hidden in God's mind from eternity and revealed in the fullness of time. St Paul affirms a continuity between the ancient covenant established by God constituting marriage as part of the very work of creation, and the definitive covenant by which Christ is united to his Church in a spousal way. This continuity of God's salvific initiative constitutes the essential basis for the great Pauline analogy about marriage.[47]

---

46 Cf. Address, 1 September 1982.   47 Cf. Address, 8 September 1982.

OLD TESTAMENT REFERENCES FOR PAULINE ANALOGY

The analogy of Christ's love for his Church, and the spousal relationship between husband and wife, has many points of reference in the Old Testament, particularly in Isaiah, Hosea, Ezekiel and the Song of Songs, which would have informed the Pauline doctrine in Ephesians. In Isaiah we see the spousal bond between God and Israel compared to the love of a man for the woman chosen to be his wife by means of a marriage alliance (cf. Is 54:4–10). There is a continuity regarding the analogy of spousal love in Ephesians 5, but with a deeper theological development. However, the redemptive perspective is clear in both analogies.[48]

The analogy of human spousal love helps us in turn to understand more clearly the total gift of Christ to his Church, and therefore the celibacy of the priest which is an image of that gift. It gives us a new insight into the mystery of grace as an eternal reality in God and as an 'historical' fruit of mankind's redemption in Christ. The 'invisible mystery' of God's plan of salvation is first made visible by Christ in his relationship with the Church, and hence by analogy in the spousal relationship of husband and wife.[49] The celibate priest is the human, historical image of Christ's love for his Church, and is, in this way, a visible guarantee of its endurance through time.

Marriage as originally constituted by God is an integral part of the 'sacramentality' of creation. As a result of original sin it was deprived of the supernatural efficacy which belonged to the sacrament of creation in its totality. Still, in spite of sin, marriage never ceased being the figure of the sacrament which Ephesians 5 refers to as the 'great mystery'.

Marriage as a primordial sacrament constitutes the *figure* (likeness, analogy) according to which the structure of the new economy of salvation and the sacramental order is constructed, which draws its origin from the spousal gracing which the Church received from Christ, together with all the benefits of the redemption. All the sacraments of the new covenant find, in a certain sense, their prototype in marriage as the primordial sacrament, as St Paul seems to imply in Ephesians, using the word sacrament in its biblical-patristic meaning, that is, with a wider connotation than that in traditional theological terminology.[50]

---

48 'For your Maker is your husband, the Lord of Hosts is his name; and the Holy One of Israel is your Redeemer, the God of the whole earth he is called' (Is 54:5); 'Husbands, love your wives, as Christ loved the church and gave himself up for her' (Eph 5:25).   **49** Cf. Addresses, 22 and 29 September 1982.   **50** Cf. Addresses, 13 and 20 October 1982.

St Paul brings together the redemptive and spousal dimension of love. Both of these dimensions will permeate the life of the spouses if they learn to discover Christ's saving love for his Church in their married life, in that special *communio personarum* to which spouses are called. The original image of marriage as a sacrament is renewed when Christian spouses open themselves to the graces of the redemption and are united 'out of reverence for Christ' (Eph 5:21).

On the basis of these considerations, man, John Paul II counsels us, should seek the meaning of his existence and of his humanity by reaching out to the mystery of creation through the reality of the redemption. It is by doing this that we will find the essential answer to the question of the significance of the human body, and of the masculinity and femininity of the human person. The union of Christ with his Church permits us to understand in what way the spousal significance of the body is completed by the redemptive significance, and this in different situations and ways of life. This applies not only to marriage but also to celibacy.[51]

CONCLUSION

In his philosophical approach to the theology of the body, John Paul II blends the truths of Thomism with the insights of phenomenology, an approach which enables him to throw new light on permanent realities and arrive at conclusions fully consonant with the perennial philosophy.[52] John Paul II's 'personalism' means that he places the person at the centre of his ethical analysis in order to see how each of our actions is in keeping with human dignity. The consequences of this approach are that the human person is seen always to merit a response of love, and can never be reduced to an object of use or treated as a means to an end.

The Pope develops the concept of personal subjectivity to arrive at an idea of the structure of the person richer than that achieved by the traditional objective approach alone.[53] He applies to the definition of person the philosophical idea of 'relation' which is fundamental to Trinitarian theology.[54] Hence integral to the reality and definition of the person is the concept of 'gift for other', which for most people finds expression in

---

51 Cf. Address, 15 December 1982.   **52** Cf. Janet Smith, *Why* Humanae Vitae *Was Right: A Reader*, San Francisco, 1993, pp 231–44.   **53** Cf. John F. Crosby, 'The Personalism of John Paul II as the Basis of his Approach to the Teaching of *Humanae Vitae*', in Janet Smith, ibid., pp 200–5.   **54** ' With the introduction of the notion of person in the *Pastoral*

spousal self-giving through marriage, but for others will be in the betrothed love of celibacy.

The encyclical *Veritatis splendor* is deeply impregnated with the personalism of John Paul II. Before becoming Pope, he had already affirmed that the metaphysics of human nature according to the Aristotelian tradition ran the risk of failing to do justice to what is distinctive about man, to what makes him a person. For him this understanding needed to be completed by developing a more personalist emphasis, that is, looking at man from the perspective of his interiority and self-giving. But John Paul II never separates 'person' from 'nature', which has the effect of estranging the person from his own body, and inevitably leads to the dualism that is at the root of a permissive sexual ethic.

As the Pope clearly affirms, 'it is in the unity of the body and soul that the person is the subject of his own moral acts'. And it is because of this coherence between the person and their sexuality that we understand the inherent moral disorder of certain kinds of sexual activity. When John Paul II articulates his Christian personalism, he is not only defending the radical embodiment of the human person, and but is also drawing out the full implications of the Incarnation.[55]

In his development of a theology of the body he concentrates on several fundamental human experiences – the need man has for union with another to complete himself; how this union is achieved in the mutual exchange of the gift of self; the attraction between the sexes; etc. In order to understand himself as a person, man has to be convinced that he can only realise himself fully through self-giving. It is out of such universal human experiences, illuminated by divine revelation, that the Pope constructs his teaching on human sexuality.

One of the basic premises of John Paul II's anthropology is that for man to respond adequately to his present 'historical' situation, he needs to know what his original condition was like 'in the beginning', in a state of innocence. By a deep analysis of specific texts from Genesis, in conjunction with others from the New Testament, he shows how God created man originally to be self-giving. However, this divine design was frus-

Constitution of the Church in the Modern World, no.24, as "achieving self by the gift of self", the notion of person as "gift", and hence as relation, has universally and constantly been offered as the core concept in all the papal pronouncements and magisterial offerings of the last 26 years since Vatican II and particularly in the last 13 years of the pontificate of John Paul II' (Robert Connor, 'The Person as Resonating Existential', *American Catholic Philosophical Quarterly*, 39, 42 [1992]). **55** Cf. John F. Crosby, 'Sins of the Flesh', *Crisis* magazine, July/August 1997, pp 25–28.

trated by original sin and the disorder introduced into man's desires as a consequence of it. Man lost the freedom to give himself according to his original specification.[56]

Nevertheless, man also needs to know that as a result of the Incarnation he has been redeemed by Christ from the consequences of the fall. This is what gives him the confidence that, with the help of grace, he can regain his original condition through 'self-mastery', the daily struggle to fight against his sinful tendencies in response to the call to holiness addressed to every Christian. It is from this fundamental perspective that a vocation to celibacy is seen as a realisable commitment and a correlative to the vocation to marriage.

---

56 Cf. Michel Séguin, 'The Biblical Foundations of the Thought of John Paul II on Human Sexuality', *Communio*, 20, Summer 1993, pp 266–289.

5

Formation for Celibacy

The nurturing of a vocation to the priesthood is essentially a work of grace. But the context in which such a call comes to fruition is normally the environment of a Christian family where the faith is lived and learned. An integral part of this formation is an education in the Christian meaning of chastity and human sexuality. It is only from this perspective that a vocation to celibacy can make sense and take root.

Up to recent decades people found little difficulty accepting that sexual activity was something essentially connected with marriage and the founding of a family. However, the 'sexual revolution' of the sixties, fuelled by the development of contraceptives, purported to get rid of outdated sexual taboos, and affirmed the right to pleasure as an end in itself. As a consequence, sex became increasingly trivialised and commercialised. Such ideas are pervasive in the media and clearly influence attitudes, especially those of the younger generation.

Because people have lost sight of the true nature and purpose of human sexuality, not even the plague of AIDS has caused legislators to rethink the lethal ideology of 'sex for pleasure'. Where basic common sense cries out for continence and self-control, all that the 'experts' can propose is 'safer sex' by means of condoms. The dignity of the human person as a being made to the image and likeness of God, endowed with a capacity for moral responsibility, is effectively ignored and the solution to the AIDS epidemic is seen as just another project in social engineering. Moral issues in relation to sexuality are thus reduced to 'problems of health', and it is under this rubric that sex education programmes are increasingly introduced into schools. The presuppositions of such education offer little that is conducive to fostering celibate vocations.

Nevertheless, the pastoral experience of the Church confirms, more clearly than ever before, that the stability of the family can only endure if couples have a solid grounding in general moral values, as well as specific moral education in sexuality during adolescence. The recently published document of the Pontifical Council for the Family, *The Truth and Meaning of Human Sexuality*,[1] is a very helpful contribution to this important task of

1 Published 8 December 1995, subsequently abbreviated to *Human Sexuality* in the text, and HS in notes.

sex education. It offers answers to fundamental questions a Christian society should be asking itself: What type of young persons do we want to form for tomorrow? What is the relationship between sexuality and the person, between sexuality and the family? What is the connection between love, sexuality and self-giving? Why is celibacy a valid and reasonable response to one's sexuality?

In other words, it provides a statement of a coherent anthropology as seen in the light of Christian revelation, and offers this as foundation or context in which a proper methodology for sex education can be established. The document reaffirms the fact that the exercise of sexuality always has a moral dimension. But it goes on to say that the recovery of this truth depends largely on the rediscovery of the relevance of the virtue of chastity.

Many years before being elected to the papacy, John Paul II wrote about the need to restore the good name of the virtue of chastity, which, he says, is 'resented' because of a distorted sense of values.[2] The document of the Pontifical Council for the Family goes a long way not only to recover its good name, but also to demonstrate the clear need for this virtue if human dignity and the stability of the family as an institution is to be restored, and if celibacy and virginity are to be appreciated for what they are.

John Paul II, in his document on the Christian Family (*Familiaris consortio*), defines very clearly that, for a Christian, sex education is fundamentally formation in the virtue of chastity, and that, consequently, the Church is firmly opposed to sex education as information dissociated from moral principles.[3] The document of the Pontifical Council for the Family provides a systematic development of the principles laid down by *Familiaris consortio*.

Human Sexuality puts the present difficulties with sex education into perspective. In the past the general culture was permeated by respect for the values of sexuality and human intimacy and, consequently, tended to protect and maintain them. However, with the decline in these traditional values in recent decades, human sexuality has been 'demythologised' and depersonalised by reducing it to the commonplace. Hence the wisdom of Ricoeur's comment: 'whatever facilitates the sexual encounter also helps it sink into irrelevance'.[4]

2 Cf. Karol Wojtyla, *Love and Responsibility*, op. cit., p. 141.   3 Cf. *Familiaris consortio*, 37, published 22 November 1981.   4 Cf. 'Sex and Despair', in *Josef Pieper: An Anthology*, San Francisco, 1989, p. 41.

FORMATION IN CHASTITY

Human Sexuality gives a very rich presentation of the virtue of chastity, establishing it as the context for a Christian sex education. Chastity has been aptly described as 'the spiritual energy capable of defending love from the perils of selfishness and aggressiveness, and able to advance it towards its full realisation'.[5] Therefore it is a virtue that can never be understood as a repressive attitude, but rather as 'the stewardship of a precious and rich gift of love'.[6]

It cannot exist as a virtue without the capacity to renounce self, to make sacrifices and to wait. So formation in chastity is not an isolated programme, but one which must be integrated into formation in other virtues such as generosity, fortitude, spirit of sacrifice, etc. As a consequence it makes for an integrated personality with a sense of self-respect, and a corresponding respect for the dignity of others. At the same time, it requires the rejection of certain thoughts, words and sinful acts, giving rise to an inner freedom. Growth in this virtue means avoiding situations which might provoke or encourage sin and, at times, in a permissive environment, it can require a heroic effort to live a chaste life. As *Human Sexuality* points out: 'the very fact that all are called to holiness, as the second Vatican Council teaches, makes it easier to understand that everyone can be in situations where heroic acts of virtue are indispensable, whether *in celibate life* or marriage, and that in fact in one way or another *this happens to everyone for shorter or longer periods of time*'.[7]

This ascetical realism, which is necessary in speaking about the commitment to acquire the virtue of chastity, reflects the spirit of the *Catechism of the Catholic Church*. Here the topic is dealt with under the heading of 'The Battle for Purity';[8] there are no illusions about the need for daily struggle in this area. The seminarian or the priest, therefore, cannot expect that living chastity according to his state will not make demands on him. We are reminded, nevertheless, that the grace of Christ is never lacking for the person who is seriously committed to living in a chaste way. Given that all are called to holiness, as we are told by Vatican II,[9] it is not surprising that interior struggle in this area is a normal part of the effort to live the Christian vocation fully.

---

5 *Familiaris consortio*, 33, quoted in HS, 4.   **6** HS, 4.   **7** HS, 19 (emphasis added).   **8** Cf. nos. 2520-27.   **9** Cf. *Lumen gentium*, 11.

CHRISTIAN PHILOSOPHY OF SEX EDUCATION

We have already seen that a Christian philosophy of sex education has to be based on a particular anthropological vision. Given that traditional Church teaching on sexual morality no longer seems credible in a world invaded by a hedonistic philosophy, such a vision is more necessary than ever today. The same solid foundation is required to underpin the argumentation for celibacy.

Since there is also much evidence to indicate that many Catholics ignore this teaching both inside and outside of marriage, the seminarian needs this deeper formation to restore credibility to the Church's teaching on sexual morality, and to communicate with conviction the idea that the Church has an eminently positive approach to human love, sexuality and marriage, and that it is essentially pro-love and pro-life.[10]

Human Sexuality develops the consequences of the fact that, since man is made to the image of God, love is the innate vocation of every human being. Realising that life is a gift received, man intuits that his existence has meaning only in so far as it is a gift to others. In this way he is capable of a higher kind of love than concupiscence, and he is freed from the tendency to selfishness by experiencing the love of others, especially the love of God as revealed in Christ. The normal way of achieving the total gift of self is through marriage, but it is also fully realised through the betrothed love of celibacy or virginity in response to a special grace.[11] The document affirms that sexuality is a fundamental component of personality, of communicating with others, of expressing and of living human love. But this is love understood as a gift of self by which one realises the meaning of one's existence.

When children are raised in an environment where they experience love as self-giving, where generosity and a spirit of service are nurtured in them from an early age, they will easily appreciate the moral implications of authentic human love. Without difficulty they will learn to have healthy relationships with God, with their parents, brothers and sisters, and their companions of the same or the opposite sex. It is in such normal Christian environments that the seeds of a vocation to celibacy take root and grow.

---

10 Cf. Vatican II decree on the training of priests, *Optatam totius*, 10. See also *Directives on the Formation of Seminarians concerning problems related to Marriage and the Family*, published by the Congregation for Catholic Education, 19 March, 1995. As we have already noted in chapter 4, no one has done more than the present Pope to establish the anthropological basis for the Church's teaching on human sexuality by his illustration of the biblical foundations, the ethical grounds and the personalist reasons behind this doctrine. 11 Cf. HS, 10–13.

CALL TO HOLINESS

Christian sex education is seen by the Pontifical Council document as an essential part of preparing children and young adults to respond to a vocation to holiness, whether in marriage or in apostolic celibacy. Parents are encouraged always to keep before them this perspective of the universal call to holiness so eloquently articulated by Vatican II.[12]

At the same time there is a clear awareness in the document that in some societies not only is marriage and the family in crisis, but so also is the vocation to celibacy and virginity. A lack of vocations to the priesthood or religious life is a natural consequence of a dilution of faith and the break-down of family life – the two are intimately related. On the other hand, *Human Sexuality* also draws out the point that it is in families where life is generously accepted, and where children are formed in the Christian view of chastity, that the hope of the Church for future vocations to celibacy and consecrated virginity lies.

John Paul II had already adverted to this in *Familiaris consortio* when he encouraged parents, discerning the signs of God's call, 'to devote special attention and care to education in virginity or celibacy as the supreme form of that self-giving that constitutes the very meaning of human sexuality'.[13]

Parents with a mature Christian spirit understand that a vocation to celibacy is a great blessing for their family. While saddened by the lapses of some clerics, they would never see this as an adequate reason for discouraging a vocation to celibacy in their children. However, what can undermine their confidence is the constant campaigning by those who keep pushing for optional celibacy and who, facilitated by a secularist media, effectively reject the frequently repeated teaching of the Magisterium on the discipline of celibacy in the Western Church.

SUPPORTIVE VIRTUES

Chastity is not an isolated virtue. Consequently, because sexuality is such an important good, it needs to be protected by the nurturing of other virtues such as modesty, temperance, a spirit of service, respect for self and others. It is in the home, too, that children learn how to reject the pres-

12 Cf. *Lumen gentium*, 11.   13 No. 37.

sures of materialism and consumerism by means of formation in generosity and self-sacrifice. The most effective example for children in this area is the generosity of parents in accepting new life. By such an apprenticeship they will easily identify and unmask the essential selfishness behind the utilitarian ethic of sexual gratification.

Formation in chastity and sexuality should be provided in the broader context of education for love and growth in the spiritual life. Accordingly, increased knowledge of human love should be paralleled by a growing love for God through prayer, frequenting the sacraments of Penance and the Eucharist, and devotion to the Mother of God. Children need to be educated in the conviction that chastity is possible, that it is a virtue which ennobles, and is a source of real joy.[14]

The document of the Pontifical Council for the Family can be regarded as the *magna carta* for Christian sex education. It is eminently positive in tone. Discussion of sex education is lifted out of the positivistic and naturalistic context in which it is normally discussed and raised to a new level. It outlines very clearly how, for a Christian, sex education only makes sense in the much broader context of formation in the virtue of chastity and the vocation to holiness to which all are called, whether in marriage or apostolic celibacy.

JOHN PAUL II AND RESPONSE TO YOUTH ABOUT CHASTITY

To achieve effective formation in chastity, it is necessary to challenge young people with the full implications of their baptismal vocation. In this context it is worth recalling the response of John Paul II to the youth of Holland who had told him they felt the Church was, to put it mildly, out of touch in its teaching on chastity. In reply to a number of questions which he was asked by these young people, the Pope said: 'You still have many prejudices and suspicions in encountering the Church. You have let me know that you often consider the Church an institution which does nothing but promulgate regulations and laws. You think that she puts up

---

14 From a Christian perspective, chastity has always been linked with happiness. It is therefore noteworthy that Allan Bloom, in his highly acclaimed commentary on the American university scene, would suggest that lack of chastity is the main cause of student unhappiness. Speaking as a secular analyst, without any religious axe to grind, he affirms that 'the world is for them [the students] what it presents itself to the senses to be; it is unadorned by imagination and devoid of ideals. This flat soul is what the sexual wisdom of our time conspires to make universal' (*The Closing of the American Mind*, op. cit., p. 134.)

barriers in many fields: sexuality, the structure of the Church, the place of women in the Church ...' Then he goes on to put their objections into context:

> Dear friends, allow me to be very frank with you. I know that you speak in perfectly good faith. But are you really sure that the idea you have of Christ fully corresponds to the reality of his person? The Gospel, in truth, presents us with a very demanding Christ who invites us to a radical conversion of heart (cf. Mk 19:3–9) ... In particular, concerning the sexual sphere, the firm position taken by him in defence of the indissolubility of marriage (cf. Mt 19:3–9), and the condemnation pronounced even regarding simple adultery of the heart (cf. Mt 5:27) are well known. And how can one fail to be struck by the precept 'to gouge out one's eye' or 'cut off one's hand' if these members are an occasion of 'scandal' (cf. Mt 5:29)? Having these precise Gospel references, is it realistic to imagine a 'permissive' Christ in the realm of married life, in the question of abortion, or pre-marital, extra-marital, or homosexual relations? The early Christian community, taught by those who had personally known Christ, were certainly not permissive. Suffice it here to allude to the numerous passages of the Pauline letters which touch upon these matters (cf. Rom 1:26 ff; 1 Cor 6:9; Gal 5:19; etc). The words of the Apostle are certainly not lacking in clarity and vigour. And they are words inspired from on high. They remain normative for the Church of every age ... Permissiveness does not make man happy ... A human being fulfils himself only to the extent that he knows how to accept the demands that have their origin in his dignity as a creature made 'in the image and likeness of God' (Gen 1:27).[15]

This is surely a powerful statement of the Gospel teaching on chastity, which is eminently positive and engages the quest for high ideals so characteristic of youth.

FORMATION OF SEMINARIANS IN CELIBACY

Celibacy is a call which is perennially valid, despite changing social and cultural conditions, because it is a gift freely given by the Holy Spirit to

15 *Address to Youth of Holland*, 14 May 1985, reported in *Osservatore Romano* (English language edition), on 3 June 1985.

those whom he pleases. Response to this gift can, of course, vary depending on the personal dispositions of those to whom it is offered and their ability to identify and appreciate it.

A vocation is a way of learning to recognise oneself, of gradually appropriating one's own identity in the light of God's grace and his will for each. It implies a recognition of life as a gift which has been allotted a particular purpose within the Father's providential plan. The discovery of a vocation to celibacy is a dialogue with grace over a shorter or longer preiod. It does not impose itself, but beckons one forward to be what God wants one to be. It is not in any way a form of self-estrangement, but is rather an exercise in self-fulfillment at the deepest level, a defining of personal identity in the presence of God.

That others may not understand one's personal commitment to celibacy is irrelevant. Indeed one may feel incapable of giving an adequate explanation for it, or experience an inability to justify one's decision in human terms. This is because the inner workings of a vocational grace generally only make sense to a spiritual director, or to those who know the person well.

As was recognised by the 1971 Synod of Bishops, celibacy at present has to cope with particular difficulties. But the same Synod, putting things in perspective, reminds us that the problems created for this charism today have been experienced by priests at other times down through the centuries. In this sense it would be short-sighted and a misreading of history to suggest that now, somehow, unique circumstances have arisen which make necessary a reconsideration of the law of celibacy in the Church.

In 1974, the Vatican document, *A Guide to Formation in Priestly Celibacy*,[16] indicated that a critical reassessment of formation in this area was necessary for several reasons. Doubtless it was not uninfluenced by the fact that the discipline of celibacy had been under sustained attack within the Church since the publication of Paul VI's encyclical, *Sacerdotalis caelibatus*, in 1967. In addition, these years witnessed a massive exodus from the priesthood by men who, in many cases, claimed that celibacy was the root cause of their departure, thus raising serious doubts in the minds of prospective candidates about the very validity or justifiability of this charism. *Pastores dabo vobis* reaffirms the 1974 norms for formation in celibacy.[17]

Consequently, seminary formators are encouraged to recognise changes in the cultural environment, both positive and negative, so that the semi-

---

16 Congregation for Catholic Education, 11 April 1974 (subsequent references to this document are abbreviated to GFPC). **17** Cf. ibid., nos.43, 44 and 50.

narian will be able to give an adequate reason for his vocation, to himself and to others. Formation of seminarians needs to take into acount the social and cultural context in which they will have to minister as priests, a context which we have attempted to outline in our introductory chapter.

A further element of modern culture, which needs to be reviewed in the training of seminarians, is the tendency to downgrade social conventions which previously provided a support for celibacy, as for example the greater formality and reserve previously demanded in relationships between men and women. We will advert to this in more detail in our next chapter.

PRESUPPOSITIONS FOR TRAINING IN CELIBACY

A candidate for the priesthood should have a basic emotional and spiritual maturity. His motivation for living celibacy should be inspired by the desire to follow Christ. A young man who has this fundamental psychological make-up will not feel hemmed in by canonical legislation which requires celibacy of aspirants to the priesthood. He will see it as giving external juridical validation to what is essentially an interior disposition, an attitude which he will in fact be cultivating for several years in the seminary before it will have juridical implications after his ordination.

Similarly the man who wants to follow Christ in the priesthood will appreciate that having a commitment to celibacy requires precautions and limitations in his life-style, out of fidelity to Christ, and not as a regime imposed from outside. Somebody who felt he could not internalise these dispositions would show that he did not have the preconditions necessary for a vocation to the priesthood, and would be advised by his spiritual director to follow another path.

A student entering the seminary with the idea that celibacy was the price to be paid for the priesthood would demonstrate that he had a seriously deficient understanding of both celibacy and priesthood, and should be counselled to change course, as he would be heading for trouble in his vocation in the future. The seminarian must acquire a deep conviction that celibacy is a state in life which is essentially related to a future life of love with the Risen Christ, where there will be no marrying or giving in marriage. Thus he needs to understand it as a charism which is directed to the salvation of souls on earth so that they can enjoy the vision of God in heaven. If his vision of the priesthood were to be limited to that of merely providing a sort of Christian social service, sooner or later his celibacy would begin to make little sense to him.

The specific elements necessary for training in priestly celibacy are interwoven with other aspects of seminary formation. The training of seminarians to be shepherds of souls after the example of Christ, Teacher, Priest and Pastor, implies a specific theological, priestly and human formation. Imitation of the Master, 'perfect God, and perfect man'[18] demands a coherent programme of Christian and human formation.[19]

FORMATION IN HUMAN MATURITY

In a candidate for Orders, human maturity relates especially to emotional maturity in the wider context of psychological and moral maturity. It is reflected particularly in a habitual capacity to act freely, and an ability to integrate human potential with habits of virtue. It will also be seen in a balanced self-control which assimilates emotional drives and subjects them to reason.

An aspirant to the priesthood will be a man who can live relatively easily in community with others, because he knows how to relate to people and enjoys the opportunity to be of service to them. This requires formation in social virtues such as affability, refinement in dealings with others, generosity and a spirit of service. All these are qualities which lead to affective maturity. In order that his ministry be as credible and acceptable as possible, his human personality should be a bridge for others to encounter Christ.[20] This should be coupled to a basic intelligence, capable of assimilating the philosophical and theological concepts essential to his priestly training, and the ability to apply himself steadily to study and work.

Human maturity implies authenticity and coherence of personality, and, therefore, formation in such virtues as sincerity, industriousness, cheerfulness, prudence and discretion, acquires a special significance as preparation for the future priestly task. In this way grace will more easily build on nature.

---

18 *Symbolum Athanasium*, DS 76.   **19** Cf. GFPC, 17.   **20** Cf. *Pastores dabo vobis*, 43. Sometimes people might complain about the absence of particular human qualities in priests. Flannery O'Connor, responding to the criticism of a friend, an intellectually 'superior' type Catholic who had a poor view of some priests, wrote in their defence: 'It is easy for any child to pick out the faults in the sermon on his way home from Church every Sunday. It is impossible for him to find out the hidden love that makes a man, in spite of his intellectual limitations, his neuroticism, his own lack of strength, give up his life to the service of God's people, however bumblingly he may go about it ...': *Letters of Flannery O'Connor: The Habit of Being*, ed., Sally Fitzgerald, New York, 1980, pp 307–8.

The acquisition of emotional and affective maturity is closely related to formation in the virtue of holy purity as befits a candidate for the priesthood. The seminarian must be convinced that the heart of the priest, like that of every human being, has been created for love. As the Holy Father forcefully affirms, 'Man cannot live without love. He remains a being that is incomprehensible for himself, his life is meaningless if love is not revealed to him, if he does not encounter love, if he does not experience it and make it his own, if he does not participate intimately in it.'[21] Consequently the candidate for the priesthood, if properly formed, will come to realise that celibacy is 'a falling in love' which is possible for someone who has integrated it into his spiritual life:

> It is a matter of choosing exclusively, perpetually, and completely the unique and supreme love of Christ for the purpose of more deeply sharing his lot by the resplendent and heroic logic of a singular and unlimited love for Christ the Lord and for his Church. By virtue of his celibacy, a priest becomes more totally a man of God. He lets himself be more completely taken over by Christ, and lives only for him. Virginal love invites him to possess God in a fuller way, to reflect him and give him to others in his fullness. The love that a priest has for others must be essentially pastoral in aim. Externally it should be shown by warm-heartedness which is indispensable in disposing people to accept the spiritual support a priest offers them.[22]

AFFECTIVE MATURITY

Education in affective maturity also implies, and requires especially today, a coherent formation in human sexuality. The seminarian needs to know the full truth about human love and chastity.[23] This means in large part educating the heart, affections and sentiments. It also requires formation in ideals of truth, beauty, goodness and generosity. Training in this virtue inculcates an awareness of the nature of temptations against purity, their source and cause, and the spiritual remedies to be used against them. Thus we are reminded in *Pastores dabo vobis*:

---

21 Encyclical, *Redemptor hominis*, 4 March 1979, no. 10, quoted in *Pastores dabo vobis*, 44 in relation to formation in Affective Maturity.   **22** GFPC, 31.   **23** Cf. *Pastores dabo vobis*, 44.

Since the charism of celibacy, even when it is genuine and has proved itself, leaves man's affections and his instinctive impulses intact, candidates to the priesthood need an affective maturity which is prudent, able to renounce anything that is a threat to it, vigilant over both body and spirit, and capable of esteem and respect in interpersonal relationships between men and women.[24]

Following this programme the seminarian will come to terms with his sexuality, seeing it in the first place as a gift from God. Sexual maturity means that he accepts himself fully as he is with his natural orientations, realising that his sexuality impinges on the whole of his personality and that consequently the genital aspect of sexuality is only one dimension of it.

At the same time, a realistic approach to this aspect of formation will point out that, as a consequence of original sin, there is an inherent disorder in man's sexual desires which requires discipline and self-control. This is not achieved without the help of grace and a daily ascetical effort. Dominating sexual passion requires a generous spirit of mortification to enable us live the life of the Spirit (cf. Rom 8:13; 1 Cor 6:9; Eph 5:6). It is the Paschal Mystery which offers us the only adequate theological and psychological basis for an asceticism which can re-establish the original harmony in man.

An indispensable aid to achieving this emotional maturity is through regular spiritual counselling. Opening one's souls to a prudent spiritual guide about all those matters which relate to the emotional aspects of one's life is one of the best guarantees of achieving that affective maturity and balance which is essential for a well adjusted seminarian and priest. On the other hand, an inclination to marriage and family life should not be regarded as a contra-indication to a celibate vocation. Celibacy is a call from God that includes the sacrifice of a normal propensity to marriage. It is a vocation to a special kind of love to be lived above all in a climate of intimacy and of close friendship with Jesus Christ. It reflects those dispositions by which one can 'reach out' to others without 'having' them – it is a particular exercise in non-possessiveness.

24 Ibid.

TRAINING IN ASCETICISM

Christian holiness, as was so often pointed out by Christ himself, demands an asceticism of self-denial, which is at the same time an ascesis of freedom. Love and self-denial complement one another, since self-denial frees us from selfishness and makes space for authentic love. Love in turn is the motivation for self-denial. The more conscious we are of the magnitude of the gift of the priesthood, and the more appreciative we are of it, the greater will be the freedom and generosity of our response.

Although self-denial is an integral part of every vocation, it is especially appropriate in the life of the seminarian who aspires to be another Christ, that Christ who was not only Priest, but Victim for sin as well.[25] However, the emphasis on priestly asceticism should not obscure the fact that there is also a real sacrificial aspect to love in marriage if it is lived out in generous response to all the demands of this vocation. The *Catechism of the Catholic Church* reminds us that all the baptised, including priests, are called to chastity.[26] Because of the normal propensity to sin in man, chastity requires an *'apprenticeship in self-mastery'*[27] which is a training in human freedom.

Living a chaste life has been eloquently described as 'a primary expression of caring for one's Baptismal identity'.[28] Fidelity to this identity requires an ascetical effort which, the *Catechism* reminds us, 'is a *long and exacting work'*, because the passions which chastity controls are among the strongest in our nature. It is clear then that chastity is never acquired once and for all; although it may demand particular effort in adolescence, it requires renewed commitment at all stages in life.[29] It is a gift which is obtained by prayer when asked for with humility.[30]

For our contemporary sex-saturated culture it seems almost incomprehensible that people would be prepared to die rather than commit a single serious sin of impurity. But that is exactly what twelve-year-old Maria Goretti did, in our own twentieth century, rather than give way to the immoral advances of a nineteen-year-old youth. Similarly, Charles Lwanga

---

25 Under the section of *Pastores dabo vobis* dealing with the formation of seminarians we read: 'It is necessary to inculcate the meaning of the Cross, which is the heart of the Paschal mystery. Through this identification with Christ crucified, as a slave, the world can rediscover the value of austerity, of suffering and also of martyrdom, within the present culture which is imbued with secularism, greed, and hedonism' (no. 48). **26** Cf. no. 2348. **27** Cf. ibid., 2339 (italics in original). **28** John Paul II, Homily, 27 September 1986. **29** Cf. *Catechism of the Catholic Church*, no. 2342. **30** Cf. Blessed Josemaría Escrivá, *The Way*, Dublin, 1968, no. 118.

and his young companions were ready to be executed in Uganda in 1886 for rejecting the homosexual approaches of a local ruler.[31]

PERSEVERANCE IN VOCATION

In seminary training the challenge and the possible difficulties in relation to perseverance in vocation have also to be dealt with adequately. As we have already seen, the priestly vocation does not eliminate the impulses of human nature. Nevertheless, a solid theological and spiritual formation will convince aspirants to the priesthood that, by responding in faith to vocational and sacramental graces, perseverance is not only possible, but offers a hundredfold even in this life (cf. Mk 10:30). Also, the example of generations of priests before them, who fought the good fight and remained steadfast to the end, is always an encouraging stimulus to perseverance.

In this context a knowledge of the fortunes of celibacy in the history of the Church is very instructive. It will come as no surprise to seminarians that down through the centuries there have been many infractions of this discipline, but it will be even more enlightening for them to identify the reasons why these failures occurred. On the other hand, the knowledge that there has been a tradition of celibacy in the Church from apostolic times will confirm them in their vocation, a tradition that, guided by the light of the Holy Spirit, Church authority has always insisted on, no matter what the difficulties and the opposition to it. Awareness of the memory of this tradition, which has produced such rich fruits of holiness and missionary zeal, will give seminarians a firm anchorage in this lived experience of celibacy and a positive conviction about fidelity to it in the future.

In an effort to attract vocations, it is important that the heroism demanded of the priesthood be not undersold. Young people have always had a capacity to respond to high ideals. It would thus be counter-produc-

---

31 In *Veritatis splendor*, John Paul II affirms how the reality of intrinsically evil acts is confirmed in a particularly eloquent way by Christian martyrdom: 'The Church proposes the example of numerous saints who bore witness to and defended moral truth even to the point of enduring martyrdom, or who preferred death to a single mortal sin. In raising them to the honour of the altars, the Church has canonised their witness and declared the truth of their judgement, according to which the love of God entails the obligation to respect his commandments, even in the most dire of circumstances, and the refusal to betray those commandments, even for the sake of saving one's own life ... Martyrdom rejects as false and illusory whatever "human meaning" one might claim to attribute, even in "exceptional" conditions, to an act morally evil in itself' (ibid., nos. 91, 92).

tive to present it as just another, though special, job with a high social content. Unless the young aspirant appreciates the essentially supernatural nature of the priesthood, it will not evince the generosity of response which such a vocation requires.

It is true that when the enthusiasm of youth wanes, when the priest is more conscious of the humanly hum-drum nature of much of his work, when looking back at what he has achieved with his life, he may perhaps feel he has not been very successful, either humanly or apostolically. There is a danger then that he may become more conscious of the loss of what he has renounced and may begin to feel that his celibacy is a burden. He may indeed undergo a crisis of faith bringing with it a distaste for things spiritual.

The priest is very vulnerable in this situation, and, as a seminarian, he needs to be alerted to its possible onset and how to cope with it. In the first place he will require the help of an experienced spiritual guide to whom he can open his soul in all sincerity, articulating his disappointments, his frustrations, his doubts, the seeming worthlessness of much of what he is doing, and his apprehensions for the future. He will also need to speak frankly about any ambiguities in his emotional life, and not be surprised at the discovery that we bear the treasure of our vocation in vessels of clay. In this way he will rediscover a sense of proportion, he will be helped see that the solution to his difficulties will inevitably require a spiritual renewal based on a solid prayer-life, and a deeper friendship with the Great Friend, Christ in the Eucharist. He should not be surprised that he will often have to rediscover many fundamental truths of the spiritual life if he is to persevere in his vocation. It is important that the point be made to seminarians and young priests that such a crisis need not arise, and in general will not, if they avail of the services of a spiritual director from the very beginning of their priesthood.[32]

CELIBACY – FORMATION IN FREEDOM

Freedom is today regarded as one of the highest goods, and rightly so. Still, there is often an ambivalence in our understanding of the true nature of this gift. As portrayed in the media and in many intellectual trends, it is frequently equated to hedonism and consumerism, 'lacking the modera-

---

[32] The nature and advantages of spiritual guidance will be developed in more depth in Chapter 6.

tion which the dignity of redeemed humanity demands of true freedom'.[33]
This emptiness as regards the purpose of existence increasingly results in
the quest for substitutes for authentic freedom.

Because of ambiguities in this area, which are part of the social and
intellectual environment, it is clearly important that the seminarian should
understand the essential nature of freedom from a Christian point of view,
and its relationship with his decision to follow a vocation to celibacy.
What emerges from much current discourse about celibacy is the deficient
understanding of personal freedom, and its correlative of personal responsibility, which exists in many quarters. Therefore a deep seminary formation in the concept of freedom, and not only in relation to celibacy, is one
of the best guarantees that the future priest will know how to fully accept
the responsibilities which are the consequences of his free choices and
commitments.

By free will we shape our own lives, and hence freedom is a force for
growth and maturity in truth and goodness. It attains its perfection when
directed towards God, our ultimate good. As wayfarers, however, we have
the possibility of choosing between good and evil. The more one does
what is good, the freer one becomes, and thus true freedom lies in the
service of the good. Consequently there is no greater freedom than in
committing one's life totally in the service of the highest good, which is
what the priest does through his celibacy in the service of Christ.

Nevertheless, human freedom is limited. The proper use of freedom is
dictated by the moral law which identifies our responsibilities to God and
to others, as well as to ourselves. The exercise of a false freedom, sin,
which means choosing self before God, produces a fundamental alienation
in man, a violation of his own freedom, which can only be recovered
through conversion and redemption.[34]

True freedom, as Cardinal Ratzinger points out, has an inherent dynamic which needs fundamental co-ordinates: it must derive *from* someone or something and be *for* something or someone. It has limits which
we need to accept if we are going to behave responsibly. Yet, the modern
approach to freedom, largely shaped by Rousseau, refuses to accept a *whence*
or a *whither*. It seems to have been forgotten that it is only the truth that
will make us free (cf Jn. 8:32), that freedom must be based on the truth
about man and be directed to his ultimate goal if it is to have any real
meaning. Man has an autonomy and freedom of his own, but within

---

33 Document, 'The Eucharist and Freedom', 6, in *Osservatore Romano*, 13 November
1996.   **34** Cf. *Catechism of the Catholic Church*, nos. 1730–42.

certain limits, limits which are set by the truth about the person, his nature and his ultimate end.[35]

To achieve true personal freedom, man needs to be redeemed, as St Paul reminds us: 'For freedom, Christ has set us free' (Gal 5:1). Because freedom is a fragile and endangered gift, it has been 'redeemed' from sin and is 'saved' by the gift of the Holy Spirit, in whom we have become children of God, freed from the slavery of sin (cf. Gal 4:4–6).[36] As the Apostle reminds us, 'where the Spirit of the Lord is, there is freedom' (2 Cor 3:17).

John Paul II has frequently pointed out during his pontificate that the problem of freedom in the world today concerns the relationship between freedom and truth, the relationship perceived by a conscience formed according to the revelation of the Gospel and the Church's teaching. However, when the link between this truth and freedom is broken or obscured, it inevitably leads to a collapse of values and a misreading of the nature of humanity, often with catastrophic results. Accordingly 'only the freedom which submits to the Truth leads the human person to his true good. The good of the person is to be in the Truth and to *do* the Truth.'[37] Personal freedom is enhanced by doing good.

Faced with the difficulty of understanding the true meaning of freedom, man must look to Christ who said he was the Truth (cf. Jn 14:6), and who affirmed that it was the truth alone that would set us free (cf. Jn 8:32). As John Paul II points out, 'the crucified Christ reveals the authentic meaning of freedom; he lives it fully in the total gift of himself and calls his disciples to share in his freedom'.[38] Consequently 'contemplation of Jesus Christ crucified is thus the highroad which the Church must tread every day if she wishes to understand the full meaning of freedom: the gift of self in service of God and one's "brothers". His crucified flesh fully reveals the unbreakable bond between freedom and truth, just as his resurrection from the dead is the supreme exhaltation of the fruitfulness and saving power of freedom lived out in truth.'[39]

---

35 Cf. Cardinal Joseph Ratzinger, 'Truth and Freedom', *Communio* 23, Spring 1996, p. 27. He continues: 'To be totally free, without the competing freedom of others, without a "from" and a "for"– this desire presupposes not an image of God, but an idol ... The real God is by his very nature entirely being-for (Father), being-from (Son), and being-with (Holy Spirit). Man, for his part, is God's image precisely insofar as the "from", "with", and "for"constitute the fundamental anthropological pattern. Whenever there is an attempt to free ourselves from this pattern, we are not on our way to divinity, but to dehumanisation, to the destruction of being itself through the destruction of the truth' (p. 28).   36 Cf. 'The Eucharist and Freedom', 2.   37 Cf. *Veritatis splendor*, 84.   38 Ibid., 85.   39 Ibid., 87.

In these striking passages from *Veritatis splendor*, John Paul II, who experienced in his own flesh the subjugation of the Nazi and Communist tyrannies, writes with uncommon insight and conviction on the relationship between true freedom and the Cross. This is the essence of Christian wisdom, and if the seminarian or priest fails to grasp and penetrate more deeply each day into this fundamental idea, he is in danger of losing sight of the real purpose of his vocation as a co-redeemer with Christ.

The more profound his appreciation of this concept, the more clearly will he understand that the Eucharist is the sacrament of the free gift of himself which Christ offered us in the Upper Room, and which was consummated on Calvary. And so, in his Mass each day, the priest will rediscover that it is on the Cross that the rehabilitation of humanity takes place, that human freedom is reborn.[40]

Christ gave himself up for us in 'a death he freely accepted' in a sacrifice of love, for only love can liberate when it loves unconditionally. Consequently, 'in the gift of his body and the outpouring of his blood, Christ affirms our liberation and redemption from sin ... , our salvation with the inner gift of the Spirit', and our hope of the resurrection. Such a hope has particular implications for freedom, teaching us patience, perseverance, self-giving and sacrifice. The risen Christ is thus the source and the measure of the fullness of freedom.[41] The Eucharist is then a celebration of freedom because the love that it encapsulates is a love that breaks down all barriers of selfishness. If we approach the altar each day in this light and with these expectations, our perception of Christian freedom will constantly mature, not just as an idea, but above all as experienced in our own lives.

FREEDOM AND CONVERSION

As we have already seen, it is our response in faith to the truth of revelation which sets us free, free not only from sin, but also in the positive sense to give ourselves to the point of offering our lives in service of others. The first fruits of assimilating the truth at a personal level is self-knowledge, which leads to conversion. Without this *metanoia* there is no possibility of experiencing Christian freedom, which begins by acknowledging our need for forgiveness. Regular experience of the sacrament of Reconciliation is a privileged means for the seminarian and priest to grasp

40 Cf. 'The Eucharist and Freedom', 4.   41 Cf. ibid., 13.

the true nature of Christian freedom at its deepest level. Indeed, John Paul II, in the section of *Pastores dabo vobis* related to the spiritual formation of future priests, tells us that 'it is necessary and very urgent to rediscover *the beauty and joy of the Sacrament of Penance*'.[42]

As a consequence of such conversion it is possible to develop the qualities inherent in one's personality which, reinforced by the gifts of divine grace, channel human freedom to its maturity. Thus freedom is fostered by human formation, pastoral care, spiritual guidance, theological education and prayer. In a word, it is holiness of life which 'constitutes the simplest and most attractive way to perceive at once the beauty of truth, the liberating force of God's love, and the value of unconditional fidelity to all the demands of the Lord's law, even in the most difficult situations'.[43] Hence we see that formation in freedom is at the same time education in holiness and priestly virtue.

By responding to his vocation the priest returns to God the freedom won for him on Calvary so that Christ can use it for his own purposes. The priest does this especially by offering the sacrifice of the Mass, and in being his instrument to bring the most radical Christian freedom to others through the ministry of Reconciliation.

Mary, in her offering of herself at the Annunciation, and again at the presentation of the Christ Child in the temple, is the great model for the Church, and for priests, in the restitution made to God of our freedom and of our commitment to be co-redeemers.[44]

FREEDOM AND ADORATION

Because of the constant barrage of sound and visual images which assail young people today, they are in danger of losing the capacity to reflect, a

---

42 No. 48 (italics in original). The Holy Father continues: 'In a culture which, through renewed and more subtle forms of self-justification, runs the fatal risk of losing the "sense of sin" and, as a result, the consoling joy of the plea for forgiveness (cf. Ps 51:14) and of meeting God who is "rich in mercy"(Eph 2:4), it is vital to educate future priests to have the virtue of penance, which the Church wisely nourishes in her celebrations and in the seasons of the liturgical year, and which finds its fullness in the Sacrament of Reconciliation. From it flow the sense of asceticism and interior discipline, a spirit of sacrifice and self-denial, the acceptance of hard work and the Cross. These are elements of the spiritual life which often prove to be particularly arduous for many candidates for the priesthood who have grown up in relatively comfortable and affluent circumstances and have been made less inclined and open to these very elements by the models of behaviour and ideals transmitted by the mass media' (ibid.). **43** *Veritatis splendor*, 107. **44** Cf. 'The Eucharist and Freedom', 23.

condition exacerbated by the accelerated pace and activism of modern living. This also has relevance for the formation of seminarians.

Hence there is a real need for reflection in the silence of prayer so that the human soul can wonder at the *magnalia Dei*, especially the mystery of the Real Presence, and learn to adore. This is the great antidote to the superficiality which characterises so much of human activity and discourse today. Only in such contemplation can one experience that true freedom which responds to God's love. It is in the worship of God in 'Spirit and truth' that we discover the deepest foundation of freedom.[45]

Today, because of a distorted sense of freedom, many need to be brought back to an authentic experience of their dignity as children of God and the freedom which derives from it. This is the role of the priest *par excellence*, especially through the sacrament of Reconciliation. Much of his pastoral activity should be directed to this objective because, as a modern spiritual writer trenchantly reminds us, the Christian who is unaware that he is a child of God is ignorant of the deepest truth about his existence.[46] The parable of the Prodigal Son is, above all, a statement of the intimate relationship between freedom, truth and conversion.

By reflecting on the Eucharist we recognise that desires, based on human freedom alone, cannot by themselves reach fulfilment in this world. The deepest aspirations of the human heart will only be satisfied in a transcendent future. The priest by the example of his celibacy, as well as by his love for the Eucharist, will be a constant reminder to his people of this great truth. He will save them from the illusion of expecting to find in this life the fulfilment of their heart's desires, and encourage them to order their lives so that they persevere with good hope in anticipation of a more definitive future.

MARY AND FREEDOM

Freedom is given to us not only for self-affirmation, but also for self-giving in love. We grow and develop by freely choosing to commit ourselves to different personal and community involvements, and by accepting all the responsibilities which these commitments bring with them. This is especially so in relation to celibacy.

The Church sees in the Blessed Virgin a model of liberation, because

45 Cf. *Veritatis splendor*, 37.   46 Cf. Blessed Josemaría Escrivá, *Friends of God*, London, 1981, no. 26.

'an attitude of fidelity in self-giving is the vital energy which Mary, the Mother of God, exemplifies in an outstanding way. For she is clearly at all times in communion with God and in solidarity with the People of God.'[47] John Paul II invites us to contemplate the one who is 'totally dependent on God and completely directed towards him', and the fact that 'at the side of her Son, she is *the most perfect image of freedom and of the liberation* of humanity and of the universe'.[48]

It is difficult to imagine a man who has a greater sense of inner freedom than the present Holy Father. It is reflected in everything he does, in everything he writes or says. This is an aspect of his personality which is recognised by the secular media, even if they don't fully comprehend why.[49] However, the French philosopher André Frossard had more insight into the origin of this unique quality. Looking at their history, he says that the Polish people in losing everything acquired a sense of freedom which owes nothing to rhetoric and everything to experience. Thus the Pope can say with conviction, 'Freedom is not "possessed", it is "conquered"'. He vigorously affirms that 'one's life as a person and a social being must be "built out of it"'.[50] This is the man whose motto all during his priestly life has been *Totus tuus*, expressing his free and total dedication to Christ through the Mother of God. He has obviously learned much from his contemplation of 'this most perfect image of freedom', and he has never ceased to encourage priests to do the same.

---

47 Cf. 'The Eucharist and Freedom', 33. 48 John Paul II, *Redemptoris mater*, 25 March 1987, no. 37 (italics in the original). 49 Cf., for example, *Time* Magazine, cover story on John Paul II as *Time* 'Man of the Year', 26 December 1994. 50 André Frossard, *Be Not Afraid!*, London, 1984, p. 24.

6

Celibacy a Way to Holiness

Priestly celibacy is a call to a special friendship with Christ. While it is true that all Christians are called to holiness as a consequence of their Baptismal vocation, priests have a greater responsibility to aspire to sanctity, and are endowed with a special grace to do so.[1] Fundamentally, celibacy makes sense to people in so far as it is seen to witness more fully to the holiness of Christ.

A vocation to holiness requires daily effort, and for the priest commitment to celibacy is an integral part of that quest for sanctity. There are many excellent books on priestly holiness in general, so it is not my purpose here to cover that well trodden ground. What I do propose is to consider some of the ascetical implications of living the virtue of celibate chastity appropriate to priestly holiness.

At the same time it is clear that the effort to grow in chastity cannot be considered in isolation from the totality of the interior struggle which is the path to holiness. Thus a man cannot be chaste without reference to the theological and cardinal virtues. In all the recent discourse about celibacy very little reference was made to the *virtue* of chastity. However, celibacy and chastity are inextricably linked and until we appreciate fully the meaning of the Christian virtue of chastity, arguments about celibacy will of necessity remain at a superficial level.[2]

A programme of formation in celibate chastity will inevitably include, among others, the following presuppositions:

- the reality of vocational grace;
- the weakness in our nature as a consequence of original sin;
- we are responsible for our actions with the freedom to say *yes* or *no* each day to actual graces;
- daily conversion and recovery are an integral part of the interior struggle;
- the need for sacramental grace to cure the wounds of our soul, especially as mediated through the sacrament of Reconciliation;

1 Cf. *Presbyterorum ordinis*, 12.   2 Cf. Chapters 4 and 5 for a detailed analysis of this aspect.

- the advantages of a spiritual guide to provide objectivity and security, and to help us be faithful to a daily programme of piety;
- the conviction that all the difficulties and temptations which arise can be overcome with the help of God's grace.

ASCETICAL FORMATION FOR CELIBACY

The chastity which goes with priestly celibacy, and which is integrally related to the virtue of temperance, is not something which is acquired once and for all; it is rather the result of a constant struggle and daily affirmation. Neither is it a virtue which is developed in isolation, but of necessity participates in the effort to acquire the other cardinal virtues of prudence, fortitude and justice. It is nourished by a spirit of self-denial, and is grounded above all on the virtue of humility. Realistically we recognise that we have feet of clay and, as a consequence, we will feel the need to have regular recourse to spiritual guidance and to the sacrament of Penance to strengthen us against temptation.

Commitment to celibacy entails acts of faith, hope and love in response to the initial grace, and to the actual graces of every day. At the ceremony of the diaconate, when he makes his solemn promise to remain celibate and consecrate his whole life to God, the candidate for Orders knows that Christ is asking much of him, but he accepts generously the consequences of his vow, secure in his friendship with the Master. Similarly when two young people get married they know there will be difficulties ahead but, in the strength of their mutual love and supported by God's grace, they are ready to face bravely an unknown future.

So too with the priest. He does not know what the future will bring, but he trusts the love of the Great Friend who has called him. He cannot be sure he will not have moments of depression or periods of great temptation. Yet, strong in love, he gives himself to Christ and accepts in advance all that his commitment will cost. A priest who draws his spiritual energy from the deep well-springs of his Eucharistic life, who safeguards his heart and avoids situations that could put his chastity at risk, will find joy and fulfilment in his vocation, even though at times he will experience the brittleness of his virtue, the tug of his passions, or the renewed attraction of married life. Deep down he is persuaded that God needs his celibacy so that he may work more effectively for the salvation of souls. His generous availability and dedication to the needs of his people will in the long run bring its own rewards – more commitment to the faith, more fidelity in marriage and family life, more vocations.

On the other hand, if a priest finds his celibacy a burden, with a consequent lack of joy or satisfaction in his ministry, a sincere examination of conscience will invariably show up ambivalence in one or other of the following areas – lack of guard of sight, indecisiveness in avoiding occasions of sin, allowing personal attachments to develop, not being sufficiently discriminating in reading or TV viewing. Habitual concessions in these areas gradually undermine that sensitivity which is a characteristic of the pure in heart, and causes one to become increasingly blind to the supernatural. Sooner or later a crisis of vocation or a crisis of faith, or at least a serious compromise of commitment is inevitable. 'The priest,' Paul VI warned, 'must consider clearly and calmly his position as a man exposed to spiritual warfare against the seductions of the flesh in himself and in the world.'[3]

PRAYER LIFE

Appreciation of celibacy as a special gift from God is something which can mature only by having a solid prayer life. Thus the man who is celibate by calling, and yet abandons prayer, is living dangerously as far as his celibacy is concerned.

As Cardinal Ratzinger has trenchantly affirmed: 'If bearing witness to Jesus Christ before men is the task of the priesthood, then it is the presupposition of this task that the priest first know him, that the priest live and find the real centre of his existence in a way of being that is in fact a being-with-him. For the man who, as priest, attempts to speak to his fellow men of Christ, there is nothing of greater importance than this: to learn what being-with-him, existing in his presence, and following him mean, to hear and see him, to grasp his style of being and thinking. The actual living out of priestly existence and the attempt to prepare others for such an existence demand growth in the ability to hear him above all the static, and to see him through all the forms of this world. To do this is to live in his presence.'[4]

The Holy Father has emphasised the point that in recent years there has been too much discussion about the priest's identity, the value of his presence in the world, etc., and too little actual praying. 'It is prayer that

3 Encyclical, *Sacerdotalis caelibatus*, 73.   4 Joseph Ratzinger, *Priestly Ministry: A Search for its Meaning*, New York, 1971, p. 9.

shows the essential style of the priest', he affirms; 'without prayer this style becomes deformed. Prayer helps us always to find the light that has led us since the beginning of our priestly vocation, and which never ceases to lead us, even though it seems at times to disappear in the darkness. Prayer enables us to be converted continually, to remain in a state of continuous reaching out to God, which is essential if we wish to lead others to him.'[5]

In an address to priests at Maynooth, John Paul II developed the same idea and concluded that 'a constant danger with priests, even zealous priests, is that they become so immersed in the work of the Lord that they neglect the Lord of the work. We must find time, we must make time', he encourages them, 'to be with the Lord in prayer ... It is only if we spend time with the Lord that our sending out to others will also be a bringing of him to others.'[6]

The wisdom of the saints makes it clear that there is no holiness without regular dialogue between the soul and its Creator. Since Christ has called the priest to an intimate friendship with himself, he rediscovers each day in prayer the meaning of his celibacy, which is a pledge of that friendship. But like all true friendships it needs to be cultivated; it cannot be taken for granted. The priest develops it by trying to avoid coming to his period of meditation with a distracted mind or an empty heart. He learns to gather up the incidents of each day and bring them to Christ to share his joys and sorrows with him, asking him to filter out the emotional ambiguities and the dross of self-interest and pride which seem to infiltrate everything we do.

The benefits of daily meditation are inevitable if we persevere despite aridity, tiredness or distractions. As Boylan points out, mental prayer has one, unique effect. Practically all the other traditional exercises of piety can be performed by a priest who still clings to his pet plans for doing his own will, whether it is a habit of deliberate venial sin, a refusal to listen to the promptings of grace, or a determination to refuse God something which God wants him to give up. Indeed 'a man may blind his conscience to the serious danger of mortal sin – he may even go farther – and still carry out all his other religious exercises and duties. *But he cannot persist in any such infidelity and still persevere in the daily practice of mental prayer. One thing or the other must give way.*'[7]

If priests don't make regular contact with the Lord in prayer, they are

5 Holy Thursday Letter to Priests, 1979, no. 10.   **6** Address, 1 October 1979.   **7** Eugene Boylan, *The Spiritual Life of the Priest*, Westminster, 1959, p. 34 (italics in the original).

in danger of becoming prisoners of their own time and surroundings. Only by regular conversation with the Good Shepherd of their souls will they avoid the risk of assimilating the values of a materialistic and sensate culture, and continue to recognise the charism of celibacy as a gift to illuminate and fulfil their lives.

'Watch and pray that you may not enter into temptation; the spirit indeed is willing but the flesh is weak' (Mk 14:38). These words of Christ are a reminder that, in the first place, prayer is essential to live a chaste life, because grace is obtained by prayer. Convinced that he cannot live celibate chastity without God's gracious help, the priest will not neglect this duty. Failures in chastity usually arise from a lack of prudence, but this is invariably preceded by neglect of the spirit and practice of prayer. The priest who prays tries to live in the presence of God. He is quick to recognise the danger of sin and is decisive in taking evasive action – he does not dialogue with temptation.[8] Prayer, John Paul II affirms, has to be the cornerstone of priestly existence: 'it will enable us to harmonise our lives with our priestly service, preserving intact *the identity and authenticity* of this vocation which has become our special inheritance in the Church as the community of the People of God'.[9]

In addition to seeing his pastoral service as an ascetical dimension of his life, and his sacramental actions as personal encounters with Christ, the priest needs to take time off for prayer to penetrate more deeply into the mystery of Christ. To have time for God, to face him sincerely and personally, is the priest's most important pastoral priority. Christ himself made the point very cogently in his last intimate conversation with the Apostles when he developed for them the analogy of the vine and the branches: 'As the branch cannot bear fruit by itself, unless it abides in the vine, neither can you, unless you abide in me ... Apart from me you can do nothing' (Jn 15:5–6). The priest needs to consciously cultivate his interior life 'because ministry without spirituality, without interior life, leads to empty activism'.[10] On the other hand, friendship with Christ in prayer has another incalculable bonus: 'ask whatever you will, and it will be done for you' (Jn 15:8). And so Cardinal Ratzinger pithily comments: 'We must learn, again and again, that we need less discussion and more prayer.'[11]

8 Cf. Leo Trese, *A Man Approved*, New York, 1953, pp. 55–6; von Hildebrand, op. cit., p. 60.   9 Holy Thursday Letter, 1987, no. 10 (italics in original).   10 Cf. Cardinal Joseph Ratzinger, 'The Ministry and Life of Priests', op. cit., p. 16.   11 Ibid.

PRESERVATION OF CHASTITY

Because of the excellence of chastity, spiritual writers tell us that the devil uses the temptations of the flesh as one of the most powerful weapons to undermine priestly holiness. St Augustine, speaking no doubt from personal experience, tells us that 'among all combats, the battle for chastity is the most demanding, because it is a daily battle'.[12] His *Confessions* point to the heroism that is necessary at times in fighting the battle to remain chaste in a society which is hostile to this virtue.

While God never allows us to be tempted beyond our capacity to resist sin, he does not, as has been pointed out, give his grace to those who voluntarily expose themselves to occasions of sin, or remain in them.[13] Consequently, one of the first means recommended by seasoned experts, who were also saints, is not just the avoidance of occasions of sins against purity, but the energetic fleeing from them.[14] St Ambrose remarks that Joseph did not stop to listen to Potiphar's wife, but fled instantly judging that there was danger in any delay.[15] As a modern spiritual writer advises: 'Get away from danger as soon as you are aware of the first sparks of passion, and even before.'[16]

However, there will always be the danger of temptation from within, no matter how much the priest is on his guard against external enticements. These will come in spite of a committed prayer life. Yet, there is never reason to be discouraged, in spite of the vehemence of the passions. The divine response to St Paul's prayer, 'My grace is sufficient for you' (2 Cor 12:9), provides the necessary hope and conviction about success in the struggle.

---

12 Homily, no. 293   **13** Cf. St Alphonsus Liguori, *Dignity and Duties of the Priest*, New York, 1927, p. 249.   **14** 'To repel the attacks of lust, take flight if you wish to obtain the victory' (St Augustine, Homily no. 293); 'How many have been cast into the mire of impurity through a presumptuous security that they would not fall; though you are a saint you are always in danger of falling' (St Jerome, as quoted in *Dignity and Duties of the Priest*, op. cit., p. 249).   **15** Cf. ibid. The book of Genesis (cf. 39:9–20) explains how Joseph overcame the advances of the wife of Pharaoh's captain. She tried to seduce him but he refused and said, 'how can I do this wickedness, and sin against God? And although she spoke to Joseph day after day, he would not listen to her to lie with her or to be with her. But one day, when he went into the house to do his work and none of the men of the house was there in the house, she caught him by his garment, saying, "Lie with me". But he left his garment in her hand, and fled and got out of the house'. To get her revenge on Joseph she used the garment he left behind to accuse him to her husband of making advances to her, and succeeded in having Joseph cast into prison. There are many lessons to be learned from this incident in Scripture.   **16** Blessed Josemaría Escrivá, *Friends of God*, op. cit., no. 182.

At the same time it is necessary to recognise that human nature is profoundly weakened as a consequence of original sin and that the sexual appetite is particularly disordered. This prevents us trusting too much in our own resources and propels us into using the graces that come from the sacraments, spiritual guidance, and a confident devotion to our Lady.

CELIBACY AND DEVOTION TO OUR LADY

Not so very long ago John Paul II posed the following question in an address to priests, 'What should we ask of Mary as "Mother of priests"?' His unequivocal reply on their behalf was: 'Today, as and perhaps more than at any other time, the priest must ask Mary particularly for the grace of knowing how to accept God's gift with grateful love ... ; the grace of purity and fidelity in the obligation of celibacy, following her example as the "faithful Virgin".'[17]

While the offering of the sacrifice of the Mass is for the priest an essentially Christocentric activity, he can never be forgetful, the Holy Father reminds him, of the Mother who gave life to the Body which is sacrificed. This daily experience should create a unique bonding between the priest and Mary and give her a special presence in his life as Mother.[18]

The priest needs to have Mary as the woman at the centre of his life to fill his heart; if he has a real devotion to our Lady he will experience her maternal warmth and support every day. In his effort to live celibacy, the priest, as one spiritual writer has put it, 'must lift his eyes and his heart to the mother, companion and bride of his Lord, to that Queen of Virgins who is not only the archetype of humanity in the divine ordering of the world, but also embodies the purest and most perfect ideal of womanhood, virgin, mother, maid and queen. It is to her, the prudent, the mighty, the kindly and faithful Virgin that the priest should turn; it is with her, the pure, gentle Mother of Christ, the Mother of divine Grace, that he should place himself under instruction ... In a fashion wholly unique she unites in herself every noble trait of womanhood, and the priest who venerates her will transfer to all her sisters something of her graciousness and nobility. In every woman he encounters in his life he will seek to discover, or awaken some glimmer, of that womanly dignity which shines forth in Mary.'[19]

---

17 Address, 30 June 1993, in *Osservatore Romano*, 7 July 1993.   **18** Cf. Holy Thursday Letter to Priests, 1995, no. 3.   **19** Josef Sellmair, op. cit., p. 210.

The passions of the human heart need to be refined and purified if we are to be able to distinguish clearly between self-seeking and self-giving. Because of human weakness we can easily confuse these two contrary dispositions in matters of the heart, and so, as Newman says, we need the 'cool breath of the Immaculate'[20] to help us be sincere with ourselves and recognise our self-seeking for what it really is.

SPIRITUAL GUIDANCE

Celibacy may become incomprehensible even to the priest if its basis, meaning and purpose are not kept clearly in mind. The more completely his meditation and prayer allow him to grasp the mystery of Christ and his Church, the more deeply rooted will he grow in his vocation, and the more fully will he sink his roots into the nourishing soil of God's grace to feed and sustain him. Without this depth and firmness, the priest is in danger of being uprooted from his vocation. If his immersion in the life of Christ is shallow and superficial he will be prey to passing theological fashions and fads, and could easily come to regard his celibacy as inappropriate, superfluous or meaningless. Personal piety is the best defence against such superficiality.[21]

Sincerity is absolutely essential to live chastity well. Sincerity with oneself, with one's confessor, and with God. On account of human deviousness, there is a strong tendency in us to self-deceit, especially in this area. If a man like David, a king and a judge of Israel who knew his moral theology, could fail to apply it to himself, and had to be confronted by the prophet Nathan before he recognised the gravity of his sin, we should not be surprised at our own blindness in this context.

In matters of holy purity there is a need to open the heart in spiritual guidance and confession with a 'brutal sincerity', as Blessed Josemaría Escrivá, an experienced director of souls, counselled.[22] Incipient attachments, lack of prudence in reading matter or TV viewing, over-familiarity with particular people, curiosity – all these should be aired, even though the priest may feel that he has no real problems. And this is precisely the point – sincerity about little failures will guarantee that there will be no big ones.

20 John H. Newman, *Discourses to Mixed Congregations*, London, 1886, p. 376.   **21** Cf. Federico Suarez, *About Being a Priest*, Houston, 1979, p. 161.   **22** Cf. Escrivá, op. cit., no. 188.

John Paul II says that, in relation to growth in holiness, it is necessary to rediscover the great tradition of personal guidance which has always given such bountiful fruits in the life of the Church.[23] Scripture tells us that 'a brother helped by a brother is as strong as a walled city' (Prov 18:19). This principle applies not only at the general level of priestly fraternity, but even more so when availing of the support that a brother priest can offer through regular spiritual guidance. Everybody needs what is so accurately conveyed by the Irish word *anam-chara*, a soul-friend in whom he can confide, with whom he can share the successes and failures of his spiritual struggle, to whom he can go for encouragement and objective advice. This is particularly so in relation to celibacy. The priest needs a guide he trusts and respects because of his experience, and also because he gives evidence of a serious commitment to holiness by his own lifestyle.

OBJECTIVE SELF-KNOWLEDGE

The priest needs to be affirmed in his celibacy as a vocation to love in a special way. He should be very clear in his mind that this commitment does not deny his sexuality, but rather, under the action of grace, enables him to love in an inclusive way.

The priesthood, as we have seen, presupposes human and emotional maturity i.e. a capacity for friendship, affection, and the sharing of confidences, while at the same time not being overdependent on them. Still, a priest with a well balanced personality will have to fight the normal daily battles to be faithful to celibacy. But these obstacles will be put into perspective by spiritual guidance and overcome with the basic ascetical means.

Nevertheless, difficulties with celibacy can at times surface for less obvious reasons. Frequently a spiritual director will first have to isolate problems of human immaturity or emotional deprivation before he can deal directly with the aspect related to celibacy. In this context, self-knowledge will often be the best service which spiritual counselling offers the priest. There may be hidden psychological or emotional scars caused by negative family bonding, overdependence on an indulgent mother, or bad school influences which the priest needs to confront with the help of a spiritual guide.

If he approaches this self-disclosure with sincerity and humility he can, with the help of grace, acquire the virtues which will enable him become

23 Cf. *Pastores dabo vobis*, 40.

humanly and psychologically secure. To achieve this he needs to put down into his soul deep roots of divine filiation, an awareness of the fatherly providence of a God who loves him more than all the mothers of this world ever could (cf. Lk 15:11–32), and which made St Paul exult on so many occasions, despite the difficulties he experienced in his own flesh. As we have already seen, the fact that we are children of a loving Father is the deepest truth about our existence.[24] Growth in this fundamental conviction is the best guarantee of achieving that emotional balance and integrity which are a necessary basis for a celibate life of fulfilment.[25]

A good spiritual director will continually open the priest's horizons on the positive implications of his celibacy. As a consequence he will become convinced of its advantages and not feel deprived in any significant way because of it. The priest will then rediscover the joy of self-giving, and of that fundamental *metanoia* which results from many small conversions each day. Spiritual counselling is an opportunity for him to acquire a conscience that is neither scrupulous nor relaxed.

One of the basic reasons for spiritual guidance is that the way we should follow in our interior life is not always clear and obvious. We are too close to ourselves to be objective in something so personal as the pursuit of holiness. The priest knows from his own experience, and from the experience of trying to guide others, the dangers of subjective self-will. This results in him often being blind to the real needs of his own spiritual life. Indeed one of the peculiar weaknesses of the human condition in matters spiritual is the tendency to allow ourselves to be over-influenced by self-regarding motives rather than by reasons which are grounded on faith or supernatural considerations. Working on the basis of human impulse alone, even heroically so, is ultimately a recipe for burn-out and disillusionment

To avoid shying away from the demands of priestly holiness, of which celibacy is an integral part, the priest needs somebody to point the way objectively, a kind and understanding mentor who will call his spiritual bluff when necessary, and help him to be sincere with himself. We all tend to work comfortably within our limits and to avoid being overstretched. A good spiritual guide will enable the priest to get the best out himself and help him keep a proper balance between work and prayer, relaxation and pastoral zeal.

24 Cf. Escrivá, ibid, no. 26.   **25** John Paul II has written penetratingly and persuasively about the rich implications of our divine filiation, especially in his encyclical *Dives in misericordia* (30 November 1980) and his apostolic exhortation *Reconciliatio et paenitentia* (2 December 1984). See also Fernando Ocariz, *God as Father in the Message of Blessed Josemaría Escrivá*, Princeton, NJ, 1994.

A spiritual director will perhaps tell him little that he doesn't know already at a theoretical level. However, his most effective contribution will be to help the priest face up to himself, to acquire a deeper self-knowledge. There will be times when the heart wants to recover the good things left behind by a vocation to celibacy. In moments of discouragement or depression, the effort to be faithful to this commitment can seem to be a form of self-delusion, and the temptation to start life again in marriage can be very strong. In such times of trial the priest needs to rediscover the love that can and should fill his heart. He will do so if he allows his soul to be guided by a prudent spiritual director, who will refocus for him the goal of his vocation, and remind him once more of the many supports of grace which are available. He will help him see that fidelity is always possible no matter how great the difficulties may seem.

In such circumstances the priest will undoubtedly have to put more effort into developing his life of friendship with Christ through prayer and a spirit of sacrifice. If he has a deep devotion to the Real Presence in the Eucharist, he will realise that no other passion can compare with it, or yield the joys which intimacy with the Tabernacle provides. In a very revealing account of his own soul, J.R.R. Tolkien, writing to his son about marriage said: 'Out of the darkness of my life, so much frustrated, I put before you the one great thing to love on earth: the Blessed Sacrament ... There you will find romance, glory, honour, fidelity, and the true way of all your loves upon earth, and more than that: death: by the divine paradox, that which ends life, and demands the surrender of all, and yet by the taste (or foretaste) of which alone can what you seek in your earthly relationships (love, faithfulness, joy) be maintained, or take on that complexion of reality, of eternal endurance, that every man's heart desires.'[26]

It is not by accident that those who have experienced the joys, but also the limitations of married love, can at times point more penetratingly and more surely to the superiority and permanent endurance of the love that the Eucharist enshrines. This human and supernatural realism is particularly relevant for a priest whose expectations of human love may frequently be more influenced by his own fantasies than by what the reality of it can deliver.

A spiritual guide will help the priest develop a solid interior life of friendship with Christ through his daily meditation, his Mass, the breviary, his Rosary, spiritual reading, examination of conscience, and a daily

---

26 J. R. R. Tolkien, *Letters*, ed., H. Carpenter, London, 1981, pp 53–4.

visit to the Blessed Sacrament. These are some of the practices of piety recommended in the recently published *Directory on the Ministry and Life of Priests*.[27] They are a solid foundation on which the priest can build fidelity to his commitment to celibacy. However, an experienced spiritual director will also have a concern to help priests acquire that unity of life which is so highly recommended by the Vatican II decree on priestly life.[28] This is a programme to achieve coherence between interior life and external activity, and thus avoid burn-out. In this way the priest's practices of piety will provide the spiritual energy necessary to turn his pastoral and ministerial activities into a means of personal holiness and fulfilment.

A logical consequence of this attitude is that through spiritual guidance a priest learns to make good use of his time, plan his work better, and fulfil responsibilities promptly. A committed and orderly work schedule, inspired by unity of life, provides a context for human and spiritual fulfilment and in this way contributes effectively to fidelity in the area of celibacy.

Overall we can see that personal spiritual guidance is an opportunity for communicating at the deepest and most intimate level of our being. It provides an awareness of being understood, supported and appreciated. This friendship is a powerful defence against the dangers of pessimism and frustration which can undermine the commitment of the priest. While psychology can provide some insights about the religious dimension of people's behaviour, discernment of spirits and the pedagogical wisdom of the saints offer us a much more profound source of knowledge for the guidance of priests and seminarians. It is the attractive profile of the saint, reflecting natural and supernatural virtues forged by grace, that should be offered as the model, rather than the narrow reductive framework of psychoanalysis which emerges from the now largely discredited Freudian interpretation of human behaviour.[29]

PRIESTLY FRATERNITY

Priestly fraternity is a great support to celibacy. As the Synod Fathers pointed out, 'there is a loneliness which all priests experience and which is com-

27 Cf. op. cit., no. 39. **28** Cf. *Presbyterorum ordinis*, 14. **29** Cf. John Farrell, *Freud's Paranoid Quest*, New York, 1996. Dietrich von Hildebrand warns us that 'Freud's thesis, on which the so-called psychoanalytic method is based, embodies a completely erroneous view of the structure of human personality, which betrays the influence of an exploded sensationalism'. One of its radical errors, he tells us, 'is that it regards the body and physiological life as the "form" of the soul, not the spiritual soul as the "form" of life and the body' (*In Defence of Purity*, London, 1937, p. 17).

pletely normal',[30] and which facilitates growth in intimacy with Jesus Christ. Still, everyone, including the priest, needs human affection and affirmation. Priestly fraternity is therefore a very important factor in the ongoing fidelity of the individual priest.

Sacramental fraternity is the basis of the human fraternity of the priesthood. It is only natural that there would be a special bond between those who are members of the same diocesan presbyterate, which provides a sense of belonging that all priests need. But this sense of being at home, of belonging, needs to be nourished by the genuine care priests show for the physical health and other material needs of their brothers. It will reflect itself also in traditional priestly hospitality, and in practical concern for those who are sick, overworked, or lonely.

The priest needs to have a minimum of comfort in his living environment, a home that is well cared for. Sometimes priests, because of financial constraints or other reasons, dispense with the services of a housekeeper and, as a consequence, end up living in very poor material conditions. It is only natural that in such circumstances a priest would tend to look for more attractive surroundings in which to relax, such as the homes of friends or parishioners. This is a type of situation which could have negative connotations for priestly celibacy, and is one which calls for constant interest and concern on the part of those with responsibility for the care of priests.

It should also be pointed out in this context that the wearing of clerical dress has its own part to play in supporting the celibacy of the priest. This is because it defines his identity in a very tangible way. It makes a statement about his commitment and how he should be responded to, in the same way that the symbolism of the marriage ring is a constant call to fidelity and facilitates it.

Priests have a special obligation to help those who may be experiencing difficulties in their vocation. They show a genuine human and supernatural affection for their brothers who are in danger of going astray by helping with 'the refined evangelical practice of fraternal correction'.[31] Are there not perhaps vocational failures in relation to celibacy which could have been avoided if priests had been more alert to the human and

---

30 Cf. *Pastores dabo vobis*, 74. The synodal document develops this idea: 'The ability to handle a healthy solitude is indispensable for caring for one's interior life. Here we are speaking of a solitude filled with the presence of the Lord who puts us in contact with the Father, in the light of the Spirit ... In this regard too, it can be said that those unable to have a positive experience of their own solitude are incapable of genuine and fraternal fellowship' (ibid.).   31 *Directory on the Ministry and Life of Priests*, op. cit, 93.

spiritual needs of their brothers? In this context it is worth noting that associations which promote priestly fraternity and holiness in the exercise of ministry are especially encouraged by the Church.[32]

GUARD OF HEART

It is frequently suggested nowadays that a priest needs a woman's friendship in order to be well-adjusted. The basis of such friendship may be a shared intellectual or cultural interest. It may even start out on a high spiritual plane but, as Boylan points out, it is difficult to keep it within such limits.[33] Indeed, common sense and the wisdom of Christian asceticism confirm the imprudence of such relationships.[34] What is often forgotten is that through normal family relationships with sisters, mother, cousins, etc, priests have all the means to develop a mature and natural attitude to women.

One single reference in the Gospel reveals to us that exceptional reserve which Christ displayed in his relationships with women. Tired after his journey the Master sat down at Jacob's well in Sichar while the disciples went into the village to buy food. It was there he encountered the Samaritan woman and had that very moving conversation with her, by the end of which this lady of compromised virtue was converted and became an evangelizer of souls (cf. Jn 4:1–30). When the disciples returned and saw him, St John tells us that 'they marvelled that he was

32 Cf. *Presbyterorum ordinis*, 8; *Directory on the Ministry and Life of Priests*, 29, 88. **33** Cf. Boylan, op. cit., p. 85. St John Chrysostom in his treatise *On the Priesthood* tells us that the priest in the world, by comparison with the monk, is confronted by more temptations: 'Though he needs greater purity, he is exposed to greater dangers, which may sully him unless he uses constant vigilance, and great attention to hinder them access to his soul. For beauty of countenance and affected airs, and studied gait, the tone of the voice, painting of the eyes and cheeks, arrangement of tresses, colouring of the hair, costly raiment, varied ornaments of gold, beautiful gems, the fragrance of perfumes and the like, which the female sex affect, are capable of making an impression on the mind, unless it be hardened by great austerity and self-restraint' (*On the Priesthood*: A treatise by St John Chrysostom. Translated by Rev Patrick Boyle CM, Westminster, 1943, p. 121). Chrysostom is above all pointing out to the priest the need for custody of the eyes so as to be able to serve God with an undivided heart.   **34** It is a matter of historical record that there have been special relationships between clerics and women such as that between St Francis of Assisi and St Clare, foundress of the Poor Clares; between St Catherine of Siena and her confessor Raymond of Capua, afterwards Master General of the Dominicans; and that between St Francis de Sales and St Jane Frances de Chantal, foundress of the Institute of the Visitation of the Blessed Virgin Mary. However, these were exceptional relationships which functioned at a very high spiritual level.

talking with a woman' and that in their surprise none of them dared ask him 'Why are you talking with her?' (Jn 4:27). It was clearly something the disciples had never seen the Master do before.

However, we know from the Gospels that Jesus had many pastoral and compassionate encounters with women – with the woman suffering from the issue of blood, with Mary Magdalen to assure her of her pardon, with Martha to chide her for being too wrapped up in her own concerns, with the mother of the sons of Zebedee for being too solicitous about their future. But he never spoke to them alone. He did so surrounded by the crowds, in the midst of his disciples, generally in the presence of someone who could give witness to the holiness of his words and the purity of his actions. Even after the Resurrection he keeps this reserve; he permits the holy women he meets on the road to kiss his feet.

In his conversation with women, the priest should exercise a prudent reserve.[35] If she is a spiritual and holy person, St Augustine says there is need for even greater prudence, because such more easily gain the affections of men.[36] However, the priest was never meant to be a man without a heart. On the contrary, he has been given a deeper participation in the sentiments of Christ's heart, which enables him to love more and with greater generosity. Precisely because of this claim which Christ has on him, the priest has a duty to guard his heart to prevent it becoming attached to particular persons.

Like any other man, the priest has a deeply felt need for love, affection and the contemplation of beauty. Hence affective maturity is reinforced by developing an interest in those expressions of beauty which enlarge the mind and refresh the spirit, whether in art or architecture, literature, music or liturgy. The deeper his appreciation of the great inheritance of Christian culture and wisdom, the more insight will he acquire about the reality and the implications of the Incarnation.

Custody of the eyes, which facilitates guard of heart, is an age-old prescription that has lost none of its effectiveness.[37] It is even more relevant in today's environment. The enticements to sensuality which are

---

35 St Bernard asks rhetorically, and with a certain irony, if being familiar with women, and preserving chastity at the same time, is not a greater miracle than raising a dead man to life? (cf. *In Cant.* s. 65). St Jerome wrote to Nepotianus: 'Do not confide too much in your past chastity; do not remain alone with a woman without a witness'.   36 As quoted in *Dignity and Duties of the Priest*, op. cit., p. 255. St Augustine attests that he knew prelates of the Church of whom he had as high an opinion as he did of Jerome and Ambrose, and yet these, by exposing themselves to such friendships, fell away from sanctity into sin (cf. ibid., p. 257).   37 Cf. Boylan, op. cit., p. 84.

purveyed by TV and advertising, by immodesty and bad example, are an opportunity for the priest, as well as every other Christian, to make constant decisions in favour of purity of mind and heart. This is not 'tridentine rigorism' or 'prudish victorianism', but the considered advice of experienced campaigners such as Augustine, Jerome, Chrysostom, and Alphonsus, men who were no mere voluntarists but intellectual giants in their own right, and who are honoured for being doctors of the Church as well as being saints.[38] In fact, guard of sight gives a new and superior type of vision, affirmed by Christ himself: 'Blessed are the pure in heart for they shall see God' (Mt 5:8).[39] There is also a strong scriptural basis for this discipline in relation to chastity.[40]

PRACTICAL CONSIDERATIONS

There have been considerable changes in the accepted conventions of social behaviour over the past few decades. Because of these mutations some of the traditional norms of reserve in priests' dealings with women have been discarded since they were considered old-fashioned and prudish.[41] Certainly some modifications were called for. However, it should give us pause that in recent years other professions have been rediscovering the importance of some of the social delimitations abandoned by priests which were aimed at ensuring their good name was not brought into question.

In secondary schools, where the exercise of professional duties involves dealing with students on sensitive issues, certain safeguards are proposed. For example, it is recommended that instances of being alone with one student should be avoided, and that doors should be left open where one-to-one contact is inevitable. The instruction to teachers recognises that

---

38 Cf. *Dignity and Duties of the Priest*, op. cit., pp. 250–2.   **39** It is not just a matter of avoiding impure images, but of having that refinement of soul which recognises that the attraction of feminine beauty and charm, which are good in themselves, can distract from fidelity to the prior claims God's love has on us as priests. As one experienced priest commented: 'Dear Lord, I find beauty and charm in everything I see! I will guard my sight at every moment, for the sake of Love' (Blessed Josemaría Escrivá, *The Forge*, London, 1988, no. 415).   **40** 'I have made a covenant with my eyes; how then could I look upon a virgin' (Job 31:1); 'Do not gaze upon a virgin, lest her beauty be a stumbling block for you ... Do not look around in the streets of a city ... Turn away your eyes from a shapely woman, and do not look intently at beauty belonging to another; many have been misled by a woman's beauty, and by it passion is kindled like a fire. Never dine with another man's wife, nor revel with her at wine; lest your heart turn aside to her' (Sir 9:5, 7–9).   **41** Cf., for example, the Maynooth Statutes of 1956 related to this – *Acta et Decreta*, p. 50.

'these safeguards may appear overly cautious'. However, it concludes that 'a due prudence requires their application'.[42]

Because of the increasing number of allegations of child abuse, the INTO has seen fit to issue a document entitled, *Guidance for Teachers: A Professional Response to Changing Times*.[43] 'As a protective measure,' teachers are told, 'it is, therefore, regrettably necessary to take particular care to minimise situations where a teacher and child are alone together and to take steps to avoid inappropriate physical contact with pupils.' When it is necessary to conduct confidential interviews with students, 'meetings with individual children should be conducted in the presence of another person, or with the door open, or with a closed door with a glass panel. Another member of staff should be told about the meeting and the reason for it.'[44]

It is scarcely surprising, therefore, that a young priest of the author's acquaintance, a chaplain in a large girls' secondary school, has decided he will no longer hear face-to-face confessions, but has provided himself with a portable confessional screen to administer this sacrament. Surely he has a right to consider that his good name is as important as that of his teacher colleagues![45]

PASTORAL RELATIONSHIP

A priest's failure to remain faithful to his commitment to celibacy damages the Church, and even more so when it becomes public knowledge. This does not happen overnight. There are warning signs which a priest may not recognise – overstepping the proper boundaries in his relationships, and a misunderstanding of the nature of the pastoral role. Strong emotional involvements can develop and he can ignore the danger signals, convincing himself that a particular relationship is somehow different.[46]

---

42 ASTI: *Guidelines for Professional Behaviour for Second-level Teachers*, September 1995. **43** Published by the Irish National Teachers' Organisation, September 1996. **44** Ibid., p. 6. **45** In light of these norms of prudence issued by teachers' organisations, and the allegations of misconduct made against priests over the past number of years, one could perhaps ask whether open confessional rooms are appropriate places to administer this sacrament to young people, and women in particular. This is a consideration which arises not only from the point of view of the priest, but also in relation to protecting the dignity of the Sacrament. In this context it is interesting to note that the Catholic hierarchy of Australia has issued instructions to the effect that glass panels should be installed in all confessionals, not only to prevent scandals, but also to reduce the risk of false allegations against priests (*Irish Times*, 26 September 1997). **46** 'There are warning signals that our

The pastoral relationship is one of trust, stemming from the confidence that people have in the probity of the priest. In sharing confidences, as in counselling or confession, the power of the priest and the vulnerability of the other person is amplified. Ordination confers a status and gives the priest a position of influence in the pastoral relationship.

Precisely because of the experience of abuses of this relationship, the Anglican diocese of Oxford recently felt it necessary to issue a Code of Practice to its ministers.[47] While the circumstances are different, and some of the recommendations do not apply, yet because there is a close parallelism in a number of areas, I think it will be instructive to summarise some of these indications below.

The priest has primary responsibility for what happens between him and the person being served pastorally. Therefore he needs to set clear boundaries to the relationship which, among others, will be influenced by the following considerations: the amount of time spent with people and the frequency of contact; while empathising with another person's situation or feelings, the need to maintain a distance appropriate to the pastoral role; avoiding seeing people late at night; not calling to houses when people are alone; avoiding anything which would cast doubts on his integrity as a priest, which is the basis of his pastoral effectiveness; being careful about expressions of consolation – to act with compassion while keeping the proper emotional and psychological distance; pastoral relationships should encourage maturity and growth, not dependency; never forgetting that he should always act in the biblical image of the shepherd (cf. Ezek 34:1–10) whose concern is to build up, protect and to feed.

There is a lot of practical wisdom encapsulated in these indications which will help the priest live his celibacy with refinement and avoid emotional ambiguities in his relationships.[48]

love may be moving away from celibacy. The first and obvious one, when the expression of one's love becomes physical. Secondly, when one feels jealous or resents others getting close to one's friend. Thirdly, when one considers the other person as ours or feels bound by a sense of duty or loyalty towards them. Fourthly, when one expects or demands certain kinds of response. Fifthly, when one's ability to reason with clarity becomes diminished leading to a lack of availability for and commitment to one's duty especially pastoral visitation, because of one's emotional involvement with another. Finally, when one's involvement with another causes us to lose our appetite for prayer' (Michael Neary, *Our Hide and Seek God: Priesthood and the Word of God*, Cork, 1990, p. 87). **47** Cf. *The Diocese of Oxford: 'The Greatness of the Trust'*: Report of the Working Party on Sexual Abuse by Pastors, Easter 1996; *The Diocese of Oxford: Code of Ministerial Practice*, Pentecost 1996. **48** In the Oxford document *The Greatness of the Trust* there is a summary of a very interesting paper entitled 'Transference –the Tie that Blinds' by Dr A. Hart (published in *Carer and Counsellor*, 5, no. 1.) which describes how emotional involvements can develop in coun-

CELIBACY AND MARRIAGE – MUTUAL DEPENDENCE

John Paul II draws a parallel between the obligations of celibacy and the commitment of married fidelity. As priests know very well through their pastoral experience, every marriage has its own trials which, if faced up to with patience, prayer and humility, invariably leads to a deeper love between the couple. But the parallel runs deeper; the fidelity of the priest to his vocation is a powerful example and has a unique sign value for those who are married. 'Married couples', the Holy Father reminds priests, 'have the right to expect from us ... good example and *the witness of fidelity to one's vocation until death*, a fidelity to the vocation that we choose through the sacrament of Orders, just as they choose it through the sacrament of Matrimony.'[49] The Church's high regard for celibacy does not imply that it devalues in any way the vocation to marriage and family life, or that it takes a Manichean view of the body and its functions. In no way, affirms John Paul II, does the pre-eminence of celibacy suggest a qualified appre-

selling situations, leading to dangerous consequences. While it is true that the relationship with the priest is somewhat different, there are common elements and thus the advice offered is not irrelevant. People, Hart says, come to a counsellor looking for help in difficult situations. When they find a receptive ear, someone who is kind, sympathetic and available to listen to their problems, a particular type of person may come to feel that the solution to their problems is not so much what the counsellor has to say as the counsellor himself! This hazard is known as transference – the client projecting unmet feelings and desires into the counselling relationship which belong somewhere else. Counter-transference, its corollary, is when the counsellor responds in a similar way. This generates emotional attachments which have the potential to become more serious, and which will go further if the counsellor does nothing to stop it. The transference and counter-transference that emerge in counselling sessions can get out of control leading to a dangerous closeness. Indications that such a situation may be developing include the following: the tendency to look forward to counselling sessions, or to extend the session time; when hidden or oblique messages are sent both ways: while on the surface it appears innocuous, at a deeper level it means something more personal – 'I really enjoy my time with you'. Hart suggests the way to deal with this situation is not to encourage it and to always stay professional. The counsellor should never share feelings with another person, not even to hint at them. He has to understand the difference between counter-transference and simple attraction. Basic attraction to women is not a concern; one can easily walk away from it. On the other hand when you allow yourself to think about someone constantly, you have a problem. One has to redirect one's thoughts and avoid fantasising. Hart recommends speaking about emotional difficulties to a close friend to develop a system of accountability. We are not only accountable to God, but we need someone to whom we are accountable and to whom we can talk freely about our feelings. The best protection against sexual temptations is to be able to speak honestly about them and to find the 'effective and affective help needed to overcome them' (pp 39–45).   **49** Holy Thursday Letter 1979, no. 9 (italics in original).

ciation of 'the love that leads a man and woman to marriage and the wedded unity of the body, forming "one flesh"'.[50]

The Holy Father returned to this idea a short time later when he wrote his great post-synodal exhortation on *The Christian Family* in 1981: 'In spite of having renounced physical fecundity, the celibate person becomes spiritually fruitful, the father and mother of many, co-operating in the realisation of the family according to God's plan. Christian couples therefore have the right to expect from celibate persons a good example and a witness of fidelity to their vocation until death. Just as fidelity at times becomes difficult for married people and requires sacrifice, mortification and self-denial, the same can happen to celibate persons, and their fidelity, even in the trials that may occur, should strengthen the fidelity of married couples.'[51]

The reverse is also true. The example of life-long fidelity in marriage is an inspiration for the priest at every stage of his vocation. This was illustrated in a graphic way by a young priest telling the story of his vocation during a Vocations Sunday homily a few years ago. He was in final year at school, thinking about the priesthood, but without having come to a definite decision. One day, on his way home from school, he dropped in to pay a visit to the Blessed Sacrament in his local church. As he knelt at the back he thought he heard the sobbing of a man up near the tabernacle. He approached him to see what was the matter, and found an old man in tears. In response to the boy's query the man explained that his wife had died a few months previously. They had been married for over fifty years and he missed her terribly, and 'now,' he said, 'I am asking God to take me because I cannot live without her.' As a result of that experience, the priest told the congregation, he was fully confirmed in his vocation to the priesthood.

A significant point was made by the bishops at the 1990 Synod when they stated that it was also necessary 'to instruct and educate the lay faithful regarding the evangelical, spiritual and pastoral reasons proper to priestly celibacy, so that they will help priests with their friendship, understanding and co-operation'.[52]

Lay people need to be reminded to pray frequently for their priests, for their holiness, and for vocations. Families who have this Christian attitude to the priesthood are the seedbeds of future vocations. Parents of such families will encourage and welcome vocations to the priesthood among their children; they will consider it as a great blessing for the whole family.

---

50 Ibid., no. 8.　**51** *Familiaris consortio*, 16.　**52** Cf. *Pastores dabo vobis*, 50.

Authentic Catholic families, where children are well formed in the truths of the faith, where every new child is a permanent witness to the dignity and the mystery of spousal love, where modesty and chastity are encouraged by word and example — all this constitutes the privileged environment where vocations to celibacy are nurtured, the experience and the memory of which will sustain the future priest in his vocation and encourage him to be faithful.

THE CROSS IN THE LIFE OF THE PRIEST

Through the Incarnation Christ introduced something entirely novel to the priesthood of the Old Testament because, unlike the line of Levi, he united in himself the role of priest and victim (cf. Jn 10:18; Heb 5:9–10). The consequences of this for the priesthood of the New Covenant are immense. It is not possible for the priest to imitate Christ unless he is also ready to offer himself as a victim for sin as Christ did.

Yet how often we tend to return to the style of the Levitical priesthood in the sense that we see ourselves as priests, but not as victims? Do we at times say Mass as if we presented a victim for sin who was totally unrelated to us, like the scapegoat of the Old Testament? Do we offer the Christ-Saviour to the Father as if we were not dying with him? If we are to be other Christs we cannot escape reproducing in ourselves the mystery enacted on the altar. On the other hand 'if we at Mass eat and drink Divine Life and bring no death of our own to incorporate into the death of Christ through sacrifice, we deserve to be thought of as parasites on the Mystical Body of Christ'.[53] Trenchant criticism that must give us pause.

If the priest seriously tries to appropriate and to reproduce in his life Christ's role as Victim, then he will with greater confidence feel that the fruits of the Redemption will be applied more effectively to his pastoral tasks.[54] If he really wants to be another Christ he will strive to subdue the

---

[53] Fulton Sheen, *The Priest Is Not His Own*, London, 1967, p. 9. Pius XII, in his Apostolic Exhortation *Menti nostrae* on the priestly life (1950), reminds the priest that 'he must strive to reproduce in his own soul what is done on the altar of sacrifice. As Jesus Christ immolates himself, so his minister should immolate himself with him; as Jesus Christ makes expiation for the sins of men, so the priest, by traversing the high road of Christian asceticism, must attain his own purification and that of his fellowmen' (no. 34).   [54] Cf. John Paul II, *Gift and Mystery*, London, 1997, pp 79–82, for a moving commentary on the 'Litany of Our Lord Jesus Christ, Priest and Victim', a devotion which he learned as a seminarian and which nourished his spiritual life during all the years of his priesthood.

passions and sinful impulses of his nature, and at the same time try to fill up those sufferings which are wanting in the passion of Christ (cf. Col 1:24). If the priest does not learn to accept the Cross in his life as an extension of his Mass, he will never understand the meaning of his celibacy or find real joy in his dedication.

MORTIFICATION

Mortification is the prayer of the body, and without it priestly prayer is incomplete. This is also a requirement to win the battle for purity of mind, and heart, and body. The rebelliousness of the flesh can be strong at times, a situation graphically and realistically described by St Paul (cf. Rom 7:14–24; Gal 5:16–23). He speaks about pummelling and subduing his body (cf. 1 Cor 9:27), and tells us that 'those who belong to Christ Jesus have crucified the flesh with its passions and desires' (Gal 5:24). This might sound like rather harsh and exaggerated language, yet it is fully in accord with the uncompromising teaching of the Master: 'If your right eye causes you to sin, pluck it out and throw it away; it is better that you lose one of your members than that your whole body be thrown into hell' (Mt 5:29).[55]

The most effective mortification is that which comes from perseverance in priestly tasks despite tiredness, the sacrifice involved in sticking to a programme of parish visitation, or the devotion of generous hours to the work of the confessional. Priests also find ample opportunity for mortification in small but regular self-denial in the areas of comfort, food and entertainment. Through mortification we need to redeem our emotional ambiguities and the often contradictory desires of the heart. This is not merely a negative enterprise in purification, but one that has an essentially positive objective – to create the space and the dispositions to share more deeply in the love of the heart of Christ.

This is a programme which is strongly counter-cultural in that the tendency today is to get rid of the cross out of people's lives. Slogans such as 'being fully human' and 'self-fulfilment' make any kind of sacrifice seem to have a debilitating effect on man. However, we are reminded by

---

55 The Curé of Ars, who did not spare his body, reminds us that 'if we want to keep intact the most beautiful of all the virtues, which is chastity, we must realise that it is a rose that only blooms in the midst of thorns, for which reason it is only to be found, as are the other virtues, in a mortified person' (Sermon on Penance, quoted in F. Fernandez, *In Conversation with God*, I, New York, 1988, p. 174).

Christ that, unless we take up his cross daily and follow him along that road, we cannot seriously claim to be his disciples.

The self-denial asked of the priest should reflect itself in sobriety and detachment. If celibacy is to be a meaningful witness to an eschatological future, to the fact that we don't have here a lasting city, then it is only natural that detachment from the things of this world should be evident in the life of the priest. This virtue will have a reference point in the type of car he drives, where he goes on holidays, how he socialises, the type of entertainment he enjoys. The implications of priestly celibacy inevitably require a certain curtailment of social involvements which will vary from person to person, and which will benefit from spiritual counselling. The priest, we are reminded, 'could hardly be a true servant and minister of his brothers if he were excessively worried with his comfort and well-being'.[56]

The lust of the flesh cannot be controlled in isolation. Because the three classical expressions of concupiscence are interconnected and influence each other (cf. 1 Jn 2:16), it doesn't come as a surprise that the struggle for purity of heart needs to be supported by a simultaneous effort to live a deep humility and a Christian poverty of spirit. The spiritual and ascetical foundations which are necessary for a committed life of celibacy can be undermined by a lack of sobriety in other areas, which could unconsciously become a substitute for what his celibacy denies the priest. If true love consists in self-giving, there is a danger of clawing it back through lack of a Christian spirit of poverty. Thus the priest needs guidance about how to develop that detachment which is the antidote to the 'lust of the eyes', and the humility and spirit of service which are the only effective defences against the needle of pride endemic in our lives.

PURITY OF CHRIST

Christ's enemies accused him of many things, of being a drunkard, a glutton, a demoniac, a blasphemer, a friend of sinners. Yet no one ever doubted the purity of Christ.[57] He could with total conviction challenge his listeners, 'Which of you convicts me of sin?' (Jn 8:46) without fear of being contradicted. All recognised the sanctity of his life.

---

56 *Directory on the Ministry and Life of Priests*, 67.   **57** Cf. Blessed Josemaría Escrivá, *Friends of God*, op. cit., no. 176. See also Xavier Tilliette, 'The Chastity of Jesus', *Communio* 24 (Spring 1997), pp 51–56.

His body, like that of his mother, was perfectly pure. His whole person inspires purity, and diffuses it like a fragrance. Yet it was the present century, a victim of its own moral blindness, which first questioned his virtue in its literature and cinematic art.

It is to the pure of heart that Christ promises the sight of God, the Beatific Vision. He preaches about chastity to the crowds eager for instruction. But it is only to the inner circle of his disciples that he speaks about the exquisite refinement of virginity and celibacy 'for the sake of the kingdom', because they 'are able to receive it' (Mt 19:12). We have to look at Christ to see what are the characteristics of a chaste, celibate life. He embraced an austere, mortified lifestyle. He was detached from the material things of this world. His life was one of untiring work and zeal for souls. That is what the priest has to aspire to in following Christ. Celibacy will be the natural complement of such a life, not an extra, unrelated dimension. We learn from Christ how to come to terms with the fact that we have a fragile nature: 'In the light of faith, we know that Christ chose to take on our nature with all its passions; he did so to teach us that they are good in themselves and become evil only through sin; and also, so as the better to redeem us from that disorder. Passions are not bad in themselves; on the contrary, when they are controlled by reason, through a firm will and directed to their right end, they are a great help in doing good. Also, by choosing to have them, our Lord healed them in us, thereby enabling man not only to control his passions but to re-order them in the service of God, and to love God passionately, with all his heart.'[58]

God has given priests the power to be dispensers of divine mysteries which surpass the privileges of his angels. The consequent responsibility to be pure of mind and body is graphically described by St John Chrysostom:

> For the office of the priesthood is executed upon earth, yet it ranks amongst things that are heavenly, and with good reason. For it was neither an angel or an archangel nor any created power, but the Paraclete Himself that established that ministry, and commanded that men yet abiding in the flesh should imitate the functions of angels. Wherefore it behoves the priest to be as pure as if he stood in heaven itself amidst those Powers ... For when you behold the Lord immolated and lying on the altar, and the priest standing over the sacrifice and praying, and all the people purpled by the precious blood, do you imagine that you are still on earth amongst men?

58 Fernando Ocariz, Lucas F. Mateo Seco, José Antonio Riestra, *The Mystery of Jesus Christ*, Dublin, 1994, p.99.

For if you consider what it is for a man yet clothed in flesh and blood to approach that pure and blessed nature, you will easily understand to what a dignity the grace of the Holy Spirit has raised priests. For by them these things are accomplished, and others not inferior to these pertaining to our redemption and salvation ... It is to priests that spiritual birth and regeneration by baptism is entrusted. By them we put on Christ, and are united to the Son of God, and become members of that blessed Head. Hence we should regard them as more august than princes and kings, and more venerable than parents. For the latter begot us of blood and the will of the flesh, but priests are the cause of our generation from God, of our spiritual regeneration, of our true freedom and sonship according to grace.[59]

Priests are called to offer to the Eucharistic Body of Christ the service which the Blessed Virgin rendered to the Body of her Child. Consequently the attempts to demythologise the priesthood, or suggest that it is a state of life no different from others, is to go against the mind of Christ and the witness of two millennia of Christian tradition. It is to be blinded to the richness of its supernatural reality. The priest is God's anointed by definition, set apart to be of service, to represent, reflect and mediate Christ and his saving grace so as to lead men to salvation.

---

59 Cf. *On the Priesthood: A Treatise,* op. cit., pp 43–4.

7

Objections to Celibacy

CELIBACY NOT A DATUM OF REVELATION

In our introductory chapter reference was made to a number of objections which are raised against celibacy today. Some of these were considered in subsequent chapters. It is now time to examine in detail the more frequently expressed reservations about this charism.

One of the principal arguments levelled against the present discipline of celibacy in the Western Church is that it is not a datum of Revelation, but rather a matter of ecclesiastical discipline and canon law. Consequently, it is suggested, the law of celibacy can be abrogated at any time. As we have already seen in our review of the history of celibacy in the early Church, there is a considerable body of evidence in favour of the argument that priestly celibacy is of apostolic origin, based on Christ's invitation to the Twelve to leave all and follow him (cf. Mt 19:29). John Paul II points out in his first Holy Thursday Letter to Priests (1979) that 'its link with the language of the Gospel is so close' that it refers back to the teaching of Christ and to apostolic tradition.[1]

What is clear from Scripture, from the early history of the Church, the writings of the Fathers, and the witness of many clerics, is that there has always been a tradition of priestly celibacy in the Church. This tradition was approved and spread by various provincial councils and Popes. It was promoted, defended and restored in successive eras of the first millennium of the history of the Church, although it frequently encountered opposition from the clergy themselves and the worldly values of a decadent society. Apart from the historical argument, the theological justification for celibacy has gained considerable ground since Vatican II, not least in the writings of John Paul II.[2] Therefore the idea that clerical celibacy is merely an ecclesiastical discipline is an argument that becomes progressively less convincing. It has also to be remembered that canonical norms cannot encapsulate or express the whole truth about the phenomenon for which they legislate. As has been pointed out, they are 'only the juridical expres-

1 Cf. 1979 Letter, no. 8. 2 Cf. ibid., nos. 8–9; *Pastores dabo vobis*, no. 29; *The Theology of Marriage and Celibacy: Catechesis on Marriage and Celibacy in the Light of the Resurrection of the Lord*, op. cit.; *Priesthood in the Third Millennium: Addresses of John Paul II*, Chicago, 1994, passim.

sion of an underlying anthropological and theological reality'[3]. Hence, although the first known canonical legislation on celibacy dates from the beginning of the fourth century, this presupposes the existence of a prior pastoral and theological phenomenon.

RIGHTS OF THE INDIVIDUAL

The objection that the Church, by 'imposing' celibacy, offends the rights of individuals has no real basis. In the first place no candidate for the priesthood has a subjective right to be ordained; the priestly vocation is a gift God can bestow on whom he pleases, irrespective of the merits of the individual. Secondly, those who are called to the priesthood accept with full freedom the discipline of celibacy laid down by the Church. This they do after six years of preparation and prayerful reflection, at an age when they are fully capable of making a mature decision.

Can the Church 'impose' celibacy? The Church responds to the guidance of the Holy Spirit who is active within her and leads her into all truth (cf. Jn 16:13). In this sense she is perfectly entitled – drawing on her experience, her tradition, and the witness of celibacy lived to the full down through the centuries – to require her priests to be celibate. Certainly, in doing so, she is asking more than is humanly justifiable.

However, the Church is not a human organisation. She has a divine origin and has been given powerful supernatural means of grace and charisms of the Holy Spirit, which justify her making the audacious claim that in the Western rite it is God's will that her ministers should be celibate, and that in giving a vocation to the priesthood the Holy Spirit also endows it with the charism of celibacy.

At the same time the point has to be made that the Church obliges nobody to celibacy. The seminary years are an opportunity for the candidate for Orders to reach a definitive judgement concerning his vocation to celibacy as a result of the specific formation he receives there. The seminary authorities have a complementary role to play in helping the student come to a conclusion about the authenticity of his vocation. There is no pressure on the candidate to go ahead. On the contrary, he will be discouraged from doing so if there is any reasonable doubt about his aptitudes or suitability.

In this context, too, it is frequently suggested that a separation between

3 John Paul II, *Address to the Roman Rota*, 27 January 1997.

priesthood and celibacy (that is, making celibacy optional) would better bring to light the richness of this charism. This approach fails to recognise the necessary interdependence between institution and charism, stemming from the teaching of Christ himself: 'if you love me, you will keep my commandments' (Jn 14:15).

Precisely because we are limited by nature, commitment to particular decisions at the human and supernatural levels means that we have to forego other possible options. Consequently charisms need to be regulated if there is to be order and effectiveness in the mission of the institution. This regulation protects the freedom of the individual and, even more importantly, it respects the freedom of the Holy Spirit to grant the charism of celibacy to whom he wills.[4]

SHORTAGE OF PRIESTS

It is often argued that the problem of the shortage of priests today could be solved by allowing married men to enter the priesthood. A discipline of optional celibacy would, we are told, attract many more young men to the priesthood. This claim is not supported either by experience or objective data. It is also a viewpoint which cannot be reconciled with a truly 'catholic' view of the Church.[5]

As we have already noted, comparison with the discipline of a married clergy in some of the Oriental Churches is not a valid one either. In this regard the comments of a Russian Orthodox bishop of the Moscow Patriarchate, in the immediate post-conciliar period, are of interest: 'For us Orthodox, the priesthood is a sacred function. For this reason we are convinced that you, Westerners, you Latins, are not on the right path where you allow the question of ecclesiastical celibacy to be debated in public, in the forum of public opinion. In our Oriental tradition, it has been possible to authorise the ordination of a handful of married men, as in any case you have done and go on doing in certain regions. But take care: in the West, *if you separate the priesthood from celibacy, a very swift decadence will set in*. The West is not mystical enough to tolerate the marriage of its clergy without degenerating. The Church of Rome (and this is her glory) has preserved this ecclesiastical *ascesis* for a whole millennium. Beware of compromising it ...'[6]

4 Cf. Karl Hillenbrand, 'The Priesthood and Celibacy', in *Osservatore Romano*, 4 August 1993. 5 Cf. Crescenzio Sepe, 'The Relevance of Priestly Celibacy Today', in *For Love Alone*, op. cit., p. 80. 6 Quoted in ibid., p. 81 (italics in original).

It is true that there has been a serious decline in vocations to the priesthood in Ireland and in other developed Western countries. Yet it does not necessarily follow that the discipline of celibacy is one of the major causes for this fall-off. Such a conclusion is not borne out by the statistics for vocations in other parts of the world. In Africa the number of seminarians increased five-fold between 1970 and 1994 (from 3,500 to 17,100). There was a similar massive increase in Central and South America in the same period (9,000 to 26,250 – a threefold increase), while candidates for the priesthood in South East Asia more than doubled (10,000 to 24,000).

The story for the Western world is very different. Seminarians in North America are now just a third of what they were twenty years ago, dropping progressively from 14,400 in 1974 to 5,700 in 1994. Although in Europe the rate of decline was less marked, numbers decreased from 34,000 in 1974 to a low of 23,000 in 1977. Nevertheless, since 1978, the year John Paul II was elected Pope, the situation has recovered with a gradual increase to 30,000 by 1994. Taking world figures as a whole, the number of seminarians dropped from 73,000 in 1970 to a minimum of 60,000 in 1975, but has been increasing every year since, reaching a total of 105, 000 in 1994.[7]

In summary, there has been an increase of 75 per cent world-wide in the number of seminarians during the past twenty years. There may be some degree of failure in celibacy in Africa and South America after ordination, but one thing is clear from these statistics: the Church's discipline of celibacy is no obstacle to the increasing numbers of young men who want to become priests, whether in Africa, or Asia or South America. Even in Europe as a whole the trend is positive. It is only in the North American continent that there appears to be a progressive and, seemingly, inexorable decline.

NORTH AMERICAN EXPERIENCE

Still, it would be dangerous to generalise about the North American experience. While many dioceses are experiencing an acute shortage of priests and a low intake of seminarians, there are others where the situation is very healthy indeed. Peoria in Illinois, Arlington near Washington DC, and Lincoln, Nebraska, have been singularly successful in attracting young men to the priesthood. Arlington, with a Catholic population of 275,000,

7 These figures, which have been rounded off for ease of comparison, are taken from the Church's annual statistics for vocations published in *Osservatore Romano*, 31 July 1996.

has nearly 50 seminarians. Since 1985 the number of priests in this diocese has increased by 50 per cent, and in 1996 alone there were 13 candidates ordained, more than in any other diocese in the United States. Bishop John Myers of Peoria, who has 50 young men preparing for the priesthood, has advised his people to prepare for the 're-priesting' of the diocese. There, one-priest parishes will soon be staffed by two, and two-priest parishes will have three.[8]

Another diocese with a very healthy seminary situation is Omaha, Nebraska. Archbishop Curtiss, the ordinary of Omaha, told the Serra International Convention in Genoa (4 July 1995), that young people 'do not want to commit themselves to dioceses or communities which permit or simply ignore dissent from church doctrine. They do not want to be associated with people who are angry with the church's leadership or reject magisterial teaching'. He urged his audience to 'take heart by what is happening in certain dioceses and religious communities throughout the world which are experiencing increasing numbers of candidates. There is a remarkable similarity in the reasons which are given for these successes: unswerving allegiance to the Pope and the magisterial teaching of the Church; adoration of the Blessed Sacrament in parishes, with an emphasis on praying for vocations; a strong effort by a significant number of priests and religious who extend themselves to help young men and women remain open to the Lord's will in their lives; and a growing number of laity who support vocation ministry.'[9]

It would therefore be misleading to draw any general conclusions about a correlation between celibacy and vocations based on the North American or the Irish experience.

INCREASE IN VOCATIONS

Paul VI said it simply was not possible to demonstrate that the abolition of ecclesiastical celibacy would considerably increase the number of priestly vocations. The contrary seems to be proven by those churches and ecclesial communities which allow ministers to marry. The cause of the decrease in vocations is, he tells us, to be found elsewhere, especially in the fact that individuals and families have lost their sense of God, and their esteem for the Church as the institution willed by Christ for the salvation of men.[10] This phenomenon is a particular expression of a much more widespread

---

8 Cf. Michael F. Flach, 'What Priest Shortage?', *Catholic World Report*, June, 1996, pp 36–41; John F. Quinn, 'Priest Shortage Panic', *Crisis*, October, 1996, pp 40–4.   9 *Origins*, 8 October 1995, p. 167.   10 Cf. encyclical *Sacerdotalis caelibatus*, 40.

condition of lack of faith and lack of vibrant Christian families. Indeed, in this post-Vatican II era, it is only when evangelization promotes Christian commitment as a vocation for all that the ground will be adequately prepared for the fostering of the particular vocation to the priesthood as well.

In a homily he gave at the ordination of priests in Rio de Janeiro in 1989, John Paul II put into perspective the argument that the abolition of ecclesiastical celibacy would bring about an increase in vocations: 'Do not be under the illusion that the prospects of a priesthood that is less austere in its requirements – such as, for example, in the discipline of ecclesiastical celibacy – can increase the number of those who intend to commit themselves to following Christ. Quite the contrary. What is lacking and must be created in our communities is rather a mentality of strong and conscious faith. Where the daily sacrifice keeps the evangelical ideal awake and raises love of God to a high level, vocations continue to be numerous.'[11]

In this context of the shortage of priests, it is often suggested that those who have left the priesthood and subsequently married should be given the option of returning to the ministry if they so desire. But this would create its own difficulties, as the Holy Father has made abundantly clear. In an address to the priests of Brazil, a country which perhaps suffers most from the shortage of priests at the present time, he put the question into context:

> People need to see, first of all, Christ's *holiness* reflected in his priests. Brazil, the whole world, *needs holy priests*, faithful to their total *consecration* to God and totally committed to their particular *mission* ... Priests, who show the immense richness of God's love, the only possible response to the infinite longing of the human heart, through the joy with which they offer their undivided heart (cf. 1 Cor 7:32-34). Priestly celibacy is not merely a Church law but it has deep meaning in the light of the theology of priesthood. The Church does not accept the attempts and pressure to reintegrate into priestly ministry those who have left it for the married life. This is not the way to solve the problem of Brazil's great lack of priests. Celibacy, dear priests, must be for each of you a joyous confirmation that you should feel chosen by the loving kindness of him who called you to a life of total, unstinting dedication to his Love. A 'man of God' transforms a community. A devout priest becomes *a promoter of au-*

11 Homily, 2 July 1989, in *Osservatore Romano*, 14 July 1989.

thentic vocations by his total dedication to God and his brothers and sisters. A priest who is faithful to his promises is the best encouragement for the family's holiness and stability.[12]

It is clear that the Church sees no meaningful future in the active ministry for those who did not persevere in their vocation. This departure from the ranks of the priesthood was, on another occasion, referred to by the Pope as 'a great sadness for the Church', a 'counter-sign' and 'counter-witness', undermining 'the great hopes for renewal aroused throughout the Church by the Second Vatican Council'.[13] To allow priests who have been laicised and married return to the active ministry would be a contradiction of the Church's history. It would be to do something that is not even allowed in the Eastern Church, where the priest may indeed marry before ordination but never after. It would amount to the Church sending contradictory signals about its understanding of the nature of celibacy.[14]

DIFFERENT CASTE

It is sometimes objected that celibacy separates priests from the laity, that it creates a kind of 'caste' which, it is claimed, does not sit well with the democratic conception of society almost universally accepted today. Apart from the fact that the priesthood is not amenable to political categorisation, this argument conveniently ignores the point that the structural organisation of all societies unavoidably leads to some kind of division or separation. Even at the natural level this form of argumentation is fallacious.

The Church is in fact much more radical in the egalitarian nature of its membership than is civil society. All the baptised are equally children of God, with an equal dignity in that all are called to holiness. Priesthood in the Church represents a differentiation of function which is not determined by man's initiative, but rather on the basis of the Holy Spirit's freedom to call whom he wills.[15]

12 John Paul II, address 13 October 1991, in *Osservatore Romano*, 21 October 1991 (italics in original).   13 Address to priests in Maynooth, 1 October 1979, in *The Pope in Ireland*, Dublin, 1979, p. 71.   14 Cf. von Hildebrand, *Celibacy and the Crisis of Faith*, op. cit., pp 83–5.   15 'To reject celibacy because it emphasises the difference between priest and laity too much and thus supposedly "divides" is to betray that the real motive to abolish obligatory celibacy is the terrible secularisation of our time, the blindness for the sacred character of the priesthood'; cf. von Hildebrand, ibid., pp 81–2.

It is not possible to grasp the fundamental nature of the priesthood if we do not realise that its very *raison d'être* is to be of service to others after the manner of Christ. As the *Catechism* explains: 'Entirely dependent on Christ who gives mission and authority, ministers are truly "slaves of Christ" (cf Rom 1:1), in the image of him who freely took "the form of a slave" (Phil 2:7) for us. Because the word and grace of which they are ministers are not their own, but are given to them by Christ for the sake of others, they must freely become the slaves of all (cf. 1 Cor 9:19).'[16] The priest, by virtue of his vocation, has to be open to all, exercising his ministry – pastoral, sacramental, catechetical – with humility (cf. Jn 13:5) and unselfish dedication to the needs of the flock (cf. Jn 10:11). It is a service which must at the same time recognise and promote the irreplaceable role the lay faithful exercise in the sanctification of the world.

Those who object that celibacy perpetuates a caste system in the Church fail to understand the rich theology of the laity articulated by Vatican II,[17] and subsequently developed by John Paul II in his document on the vocation and mission of the laity.[18] The laity incorporated in Christ by Baptism participate in his priestly, prophetic and kingly office by striving for personal holiness, and by bringing Christ to others through the witness of their lives. They enjoy full membership of the Church and a full participation in its mystery. With priests they participate in the same life of grace and holiness. They have the same honour and dignity. The special nature of the lay vocation is that it can make the Church present and active in those places where it is only through them that she can be the salt of the earth – by the renewal of the temporal order.[19] Their baptismal vocation has an essentially secular character which empowers them to impregnate all human realities with the spirit of the Gospel, sanctifying the world from within.[20]

The application of the democratic model to the Church with a view to 'levelling down' the ministerial priesthood would not arise if the full implications of the common priesthood of the faithful were taken seriously. Both priesthoods derive from the priesthood of Christ and participate in it. They mutually support each other.

But, as Vatican II emphasises, there is an essential difference between the two and not just one of degree only.[21] This difference is characterised by the *sacra potestas* (sacred power) with which the priest is endowed by

---

16 *Catechism of the Catholic Church*, no. 876.   **17** Cf. *Lumen gentium*, 30–42; decree on the lay apostolate, *Apostolicam actuositatem*.   **18** Apostolic Exhortation *Christifideles laici*, 30 December 1988.   **19** Cf. *Lumen gentium*, 33.   **20** Cf. ibid., no. 31; *Christifideles laici*, 15.   **21** Cf. *Lumen gentium*, 10.

sacramental ordination, and which enables him to perform the Eucharistic sacrifice *in persona Christi*.[22] A reductionist approach to priesthood and celibacy also arises because of certain ambiguities which result from the participation of the laity in pastoral roles. The point has been well made that 'to the extent that this participation is presented as a "promotion" of the laity, we risk losing sight of the proper mission of the laity played out at the heart of the world, in the spheres of work, family, economy, communication, and politics. The laity have no need to become clericalised in order to be appreciated. To see their promotion in pastoral roles is a final residue of clericalism.'[23]

CELIBACY AS ISOLATION

The objection that the priest as celibate is an outsider or alien to the world he has to evangelise, is effectively an argument from the perspective of lack of faith, nourished by the criteria of a sensate culture. Jesus, the proto-evangelizer, lived a life of celibacy and taught very clearly that, for the sake of the kingdom of Heaven, one must be willing to abandon home, parents, wife or children (cf. Lk 18:29-30). Down through the centuries, starting with the young apostle John, there have always been men ready to respond generously to this invitation of Christ, and who have had a profound effect on society, not only at the level of the faith, but also on the important social and cultural issues of their day.

Another variation of this argument is that man has changed so radically in the past century that the revelation of Christ needs to be presented in a new language and reformulated in a way which 'modern' man will understand, and that this has implications for celibacy.

It is true that there have been immense changes in man's external environment as a result of technological development. It can also be admitted that the intellectual and cultural climate of the twentieth century is very different from that of previous centuries. These, however, are trends of the historico-social order which can change at any time, and which do not affect man in his ontological structure, in his character of *imago Dei*. To suggest otherwise is to substitute for the truths of divine revelation an amorphous flux of the 'spirit of the age'. It is to make history the source of revelation, rather than the Gospel and the traditional teaching of the Church.

22 Cf. ibid.   **23** Fr Marc Ouellet, S.S., 'Priestly Ministry at the Service of Ecclesial Communion', in *Communio* 23 (Winter 1996), p. 680.

AFFECTIVE NEEDS

It is frequently suggested nowadays that celibacy is against nature because, we are told, it excludes the fulfilment of lawful physical, psychological and affective needs.

The fact of being endowed with a sexual faculty, which makes human procreation possible, does not make the sex act necessary *per se*. Even so, due to a mistaken concept of sexuality promoted by a hedonistic culture, the priest can be influenced by the widely held view that human beings are biologically determined.[24]

As Paul VI aptly reminded us, man, who is created in God's image and likeness, is not just flesh and blood, nor is his sexual instinct all that he has. On the contrary, our nature is constituted primarily by our capacity for understanding and freedom of choice. As a consequence of these powers, man is superior to the rest of creation, and, with the help of God's grace, he is master of his physical, psychological and affective drives. The choice of celibacy does not imply ignorance of or disdain for the sexual instinct and human affectivity. Rather it demands a deep appreciation of their role in God's plan for the individual and for human society, and how, within the context of marriage, conjugal love is a good and noble thing, and a way to holiness.[25]

---

24 'The erroneous notion, that the male is in a sense compelled to sexual activity by virtue of the very fact of being male, is becoming stronger and stronger. People even think that the sexual act "proves" one's virility; that without it a man is in some sense disabled, unrealised' (Wanda Poltawska, 'Priestly Celibacy in the light of Medicine and Psychology', in *For Love Alone*, op. cit., p. 99).   **25** Cf. encyclical, *Sacerdotalis caelibatus,* 50–4. James Hitchcock has some pertinent comments in this context: 'The celibacy issue within the Roman Church is therefore a crisis much broader and more profound than is generally recognised, because celibacy is a symbol of the first importance to the whole Church and because what is involved is not solely the personal happiness or personal rights of individual priests. The Church could easily concede the right of marriage to priests involved in active ministries, while retaining the celibate discipline in cloistered and semi-cloistered orders. The abrogation of the present celibacy law, however, is being demanded by many priests precisely because they cannot live "fulfilled" lives as celibates. To accede to their demands at the present time would tend to reinforce the prevailing cultural notion that personal fulfilment is impossible without an active sex life. It would also obscure even further the traditional association between asceticism and transcendental spirituality. If activist priests alone were restive under celibate discipline there would be less cause for concern. The fact that Trappists have also not been immune to the scent of orange blossom suggests that what are being repudiated are the most fundamental Catholic assumptions concerning the spiritual life ... Loss of belief in the celibate vocation is intimately related, for many priests, to a loss of confidence in their ability to witness to a transcendental spirituality and their consequent determination to immerse themselves as deeply as possible in the world' (*Years of Crisis: Collected Essays* 1970–1983, San Francisco, 1985, pp 271–2).

Celibacy does not, however, limit or stunt the human affectivity of the priest. It raises it up to a new level. By divine gift he finds that the love of his heart is reciprocated completely in the love of the heart of Christ. As a result of his training the priest does not lack knowledge of the human condition. Indeed, through his pastoral ministry, especially in his work as confessor, the priest is much more likely to have a deeper knowledge of the secrets of the human heart. Also, because he loves with less self-interest, he will be more inclined to see people as God's gifts, as temples of the Holy Spirit.

PRIEST AND PEOPLE

Historically the Catholic faithful have always had an instinctive perception of the self-sacrificing and disinterested love represented by the celibate priest, especially where holy priests were concerned. His celibacy was never a barrier to people seeking advice about difficult human situations, even in relation to problems in conjugal life. Precisely because they recognised in the priest the image of the Good Shepherd and the Divine Physician, they were ready to unburden themselves with confidence and follow the advice received. We find confirmation of this from an unlikely source:

> Today we see clearly that Luther was fatally limited, superficial and imprudent ... He gave back sexual intercourse to the priest: but three-quarters of the reverence of which the people are capable (and particularly the women of the people) rests on the belief that a man who is exceptional in this regard will also be exceptional in other matters. It is precisely here that the popular belief in something superhuman in man, in the miraculous, in the saving God in man, has its most subtle and suggestive advocate. Having given the priest a wife, he had to *take from him* auricular confession. Psychologically this was appropriate, but thereby he practically did away with the Christian priest himself, whose profoundest utility has ever consisted in being a sacred ear, a silent well, a grave for secrets.[26]

---

26 F. Nietzsche, *Die Fröhliche Wissenschaft*, p. 358, as quoted in Hans Urs von Balthasar, *The Office of Peter and the Structure of the Church*, San Francisco, 1986, pp 38–9 (italics in the original).

The testimony of a modern writer, with a lot of experience of life behind him, is also of interest in this regard. 'It is objected', writes Paul Johnson, 'that a celibate priest, who has not known human love, is not a fit person to minister to souls: he may be all right in a monastery, praying, but he is unsuited for pastoral work. It is particularly objected against the present Pope John Paul II, that being celibate, he ought not to pronounce, *urbi et orbi*, on such important questions as family planning, divorce and sexual sin.'

Johnson criticises what he sees as the feeble claim that experience of married life would be the chief qualification to preach God's will on sexual matters, and says that there is more than one way of acquiring sexual knowledge and expertise:

> The average husband and wife, who remain faithful within mar-
> riage, may be – probably are – happy sexually, but they cannot be
> described as particularly experienced. The average celibate priest, by
> contrast, acquires through the confessional an insight into the vari-
> ety and power and problems of sexuality denied to most married
> couples, indeed to many psychiatrists ... Priests have often told me
> that the very absence of direct experience in sex, which can be con-
> fusing and lead to prejudices, can make their approach to dealing
> with sexual problems of parishioners more objective and successful.
> But a point far more important than any of these is that the particular
> concentration on devotion to God made possible by celibacy also
> makes it far more likely that a priest can reciprocate God's love with
> its own intensity, and so inevitably receive more in return. And the
> love which God gives us is the source of all grace and wisdom. The
> more we are capable of receiving, the more likely it is that we will
> take right courses and lead others along them. So what the celibate
> priest loses in direct experience of sexual love – and that loss, as I say,
> may not be great – he more than makes up in the wisdom and
> patience and understanding God imparts to him.[27]

27 Paul Johnson, *The Quest for God: A Personal Pilgrimage*, London, 1996, pp 56–7. After a bohemian youth in Paris (cf. ibid., p. 181), he returned to more conventional ways and had a very happy marriage. He speaks frankly, though not uncritically, of his love for the Church, which he would like everybody to be a part of 'because I am acutely conscious of the comfort and security, the stability and certitude, the happiness and the wisdom –yes, and the freedom –which being a Catholic has brought to me'(ibid., p. 112).

CELIBACY THE PRICE OF PRIESTHOOD

In the current debate about optional celibacy one often comes across an argument, usually articulated by priests, which runs along the following lines. Celibacy was part of the bargain of priesthood; it was, they say, the price to be paid for ordination, and this was accepted at the time without too much questioning. Subsequently some priests discover, with experience of life and a deeper awareness of the demands of celibacy, that the price was too high, and find themselves trapped. Consequently, the conclusion runs, in order to avert these difficult situations, celibacy should in future be optional for the priesthood.

A first response to this argument is that presenting for ordination with this approach shows a very inadequate appreciation of the nature and purpose of celibacy. In truth it sounds more like a *post factum* rationalisation than a serious argument for optional celibacy.

The only adequate reason for choosing celibacy is a response of faith to a call to imitate Jesus Christ. It is a commitment that must be renewed repeatedly, especially when alternative options present themselves. With good reason it has been pointed out that a priest needs positively to *choose* celibacy rather than merely *accept* it, because to do otherwise 'quite frequently leads to cynicism, resignation and compromise which inevitably manifests itself in living one's priesthood as a bachelor rather than a celibate'.[28]

Great care is taken in the seminary to ensure that the future priest understands the celibate vocation and that his decision in responding to it is totally free and unconditional. Ultimately, admission to the priesthood is a matter for the bishop to decide, since no one has a *right* to be ordained. Charisms in the Church from the time of the Acts of the Apostles require institutional validation to protect the rights of God, the preservation of order in the Church, and the supreme good of the sanctification of souls.

Those who are unhappy with celibacy emphasise the negative aspects which entail self-denial – the renunciation of conjugal life, intimate companionship and having a family of one's own. In Scripture, on the other hand, it is not the sacrifices related to celibacy that are stressed, but rather the joy of finding the pearl of great price, and the hundred-fold guaranteed even in this life (cf. Mt 19:29; Lk 18:29–30).

28 Michael Neary, op. cit., pp 89–90.

PERSONAL RESPONSIBILITY

There is a tendency nowadays not to accept responsibility for one's situation, but rather to cast the blame for personal difficulties on society or the Church. This attitude has affected some priests as well. Certainly there are situations where individuals are hurt by the system, but in general personal happiness or discontentment is largely of our own making.

We are essentially responsible for the thrust of our own lives, but the tendency to shuffle off accountability for failure or error is deep-rooted in human nature. Shakespeare, who was a keen student of the human condition, portrayed the phenomenon with some hyperbole, but not a little truth: 'This is the excellent foppery of the world that, when we are sick in fortune, – often the surfeit of our own behaviour – we make guilty of our disasters the sun, the moon and the stars: as if we were villains by necessity; fools by heavenly compulsion; knaves, thieves and treachers by spherical predominance; drunkards, liars and adulterers by an enforced obedience of planetary influence.'[29] But he also identified the fallacy of the argument: 'The fault, dear Brutus, is not in our stars, but in ourselves, that we are underlings.'[30]

The linking of personal problems, moral or otherwise, to maladjustments and to forces beyond the control of the individual may frequently be justified. Nevertheless, there are adjustments at the spiritual level which we all have to make to oppose our own sinful tendencies, and to persevere in fidelity to commitments. As the Master reminds us, it is by perseverance that we shall gain possession of our souls.

The philosophy of excuse is not a valid substitute for the philosophy of responsibility and accountability. For the Christian, and especially the priest, faith opens up new horizons of hope. Like the distraught father in the Gospel who prayed humbly for help, he will be encouraged by the response of Christ, 'all things are possible to him who believes'(Mk 9:23).

LACK OF FORMATION

The point has been made that seminary training in the post-Vatican II era did not prepare priests adequately for the difficulties of a celibate life, which they would have to face after leaving the seminary. It is suggested that this may be in part the cause of the crisis today.

29 *King Lear*, Act I, Scene II, line 189ff.   **30** *Julius Caesar*, Act I, Scene II, line 140–1.

While there may be some substance in this complaint, I think it has also to be said that the general moral and spiritual formation imparted in the seminary provided the appropriate means to cope with the basic demands of celibacy. Very much aware of the new challenges in this area, the Vatican published a comprehensive document on seminary formation in priestly celibacy in 1974,[31] and John Paul II recommended this text to all seminarians in *Pastores dabo vobis.*[32]

If priests after leaving the seminary continue to have regular spiritual guidance, the chastity demanded by celibacy will not become a problem but will continue as one of the elements in the normal struggle to try to achieve that holiness of life to which all Christians are called. It is worth remembering, as we have already noted, that the teaching of the *Catechism of the Catholic Church* on chastity is given under the rubric of 'The Vocation to Chastity'[33] and 'The Battle for Purity'.[34] This virtue is a call and a struggle, both of which elements are necessary to approach it with Christian realism.

FORMATION IN FIDELITY

Celibacy, which calls into question the reductionist philosophy of man spread abroad by our culture of scientism, is also a challenge to that incapacity to make a permanent commitment which seems to be characteristic of younger generations. This inability to commit oneself irrevocably is demonstrated, particularly in the Western world, by the increasing rate of marriage breakdown and divorce, as well as by the rise in the number of couples living together without any binding commitment, civil or ecclesiastical. This is the result of a collapse in basic social relationships where values such as loyalty, friendship, and a spirit of service have less and less significance. Love as self-giving is replaced by love as possession, where the other is regarded as an object of sexual fulfilment rather than a person to be cherished for themselves.[35]

Clearly, education has a decisive role in determining the type of people our society produces. If children learn little about self-denial or a spirit of service through self-giving to others, they will have little predisposition to

---

31 Congregation for Catholic Education, *A Guide to Formation in Priestly Celibacy*, 11 April 1974. **32** Cf. *Pastores dabo vobis*, 50, and Chapter 5 of this book. **33** Cf. nos. 2337–50. **34** Cf. nos. 2520–27. **35** The human tragedy, which such evasion of responsibility creates, is described in all its moral bleakness by Allan Bloom in his commentary on the American university scene; cf. *The Closing of the American Mind*, op. cit., pp 109–137.

understand and accept the sacrificial love which is required to live celibacy, or to respond generously to the full implications of marriage as a Christian vocation and a way to holiness.

Many of the current criticisms of celibacy derive from this climate of insecurity, which regards with suspicion any expression of irrevocable fidelity and commitment. It is only natural that from this perspective of the consumerist ethic, which promotes the gratification of desire, celibacy appears to be an inhuman imposition and, indeed, an impossible commitment. All the more so if there is a lack of Christian faith, that is faith in a God who is fidelity *par excellence*, who became incarnate in Jesus Christ and remains with us in his Church and in his sacraments.

Fidelity is a characteristic that marks the whole of the personality, in the same way that infidelity cannot be confined to just one of its vital areas of influence. It is fidelity that brings to light the moral quality that lies at the core of the human person. Accordingly, as we have already seen, education for celibacy, or for chastity in general, cannot be confined within a narrow band of the overall educational enterprise. It is essentially formation in the full truth about the human personality, that truth which leads to a profound appreciation of authentic freedom (cf. Jn 8:32). As St Thomas points out, the reason for chastity is to facilitate growth in charity and the other theological virtues which unite the mind to God.[36]

The fidelity of which the human person is capable is not so much a linear, inflexible fidelity all through life, as one around which there are oscillations – advances and regressions.[37] Advances which are achieved as a result of God's grace, and regressions like that of the Prodigal Son which, forgiven by the Father of all mercies, refocus the heart and cure the deviations of the senses. Only the person whom God binds to himself and to his infinite love can be truly faithful. His is a love which elevates us without uprooting us from our human condition, and which frees us by attaching us to himself with bonds anchored in immutable Truth, Goodness and Beauty.[38] Only God through Jesus Christ can insert in our creaturely life a dimension of eternity which makes us capable of a fidelity that is at once dynamic and secure.

---

36 '*Ratio castitatis consistit in caritate et in aliis virtutibus theologicis, quibus mens coniungitur Deo*' (*Summa Theologiae* II-II, 151, 2).   **37** We are referring here to the normal ups and downs of the Christian quest for holiness. Obviously there are aspects of life where an unconditional fidelity is asked for – fidelity to the faith, to our particular vocation, etc. It is precisely because of their inflexible loyalty to Christ and his teaching that the Church honours the martyrs.   **38** Cf. J. B. Torelló, 'Las ciencias humanas ante el celibato sacerdotal', in *Scripta Theologica*, 27 (1995/1), 269–83.

Celibacy offered to God in this way is, of course, a challenge to human beings in the exercise of their freedom. To reach its maturity, it needs a bonding and even a death, in a way that the greatest freedom of all, liberation from sin, was achieved at the price of a death. Since then, authentic freedom and the Cross have been inevitably intertwined, just as the most authentic human love finds expression in the sacrifice of self. Unfettered freedom, without some responsibility, is a contradiction, because flight from every restriction or tie engenders anguish and a sense of guilt. Frankl sees in committed freedom that quality of the human spirit which enables the individual to transcend his biological, psychological and social conditioning.[39]

FRUSTRATIONS

But what about the frustrations which unfulfilled ambitions and desires engender? Every decision entails the inhibition of some of our desires in the sense that our choices, which commit us to particular lines of action, eliminate other possible options, since we are limited in what we can do.

There are people who feel frustrated because they are not married, and others because they are. As one psychiatrist who is also a priest has pointed out, 'the celibate is not more exposed to difficulties than is the married person, and one must also mention that the frustrations imposed by marriage are generally less readily accepted than those which celibacy brings with it. The key factor in any sexual question will be the spiritual and religious interior disposition that looks beyond changing situations and values which are provisional and reversible, and seeks instead factors that are final and irrevocable, as a clear sign of the specific dedication that is freely chosen and which brings fulfilment.'[40]

Authentic freedom embraces what is irrevocable, whereas those who have little interior freedom tend to choose only what is provisional or transient. At the same time we have our own fads and fancies which are part of normal life, but which the wear and tear of human interaction helps us to even out. Yet, by holding on to the reality of God and his providence, and by living a freedom that is conditioned by commitment, we avoid the dangerous trap of confusing fantasy with reality.

As we have already seen, Christian anthropology tells us that man is

---

39 Cf. Victor Frankl, *Man's Search for Meaning*, London, 1964.   **40** J.B. Torelló, 'Celibacy and Personality', in *Osservatore Romano*, 18 January 1973.

constituted both by interiority and openness to others. However, if he turns in on himself and focuses exclusively on own emotional equilibrium, his well-being and personal fulfilment, he stifles his capacities for growth and maturity. He mistakes effect for cause, not realising that self-fulfilment comes as a consequence of the effort to transcend oneself through love and a spirit of service. If the effect is treated as an end in itself, it escapes and is dissipated because it undermines the very capacity of man to transcend himself.[41]

The human person is essentially open to the other, to something or someone beyond himself—the world, one's neighbour, God. This is what St Thomas More tried to teach Richard Rich, who was intent on pursuing a career in search of self-glorification. 'Why not be a teacher?', he encourages him, in Robert Bolt's dramatisation of the scene. 'You'd be a fine teacher. Perhaps − a great one.' 'And if I was', Rich queried, 'who would know?' 'You', replied More, 'your pupils, your friends. God − not a bad public, that!' But, as we know, Rich insisted on his fantasy with disastrous personal results.[42]

Man fulfils himself if he lives openness of love and service to others as a way of being. In this going out of himself, in his surrendering of himself, he discovers the real meaning of his life and experiences self-fulfilment and happiness. Hence we appreciate the significance of those words of Christ: 'For whoever would save his life will lose it; and whoever loses his life for my sake and the gospel's will save it' (Mk 8:35). If all human life is fulfilled through generous love and service, how much more should not this be true of those who by sacramental consecration are committed to a service which should bear no trace of selfishness, or desire for recognition or personal success?

MEDIA PRESENTATION OF CELIBACY

For some time there have been insistent calls for the abolition of 'compulsory' celibacy in editorials and feature articles in the print media, and in TV and chat show commentary. Underlying much of this crusade is the assumption of a direct causal link between celibacy and sexual deviance. Yet at no time has any solid scientific or statistical evidence been offered to substantiate this claim.[43] Nevertheless, as a result of saturation coverage

---

41 Cf. Torelló, 'Las ciencias humanas,' op. cit., p. 279.   42 Cf. Robert Bolt, *A Man for All Seasons*, Act I, Scene I, London, 1960, p. 4.   43 Cf. Philip Jenkins, *Pedophiles and*

in the media of some clerical sexual scandals, many people seem to have been persuaded into thinking that there must be some intrinsic connection between celibacy and sexual immorality, and that it is widespread among the clergy.[44] Indeed Pope John Paul II refers to 'a systematic propaganda which is hostile to celibacy' and 'which finds support and complicity in some of the mass media'.[45]

With few exceptions the secular media seem to be incapable of making a balanced judgement about celibacy due to their hostile attitudes to the discipline and order of the Church. Since priests are subject to the normal human reactions, they are affected by incessant negative 'news' and comments concerning celibacy. It is therefore understandable that they should experience doubts about the validity of celibacy as a life-style for the priesthood.

Fr Avery Dulles, the American theologian, has identified a number of reasons for the tension between the secular media and the Church:

- the Church's message is a mystery of faith, to be approached with an attitude of reverence, whereas the press tends to be investigative and iconoclastic, revelling in exposing what it considers false and pretentious.
- the teaching of the Church is eternal and seeks to maintain continuity with its past, whereas the press feeds off novelty, and thrives on the ephemeral. In reporting, it accents what is new and different.
- the Church seeks to promote unity and reconciliation, whereas the news media specialise in conflict and disagreement.
- the main work of the Church is spiritual, preparing souls to receive grace with a view to eternal salvation. Media comment concentrates on more empirical phenomena, and selectively reports Church teaching as though the Pope were chiefly interested in sex, politics and power.

Priests: Anatomy of a Contemporary Crisis, Oxford, 1996, where he demolishes a number of myths created by the media about priests and pedophilia. **44** The demonising effect of the media was graphically illustrated by the experience of a priest friend who called to a children's hospital to visit a young parishioner during a period of relentlessly hostile reporting of a particular scandal. His arrival was greeted in the ward by clear signs of panic among the nurses. He was then escorted to the patient, and was kept under direct observation for the duration of the visit. The bias and imbalance in the reporting on this issue has been critically examined by journalist David Quinn – cf., among others, his articles in the *Sunday Business Post*, 18 November 1994, 9 July 1995, and the *Irish Catholic*, 5 December 1996. **45** Address, 27 October 1990.

- in a democratic society the media have great difficulty in coming to terms with the hierarchical structure of the Church, in which its leaders hold authority from Christ and not from the people. Journalism has an inbuilt bias against the authoritative teaching of popes and bishops, and tends to favour the dissident priest or theologian as champions of freedom.
- Church teaching on matters of belief and moral practice is often complex and subtle, whereas the press and the electronic media are hungry for stories that are short, simple and striking.
- the Church aims to persuade its hearers of the truth of Revelation, and seeks to arouse a firm commitment to following Jesus Christ. Journalism, by contrast, reports facts in such a way as to make them accessible to people of any or no religious belief.[46]

Another reason could also be added for this tension: the media increasingly focuses on personalities, not on issues or institutions, as a way of covering stories, whereas the Church believes that its message and purpose transcend the fallibility of the individual person.[47]

If the priest is aware of these adversarial relationships between the media and the Church, he will not be unduly worried about what is reported in so far as it affects himself. He will, however, be concerned at the possible negative effects which media reports and comments could have on a less discriminating reader, viewer or listener.

There are, as we have said, striking exceptions to the general rule. In the middle of unrelentingly hostile reporting of the Church's stand on celibacy, related to a recent clerical scandal, one English Sunday newspaper got to the core of the issue. While condemning the hypocrisy and deceit of the man at the centre of the scandal, it went on to say that the discipline of priestly celibacy did not, in the long run, depend on practical arguments such as greater availability, etc. Rather 'it derives from something that reasonable, secular man cannot understand: the tradition of asceticism that is central to Christianity. The Church has always regarded celibacy as sanctioned by Christ's own words about those who "make themselves eunuchs for the kingdom of heaven's sake", and by his own choice of the single life.' It comments that self-denial, humility, and pov-

---

46 Avery Dulles, SJ, 'Religion and the News Media: A Theologian Reflects', *America*, 1 October 1994, pp 6–9. **47** Cf. Madeleine Bunting, 'The Media and Religion', a lecture given at Gresham College, London, 11 November 1996, and reported in abbreviated form as 'God's Media Image', in *The Tablet*, 16 November 1996.

erty of spirit are ideals which have always been central to Christian teaching, and that celibacy for priests is one attempt to turn these ideals into reality. The editorial concludes: 'It would be wise for the Church to remind people of all this. It is true that the whole Christian package, if fully understood, is likely to be repulsive to the secular mind. But it cannot even be understood unless it is frankly preached.'[48]

History indicates that the issue of celibacy can generate a level of hostility which is difficult to explain in human terms alone. It was particularly evident at the time of the Reformation. Again, after the French revolution, hatred of celibacy emerged in a particularly perverse way in the effort to try to force priests to marry. Consciously or unconsciously, celibacy has frequently been perceived by the tyrant or the sensualist as a reproach to his own immorality. It makes him uncomfortable, and his tendency is to try to undermine it or destroy it. The same destructive pride was at work in the attacker of Maria Goretti and the execution of the youthful Ugandan martyrs.

CELIBACY AND ANTHROPOLOGY

John Paul II counsels us that 'we should not be too surprised at all the objections and criticisms which have intensified during the postconciliar period. Did not Jesus Christ, after he had presented the disciples with the question of the renunciation of marriage "for the sake of the kingdom of heaven", add these significant words: "Let anyone accept this who can"?[49]

'None of the reasons', John Paul II continues, 'whereby people sometimes try to "convince us" of the inopportuneness of celibacy corresponds to the truth, the truth the Church proclaims and seeks to realise in life through the commitment to which priests oblige themselves before ordination. The essential, proper and adequate reason, in fact, is contained in the truth that Christ declared when he spoke about the renunciation of marriage for the sake of the kingdom of heaven, and which Saint Paul proclaimed when he wrote that each person in the Church has his or her

---

48 *Sunday Telegraph,* 22 September 1996. Commenting on the Bishop Wright case, Paul Johnson said his transgressions 'have been exploited by the enemies of the Catholic Church – mainly, it must be said, garrulous journalists and television pundits not remarkable for their celibacy, sobriety and disinterestedness – to badmouth the entire priesthood and to predict that the rule of sacerdotal celibacy will soon have to be scrapped. Nothing could be further from the truth' (*The Spectator,* 28 September 1996). **49** Holy Thursday Letter, 1979, no. 8.

own particular gifts (cf. 1 Cor 7:7). Celibacy is precisely a "gift of the Spirit".'[50]

From the standpoint of the Pope the objections to celibacy 'appeal to criteria alien to the Gospel, to Tradition and to the Church's Magisterium,' and are based on defective anthropological considerations of very dubious and relative value.[51] What precisely he meant by 'dubious anthropology' was made abundantly clear when, in September 1979, he began his series of weekly talks on human intimacy and the 'nuptial meaning of the body'.[52]

Many of the arguments against celibacy derive from the secular and Freudian idea that unless a person enjoys sexual fulfilment he is somehow diminished or is likely to be emotionally or psychologically unbalanced, a sort of freak in the modern hedonistic culture. In a world where the definition of man is strongly influenced by such presuppositions, and where more importance is given to psychological and sociological models than those drawn from biblical revelation, there is a real need for John Paul II's articulate statement of a Christian anthropology. It is only in the light of divine revelation, culminating in the Incarnation of the Word, that we can fully appreciate the unique value of the call to celibacy, and have the audacity to proclaim it as a great good, and the courage to aspire to it.

Priestly celibacy, the present Pope tells us, 'is for the Church a treasure to be carefully guarded and to be presented especially today as a sign of contradiction for a society which needs to be called back to the higher and definitive values of life'.[53]

In the living of celibacy, John Paul II, perhaps more than anybody else, is well aware of the difficulties which priests are confronted with at the subjective and objective levels. But he is convinced that if the necessary conditions of interior life, human balance, fraternity and formation are established, all these difficulties can be overcome.[54]

50 Ibid. 51 Cf. ibid. 52 Cf. chapter 4. 53 Address, 22 October 1993. 54 Cf. Address, 17 July 1993.

8

Witnesses and Testimonies to Celibacy

An awareness of the historical, scriptural and theological foundations for celibacy deepens our conviction about the validity and the appropriateness of this charism in the life of the priest. Yet at the same time the witness or the experience of individual priests adds significantly to our appreciation of the value of this gift of the Holy Spirit. One has only to reflect on the many vocations to celibacy which were inspired by the example of good priests.

One could draw on many personal testimonies, and several different sources, to illustrate the fruitfulness of celibacy in the life of the Church. However, a brief selection of witnesses to this charism is all there is space for. The following testimonies will, I feel, throw light not only on the value of celibacy in itself, but will also underline the deep appreciation of this charism which takes root in the minds of the faithful when they experience the generous service of the priest in their own spiritual lives.

NEWMAN AND CELIBACY

It is universally recognised that intellectual honesty was one of the outstanding characteristics of John Henry Newman. But, he was also possessed of a much rarer quality, a unique *emotional* honesty, which is instructive and revealing for what he has to say about celibacy and how it influenced his own affective life.[1]

At fifteen he had a first intimation that his vocation was to be a celibate one. Three years later it became a definite commitment based on strong supernatural convictions.[2] His journal and diaries testify to his deep appreciation of the virtue of holy purity which he acquired as the result of daily struggle. As a boy of fifteen he wrote: '*Fac me temperatum, sobrium, castum.*'[3]

---

1 Cf. Meriol Trevor, *The Pillar and the Cloud*, London, 1962, p. 95. See also Jaki, op. cit., pp 159–170. With reference to his *Essay on the Development of Christian Doctrine*, Jaki refers to 'Newman's profound conviction about celibacy as an indispensable, integral part of the priesthood, and indeed of the entire system of Christian dispensation and doctrine' (ibid., 163–4).   2 Cf. Ian Ker, *John Henry Newman: A Biography*, Oxford, 1990, p. 5.   3 'Make me temperate, sober, and chaste'.

Later, at twenty three, around the time he received Anglican orders, he would note in his diary: 'Pray for purity, sobriety – chastity – temperance – self-denial – simplicity – truth – openness.'[4] It should also be mentioned that he did not consider sins against purity lightly.[5]

As is clear from his letters, Newman had a capacity for deep affection. This is reflected in his relationships with family and friends, Oxford colleagues, and fellow Oratorians. One of the great sorrows of his life was the death of his youngest sister, Mary, at the early age of nineteen. The depth of his feeling is evident from what he wrote about her afterwards: 'She was gifted with that singular sweetness and affectionateness of temper that she lived in an ideal world of happiness, the very sight of which made others happy.' He did, however, have an intuition that Mary's would be a short life: 'I was led to this by her extreme loveliness of character, and by the circumstance of my great affection for her. I thought I loved her too well, and hardly ever dared to take my full swing of enjoyment in her dear society.'[6] For the rest of his life he could not speak about her without tears coming to his eyes.

There are many such recorded instances of his affection for friends and the families of his friends. While he was careful to distinguish affection from its overflow into unchastity, he always maintained that 'man is made for sympathy, for the interchange of love'.[7]

As an Anglican, Newman understands celibacy in the context of Christ who was born of a virgin and who remained a virgin. But such a choice then, as now, was strongly counter-cultural: 'the way of the world at present', he commented, 'is to deny that there is such a gift'.[8]

His appreciation of celibacy grew after he became a Catholic, as also

---

4 Joseph Tolhurst, 'The Interchange of Love: John Henry Newman's Teaching on Celibacy' in *Irish Theological Quarterly*, 59, no. 3, 1993, p. 218.   5 'I had a strong persuasion that offences against the rule of purity were each of them visited sharply and surely from above' (*Apologia pro Vita Sua*, London, 1886, p. 147). In one of his discourses he goes to the root of the hostility to chastity which is evident in today's world also: 'The Church is built upon the doctrine that impurity is hateful to God, and that concupiscence is its root; with the Prince of the Apostles, her visible Head, she denounces "the corruption of concupiscence which is in the world", or, that corruption in the world which comes of concupiscence; whereas the corrupt world defends, nay I may even say, sanctifies that very concupiscence which is the world's corruption ... ; it deifies and worships human nature and its impulses, and denies the power and the grant of grace. This is the source of the hatred which the world bears to the Church; it finds a whole catalogue of sins brought into light and denounced, which it would fain believe to be no sins at all' (*Discourses Addressed to Mixed Congregations*, London, 1890, pp 149–50).   6 Cf. Ker, op. cit., p. 30.   7 Placid Murray, *Newman the Oratorian*, Dublin, 1969, Paper no. 18, p. 277.   8 *Parochial and Plain Sermons*, VI, London, 1875, p. 187.

did his esteem for marriage.[9] As an Anglican he had to justify celibacy in light of a particular dedication, but afterwards he felt free to speak about a 'nobler state of life'. This he did eloquently in a homily preached on virginity and celibacy in 1852, at a time in England when celibacy was under constant fire from non-Catholics.[10] Newman responds to these vulgar attacks with a calm and dignified statement of Christian virginity and celibacy, drawing on the wisdom of Scripture and the Fathers of the Church. It is this composure, combined with his deep appreciation of the role of human love in marriage, which gives particular relevance to his insights in the context of the present polarisation of ideas about optional celibacy.[11]

Reviewing the divine plan of redemption, he recalls how God came to meet us in Christ as the Word Incarnate, not as Judge but as Lover of souls: 'He has married himself to his Church, and to every elect soul in it, giving himself for it.' Reflecting on the nature of man, made of body and soul, and how it was not good for him to be alone, he recalls how a helper was created for him. Because of his expansive nature, his capacity to love many things, he must begin from some fixed points. It is a law of our nature, Newman affirms,

> to have one central and supreme attachment, to which none other can be compared. An affection, one, mutual, sovereign, unalterable, is earthly happiness and his earthly strength. Two mortal creatures of God, placed in this rough world, exposed to its many fortunes, destined to suffering and death, join hands, and give the faith to each other that each of them will love the other wholly until death. Henceforth each is made for the other – each has possession of the affections of the other in a transcendent way; each loves the other better than anything else in the way; each is all in all to the other; each can confide in the other unreservedly, each is the other's irreversibly. There is but one mind, one aim, one course, one happiness, between two. Each is reflected in the other; each reads his own thought in the other's face; each feels for the other more than himself. Such is the fountain head of human civilisation, the guardian of religion,

9 This is evident if, for example, we compare what he wrote on these topics after his severe illness in Sicily in 1833 with his homily of 1852; cf. Ker, ibid., pp 196–7.   **10** Cf. Murray, op. cit., pp 270–81. This was a homily delivered at the religious profession of Mary Anne Bowden, daughter of his oldest friend, John Bowden, from Oxford undergraduate days. **11** With reference to *An Essay on the Development of Christian Doctrine* and the *Apologia pro Vita Sua*, Cholij affirms that Newman considered celibacy to be of apostolic origin; cf. Cholij, op. cit., p. 70.

and the norm of philanthropy, and the sanctification of mankind. There is no such union elsewhere in this natural world ... Conjugal duty is indestructible: and in its ardour and its security it may seem (if I may speak the word with reverence) to recall to us the everlasting ineffable love with which the Father loves the Son who is in his bosom and the Son the Father who has from all eternity begotten him.[12]

Such he says was the blessedness of man in his own nature and without reference to grace. It may seem a somewhat idealistic view of marriage but it is the background against which he defines and delineates that other irrevocable commitment of celibacy. With the preaching of the Gospel our Lord himself, the 'Crown of Virgins', the Blessed Virgin, and St John the Baptist set the pattern for the new disciples. In putting celibacy before us as 'the higher state', Newman affirms that Christ did not deprive us of some essential blessing: 'The Gospel recommends celibacy, but observe how it draws around it the choicest blessings of human nature, while it seems to be giving them up ... Henceforth a system of grace came in, which raised man above himself, and without repealing the laws by which he was naturally governed, put before his eyes a nobler state of life and counselled him to do that which came to him on no obligation.'[13]

To put this Gospel view in perspective he recalls the celibacy recommended by the philosophers, which he says 'does but harden the heart' and is of a 'forlorn, haughty and repulsive nature'. Thus, he continues, to make a single life its own end, to adopt it simply and solely for its own sake:

This is not the Virginity of the Gospel – it is not a state of independence or isolation, or dreary pride, or barren indolence, or crushed affections: man is made for sympathy, for the interchange of love, for self-denial for the sake of another dearer to him than himself. The Virginity of the Christian soul is a marriage with Christ ... O transcending condescension that he should stoop to be ours in the tenderest and most endearing way – ours to love, ours to consult, ours to minister to, ours to converse with, ours to joy in. Ours so fully that it is as if he had none to think of but each of us personally. The very idea of matrimony is possession – whole possession – the husband is the wife's and no other's, and the wife is the husband's and none but his. This is to enter into the marriage bond, this is the

12 Murray, ibid., pp 275–6. 13 Ibid., p. 276.

force of the marriage vow, this is the lesson of the marriage ring. And this is to be married to Jesus. It is to have him ours wholly, henceforth and forever, – it is to be united to him by an indissoluble tie – it is to be his, while he is ours – it is to partake of that wonderful sacrament which unites him to his Blessed Mother on high – *Dilectus meus mihi, et ego illi, qui pascitur inter lilia* (Song of Songs 6:3).[14]

So Newman would affirm that it is not possible to understand celibacy except viewed from a supernatural perspective. Nor could it be a rule of life unless supported by grace. In a fine passage from his discourse on *The Glories of Mary* he shows how the Blessed Virgin is the 'pattern of purity' and reveals to us something of his own personal struggle in the quest for this virtue:

> Above all, let us imitate her purity ... What shall bring you forward in the narrow way, but the thought and patronage of Mary? What shall seal your senses, what shall tranquillise your heart, when sights and sounds of danger are around you, but Mary? What shall give you patience and endurance, when you are wearied out with the length of the conflict with evil, with the unceasing necessity of precautions, but a loving communion with her! She will comfort you in your discouragements, solace you in your fatigues, raise you after your falls, reward you for your successes. She will show you her Son, your God and your all. When your spirit within you is restless and wayward, when it is sick of what it has, and hankers after what it has not, when your eye is solicited with evil and your mortal frame trembles under the shadow of the Tempter, what will bring you to yourself, to peace and to health, but the cool breath of the Immaculate and the fragrance of the Rose of Sharon? It is the boast of the Catholic religion, that it has the gift of making the young heart chaste; and why is this, but that it gives us Jesus Christ for our food, and Mary for our nursing Mother?[15]

When Charles Kingsley attacked Newman's personal integrity, he responded in the *Apologia* with that classic defence of himself and of the Catholic priesthood in general, vindicating also the discipline of priestly celibacy. He had already suffered the indignity of the notorious Achilli trial in the same cause. For his efforts he received the universal gratitude of

---

14 Ibid., p. 277. 'I am my beloved's and my beloved is mine; he pastures his flock among the lilies' (Song 6:3). **15** *Discourses to Mixed Congregations*, London, 1886, pp 375– 6.

the priests of England. Priests today can also be thankful to Newman not only for his deep theological insights into celibacy, but especially for revealing to us how the practice of it was reflected in the intimacy of his own soul.

BISHOP ALVARO DEL PORTILLO

As we have already noted, the Vatican II document on the ministry and life of priests deals with the question of priestly celibacy in some detail.[16] Bishop Alvaro del Portillo was secretary of the commission which prepared this document, and consequently he was in a position to be well informed about the thinking of the conciliar Fathers on the topic of celibacy. It is his opinion 'that no ecumenical council had ever tackled the subject of priestly celibacy with such directness, in as large and representative an assembly, and none was as well-furnished with working data'.[17]

In previous chapters we have referred to some of the reasons why Monsignor del Portillo, drawing on the insights of Vatican II, considers celibacy appropriate to the priesthood. Writing out of a background of wide theological and pastoral involvement, and drawing on his experience of preparing and calling hundreds of young men to the priesthood, his observations on celibacy have a particular significance.

> Celibacy makes the priest a special representative sign of the virginity and fruitful love of the Spouse of Christ and makes him also a prophetic witness, in time, of that future world where justice dwells (cf. Pet 3:12), and in which the redeemed will be like to God since they will see him as he is (cf. 1 Jn 3:2). Similarly everyone can see how perfect and perpetual continence for the sake of the kingdom of heaven reinforces and shows forth to men the escathological calling which is inherent in Christ's mission, and especially in the evangelising ministry of the priest, the restless witness of eternity. This sign is particularly powerful in the crisis of faith which materialism has provoked in the world today.
>
> All the reasons which show celibacy to be appropriate to the priesthood are founded on the mystery of Christ and on his mission;[18] they are therefore reasons which the Church discovers as she deep-

---

16 Cf. *Presbyterorum ordinis*, 16. See also the Vatican II decree on the training of priests, *Optatum totius*, 10.   **17** del Portillo, op. cit., p. 39.   **18** Cf. *Presbyterorum ordinis*, 16.

ens her knowledge of the theology of the priesthood. Christ's spouse senses that certain intimate tensions unite the mystery of undivided love and the mystery of the priesthood of the New Covenant; and this is why she teaches that these reasons, which are not absolute, but are definitely appropriate, are integrated into a spirituality which is clearly sacerdotal, tending towards the mystical transformation of Christ's minister into the high priest himself whom he represents through the character he receives in the sacrament of Order.[19]

Bishop del Portillo goes on to point out that one of the objectives of the council Fathers was to avoid the possibility of misunderstanding priestly celibacy by linking it with virginity as practised in the religious state. Hence the reasons given by Vatican II for the appropriatenes˘ of priestly celibacy do not refer to the intrinsic value of continence, nor are they based on the advantages of celibacy to the priest as a means to achieve personal holiness. Rather, the council teaching grounds itself on the premise that celibacy is appropriate because it strengthens the intimate sacramental link between the priest and Christ whose image he is, and thus makes his mission more effective. Consequently

the link between celibacy and priesthood is not something artificial and ephemeral. Although it is not part of the fundamental constitution of the church, the celibacy of priests is not a 'superstructure' which has no basis, nor is it a hang-over from some particular historical period. It is a result of the action of the Holy Spirit – and therefore a lively sign of the development of the seed which is growing into a fruitful tree (cf. Mt 13:21–32). Before the theologians deduced its christological and ecclesiological appropriateness, the *sensus fidei* of the people of God had begun to intuit the deep spiritual and pastoral connection between celibacy and priesthood. Thus, the supernatural instinct of the prophetic community anointed by the Holy One (cf. 1 Jn 2:20) anticipated the successive acts of the magisterium which first recommended celibacy to all the clergy and eventually established, in the Latin church, a legal obligation whereby all who were ordained had to be celibate ...

Priests who must guard this divine gift, and all the community of the faithful, for whose life priests give their own life in sacrifice, have

19 This and subsequent quotations are extracts from Chapter 4 of his *On Priesthood*, op. cit., 'The Celibacy of Priests in the Decree *Presbyterorum ordinis*', pp 49–56.

a duty humbly and continually to ask the Father, in Christ's name (cf. Jn 14:13) not to refuse his people an abundance of this grace. Therefore the Council asks 'that not only priests but all the faithful would cherish this precious gift of priestly celibacy, and that all would beg God always to lavish this gift abundantly on his Church'.[20]

It is only through prayer, in the intimacy of that direct and personal dialogue with God, that one's heart and intelligence are opened (cf. Acts 16:14), so that the man of faith can deepen his understanding of God's will for him. If priests, as educators in the faith,[21] teach this to the faithful generally, one can well understand why the Council reminded them to meditate and pray themselves so that they can be faithful to their own vocation and to the gifts they have received along with it. The love-reason of celibacy can be understood only by an intellect illuminated by the scandal, the madness and the fruitfulness of the Cross (cf. 1 Cor 1:23; Jn 12:32).

Only by reasoning which is not 'intellectualist' or abstract – which does not evade the sincerity of personal response to God who calls each by his name (cf. Is 43:1) – can a priest immerse his soul in the 'great mysteries that are signified and fulfilled in it'.[22]

By this spirit of prayer and worship, with which the priests 'will pray in union with the Church for the grace of fidelity which is never denied to those who ask',[23] the priest's existence is opened to a full understanding of the difficulties which the custody of the gift of perfect continence entails for a man who is psychologically and physiologically normal, and he will have a refined sensitivity for using the necessary natural and supernatural means and ascetical practices 'which are approved by the experience of the Church and are as necessary as ever in the modern world'.[24]

The celibacy of priests does not exclude, even here on earth, human joy and happiness (cf. 1 Cor 7:40). However, like all radical, definitive decisions which affect the entire life of a man, celibacy is a difficult bond of love. Therefore, just as in human love, the fullness of love which celibacy involves calls for a renewal every day in a joyful renunciation of one's self. Only in this way can one overcome the difficulties which can develop as time goes on, and which can

---

20 *Presbyterorum ordinis*, 16.   **21** Cf. ibid., no. 6.   **22** Ibid., no.16.   **23** Ibid.   **24** Ibid.

result from routine or from the resistance which one's sacrificed flesh makes (a resistance which is understandable in any normal personality). Celibacy is a normal possibility for a well-balanced nature, but it cannot be observed by human efforts alone: 'I believed that continence was to be achieved by man's own power, which I knew that I did not possess. Fool that I was, I did not know that no man "can be master of himself except of God's bounty" (Wis 8:21), as your Bible tells us. And you would have given me this strength, if I had allowed the cries of my soul to beat upon your ears and had had faith firm enough to shed my troubles on to you.'[25]

MOTHER TERESA

Mother Teresa of Calcutta was by any standards a remarkable woman. She received international recognition, including the Nobel Peace Prize, for her outstanding work with the outcasts of society, not just in India but all over the world.

Her whole life was shot through with a deep Christian faith, and at every opportunity she defended the teaching of the Church, especially in relation to contraception and abortion. She has spoken and written persuasively about many aspects of the faith, including priestly celibacy.

She develops, very penetratingly, the Christological aspect of celibacy beyond the merely theological as follows:

There is no comparison with the vocation of the priest. It is like a replacing of Jesus at the altar, at the confessional, and in all the other sacraments where he uses his own 'I', like Jesus. How completely the priest must be one with Jesus for Jesus to use him in his place, in his name; to utter his words, do his actions, take away sins, and make ordinary bread and wine into the Living Bread of his own Body and Blood. Only in the silence of his heart can he hear God's word, and from the fullness of his heart can he utter these words: 'I absolve you' and 'This is my Body'. How pure the mouth of the priest must be, and how clean the heart of a priest must be to be able to speak, to utter the words, 'This is my Body', and to make bread into the living Jesus. How pure must be the hand of the priest, how com-

25 St Augustine, *Confessions* 6, 11.

pletely the hand of Jesus must be the hand of the priest, if in it, when the priest raises that hand, is the precious Blood of Jesus.

You, as God's priest, are to be his living instrument, and so you must ever give him permission to do with you exactly as he wills for the glory of the Father. The same Spirit will invite you to live an ever closer *oneness with Jesus* – in mind, heart and action – so that all you say and do will be for him, with him and to him. As he is one with the Father, so you too must be one with Jesus. As it is with his own priesthood that you have been sealed, so he must be the one to live that priesthood within you. *Nothing and nobody must separate you from Jesus*, so that you can say with St Paul: 'It is no longer I who live, but Christ who lives in me.'

So, therefore, every priestly vocation is not just to do this or to do that; a priest has been created to belong totally – body, soul, mind, heart, every fibre of his body, every fibre of his soul – to God because he has called him by his name. A priest is very precious to him, a priest is very tenderly loved by God, by Jesus who has chosen him to be his 'second self'.

You are to be *a radiance of Jesus himself.* Your look must be his, your words his words. The people are not seeking your talents, but God in you. Draw them to God, but never to self. If you are not drawing them to God, then you are seeking yourself, and people will love you for yourself, not because you remind them of Jesus. Your desire must be to 'give only Jesus' in your ministry, rather than self. Remember that it is only your communion with Jesus that brings about communication of Jesus. As Jesus was so united to the Father as to be his splendour and image, so by your union with Jesus you become his radiance, a transparency of Christ, so that those who have seen you have in some way seen him.

Yes, the world is in great need of priests, of holy priests, of priestly celibacy, for the world is in need of Christ. To doubt the value of one's priesthood and one's priestly celibacy in today's world is to doubt the very value of Christ and his mission – for they are one.[26]

These are not just challenging thoughts on the implications of celibacy; they are also a profound statement of the very nature of the Catholic priesthood.

---

26 'Priestly Celibacy: Sign of the Charity of Christ', in *For Love Alone*, op. cit., pp 213–18 (italics in the original).

DISADVANTAGES OF A MARRIED CLERGY

Some people argue that a married clergy would solve many of the Church's problems. A married clergyman with the Church of England, who recently converted to Catholicism, begs to differ, and offers his comments on the advantages of the discipline of celibacy in Catholic Church:

> How is the compulsory celibacy of the Catholic clergy to be defended, as the Church approaches the end of the second millennium? In an age which is in the grip of what C S Lewis –writing, incredibly, in the pre-sexual-liberation forties – called even then 'the erotic obsession of the twentieth century', the Catholic Church's denial of sexual relations to its clergy is bound to seem peculiar, even perverted.
>
> But that is no reason, by itself, for change. Nor is another reason – in my opinion wholly bogus – currently being widely argued. The current agitation in these islands has been largely animated by a number of cases of breakdown of discipline among the clergy – priests molesting children and having affairs with women who come to them for counselling. But this is not only a Catholic problem. Such cases occur with the same frequency in Protestant countries, and among married clergy ...
>
> There is in the Catholic clergy a particular kind of dedication to the purposes of God, and the Catholic laity has come to take it for granted. This dedication is, in the overwhelming majority of cases, total and uncompromising; and its special character derives from the renunciation of so much that in our society and at this juncture in our cultural history we take for granted as being essential for normal human happiness. It is the renunciation of self which that sacrifice represents, it seems to me, that makes celibacy such a precious possession of the Catholic Church. It is one of the jewels in our crown: we would be fools thus lightly to throw it away.
>
> Of course there are those for whom the sacrifice is too great, who crumble beneath the strain. But what is more striking is the vast majority of bishops and clergy who remain faithful to their vows. It is a majestic record of heroic service; and it makes the priesthood of the Catholic Church something for which and in which I, as a Catholic layman, have a deep sense of gratitude and pride. I may add, as an Englishman educated in Ireland, a country for which I have had a deep and abiding love for over thirty five years, and whose Church

and culture had a profound influence on my own conversion to Catholicism, that I am certain that the current mood of brutish anti-clericalism in certain quarters in Ireland will be rejected by future generations with shame and loathing.

The Church should be less defensive about the virtues of celibacy. Because it is largely celibate, the ordained ministry of the Catholic Church is unique. A priest is a person set apart for the purposes of God alone. A married clergyman has to balance his commitment to his people with his commitment to his wife and children. A husband and father has to give his wife and children first priority. His vocation has to be a career; he has to consider where he will go, whether the house is suitable, what the local schools are like. There is also a much greater temptation to think about the prospects of advancement. Furthermore, many places of great spiritual need, like the inner cities, are ruled out as places where he can exercise his ministry.

Churches with a married clergy have their own problems. A celibate priesthood may be demanding; but so is the life of a married clergyman. There is a high rate of marriage breakdown among married clergy. The life of clergy wives and children is often isolated and stressful. Those in the Catholic Church who think that getting rid of clerical celibacy is the panacea for all our problems are simply ill informed about the alternatives. Protestant Churches too have a crisis of vocations.

In the end, the real reason for retaining a predominantly celibate clergy is that it is one of the Catholic Church's most singular glories. It is what the Pope calls 'a sign of contradiction', an indication that the Catholic Church has its own agenda. It is a powerful sign in an age when so many churches have come to do no more than mirror the fashions of the passing age – that the real business of the Church is God's business and not that of the rulers of this world.[27]

UNDER THE CHINESE COMMUNISTS

The value of celibacy shines out in a special way when it is put to the test under persecution. In a world which prides itself on its appreciation of freedom, but which is often enslaved by materialism and sensuality, the following three episodes from history shed their own light on the value of

27 William Oddie, *Irish Catholic*, 21 November 1996. See also L.F. Martin, 'When Clergy Marry: An Insider's View', in *Homiletic and Pastoral Review*, June 1997, pp 29–32, 45–47.

celibacy as a witness to love of God in the world. The first was recorded by the Archbishop of Canton.

Dominic Tang Yee-ming was ordained in Shanghai in 1941, and in 1950 was appointed apostolic administrator of the Canton diocese. These were years when the Communists had come to power and Catholics were undergoing intense persecution. Because of his refusal to recognise the breakaway Patriotic Church he was denounced publicly on several occasions. In 1958 he was imprisoned for twenty-two years, during seven of which he was placed in solitary confinement. It is from this background that he reflects on priestly celibacy, which he describes as 'the heart of a priest's identity and commitment'.

'During the Cultural Revolution in China', Archbishop Tang Yee-ming tells us, 'many of the clergy were forced into marriages. This was one way the Communists attacked the Church and its ministers. They did not understand celibacy, belittled it and wanted to do away with it. There were priests who got married. However, over the years the Communists have come to realise that Catholics will not accept these married priests as their ministers. They strongly oppose having any Catholic priest who is married to act as their spiritual leader. I do not believe they were passing personal judgement on these priests, but what they are saying, it seems to me, is that they want celibate priests who can dedicate their whole lives to the Lord and to his people.'[28] The opposition to married priests was so strong that the Communist authorities were forced to change their policy.

While the demand for celibate priests owes a lot to the tradition the people were used to, at the same time the Archbishop believes that the reason goes deeper. He is convinced that the Chinese Catholics recognised instinctively that a celibate person was somebody totally set apart for the service of the Christian community, and as a consequence they felt they could trust him more. Hence they insisted on having a priest determined to serve the Lord completely, who would in turn lead them to know and follow Christ.

Before he was released, after twenty two years of imprisonment, the Chinese authorities tried one last effort to separate him from his loyalty to the Holy See. Having failed, he was eventually set free. Among the reasons given for his release was the fact of him 'never having played around with women'. It was, in the view of the Archbishop, a negative testimony by the authorities to the good of celibacy.

28 Archbishop Dominic Tang Yee-ming, 'Celibacy: Fidelity to one's Priestly Identity', in *For Love Alone*, op. cit., p. 148. The remainder of this testimony is taken from this article.

THE LOST CHRISTIANS OF NAGASAKI

Christianity flourished in Japan after the missionary efforts of the sixteenth century. However, a bitter persecution of Christians broke out in 1614, lasting for thirty years and carried out with incredible violence. By the time it ended over a thousand missionaries and 200,000 Christians had shed their blood for the faith, including the Nagasaki martyrs of 1622. Apostasies were comparatively few.

Japan then cut itself off from the rest of the world for over two hundred years, mainly to keep out missionaries, thinking that by doing this Christianity would die a natural death. Nevertheless, in the 1860s Japan once again opened up to the outside world in the interests of trade. Missionaries were able to return, although the laws against Christianity remained in force: it was banishment or death for any native to embrace the Catholic faith. In 1863 French missionaries arrived in Nagasaki to look after the needs of European Catholics, but no progress was made with the native Japanese.

A small church was built, and out of curiosity a number of Japanese often visited it and were even present for Mass. On 17 March 1865 a group of fifteen men, women and children approached the church, tentatively, and made themselves known to Père Petitjean as Christians. But before doing so they confirmed that he was a Catholic priest by asking some specific questions.

After the persecution of two hundred years previously the missionaries had promised to come back, and part of the tradition that had survived among the thousands of secret Christians who lived in the hills around Nagasaki was that these long hoped-for priests, when they returned, would be recognised by the fact that they would honour the Blessed Virgin, they would be sent by 'the great White Father of the West' (the Pope), and they would be celibates.

It seems that some time before, a group of Protestant missionaries had arrived but, when they found they were married, the Japanese Catholics knew they did not fit the tradition of the faith handed down to them. Having confirmed the first two elements for authenticity they now put the final test question to Père Petitjean – did he have children? When the little group discovered that he was a celibate Catholic priest, they bowed to the ground and thanked God.

How fifty thousand people managed to keep the faith without priests over a period of two hundred years, in constant danger from hostile authorities, is one of the most moving stories of recent Church history.[29]

LOVE FOR CHRIST

Apart from reasons of availability, Christ invited the apostles to leave everything behind so that they could share in a special way in his friendship (cf. Mk 3:13; Jn 14:15). The experience of this friendship, through the special love born of celibacy, has inspired, and continues to inspire, generosity and heroism in the service of the Master.

In this context the celebration in Rome of the Holy Father's Golden Jubilee as a priest comes to mind, and the witness of some of his fellow jubilarians on that occasion. One recalls particularly the testimony of Fr Anton Luli from Albania, who spent forty-two of those fifty years of his priesthood imprisoned under the harshest Communist dictatorship in Europe.

It was a life spent in chains and every kind of torture. He lived in solitary confinement for seventeen years. His first prison, in a freezing December of 1947, was in a lavatory, where he stayed for nine months forced to crouch on hardened excrement, and never allowed to stretch because the space was so small. On Christmas night of 1947 he was dragged to another lavatory, forced to strip, and was hung up by a rope passed under his arms. He was naked and could barely touch the ground with the tips of his toes. Slowly and inexorably he practically froze to death, until he gave a desperate cry alerting his gaolers. They pulled him down and practically kicked him to death. That night, he commented, 'in the solitude of that first torture, I experienced the real meaning of the Incarnation and the Cross'.

'But in this suffering', he recalls, 'I had beside me and within me the comforting presence of the Lord Jesus, the Eternal High Priest. At times his support was something I can only call "extraordinary", so great was the joy and comfort he communicated to me'. He never felt resentment for those who humanly speaking had robbed him of his life, until he was released in 1989 when he was seventy-nine years old.

'The priest', he continued, 'is first and foremost someone who has known love; he is a man who lives in order to love. To love Christ and to love everyone in him, in all life's circumstances to the point of giving up his life'. Thus, he concludes, 'everything can be taken from us, but no one can wrench from our hearts our love for Jesus or our love for our brothers and sisters. In this regard, today as in the past and as it always has been, we can say with conviction and with joy, in Paul's words, "Who can separate

29 Cf. Francis J. Bowen, *Pioneers of the Faith*, London, 1938, pp 17–38.

us from the love of Christ? Shall tribulation, or distress, or persecution, or famine, or peril, or sword?"(Rom 8:35). Holy Father, today as in the past, this is the deep conviction that we priests present here profess before you. This is the gift we offer to the Lord and to Your Holiness on this day blessed by the Lord.'[30]

For this heroic priest 'it is in the heart of God, in his love for humanity, that Christ's priestly mission was born, and it is in the loving heart of Jesus our Saviour that our own priesthood flowers'.[31]

JOHN PAUL II ON CELIBACY

As we have already seen, John Paul II has written much on celibacy and has made his own original contribution to the Church's self-understanding of this charism. His ideas have been a constant point of reference all through this book, and so it would seem appropriate to finish our considerations with an extract from an address which he gave to members of the Canadian hierarchy a few years ago, and which constitutes a summary of much of this teaching:

> At this time, when some question the desirability of maintaining the discipline of priestly celibacy, *Bishops must courageously teach the fittingness of linking this 'sign of contradiction' with the ministerial priesthood.* On the basis of her experience and reflection, the Church has discerned, with growing clarity through the ages, that priestly celibacy is not just a legal requirement imposed as a condition for ordination. It is profoundly connected with a man's configuration to Christ, the Good Shepherd and Spouse of the Church. As *Pastores dabo vobis* states: 'Certainly it is a grace which does not dispense with, but counts most definitely on, a conscious and free response on the part of the receiver. This charism of the Spirit also brings with it the graces for the receiver to remain faithful to it for all his life and to be able to carry out generously and joyfully its concomitant commitments' (no.50).
>
> Cultural considerations, and the scarcity of priests in certain regions, sometimes give rise to calls for a change in this discipline. *To give decisive weight to solutions based on criteria deriving more from certain*

30 Testimony, 7 November 1996, at the Vespers service celebrated in Rome for the Holy Father's Jubilee, *Osservatore Romano*, 27 November 1996.   31 Ibid.

currents of anthropology, sociology or psychology than from the Church's living tradition is certainly not the path to follow. We cannot overlook the fact that the Church comes to know the divine will through the *interior guidance of the Spirit* (cf. Jn 16:13), and that the difficulties involved today in keeping celibacy are not sufficient reason to overturn the Church's conviction regarding its value and appropriateness, a conviction constantly reaffirmed by the Church's Magisterium, not least by the Second Vatican Council (cf. *Presbyterorum ordinis,* 16). Like the Church in other countries, the Church in Canada is called to face this situation *with* faith and courage, trusting 'in the Spirit that the gift of celibacy ... will be generously bestowed by the Father, as long as those who share in Christ's priesthood through the sacrament of Orders, and indeed the whole church, humbly and earnestly pray for it' (ibid.).[32]

---

32 Address, 8 November 1993, in *Osservatore Romano,* 17 November 1993 (italics in original).

Epilogue

Looking back over the complex history of priestly celibacy in the Church, we see that there is one central idea which is common to East and West, and it is this: that, for clerics who exercised the service of the altar, continence is required because of their unique function as mediators between God and man. Even the Council of Trullo, which introduced a serious element of discontinuity in the tradition, is essentially motivated by this theological perspective.

Of all the Old Testament prescriptions and rites related to the purification of priests, it is surely striking, as Cochini has pointed out, that the one element which has transferred into the priesthood of the Christian tradition is the memory of the divine law which required of the Levites that, in order to accomplish worthily their Temple duties, they should abstain from conjugal relations with their wives.[1]

Not only did the early Church authorities and the Fathers see it as a distinctive mark of the priesthood founded on Christ, but they gave it a deeper significance and scope by demanding daily conjugal abstinence. It would, nevertheless, be inadequate to try to justify theologically priestly celibacy as the ultimate stage of the development of the temporary continence of the Levitical priesthood. That would be tantamount to anchoring celibacy primarily within the context of ritual purity and separate it from its primary and essential theological explanation and function: its ontological participation in Christ's own priesthood and his spousal love for his Church.

The memory of the early Church and the testimony of the Fathers is that the Apostles, whatever their marital situation after being called by Christ, lived perfect continence thereafter. This conviction was to be a constant reference point for subsequent Church leaders in determining celibacy (or perfect continence) as one of the requirements necessary for exercising the priestly ministry, and for keeping intact the essential identity of the priesthood as it was transmitted from one generation to the next.[2]

---

1 Cf. Cochini, op. cit., p. 429.   2 Cf. ibid., p. 438.

It has also to be noted that from the beginnings of the Church, but independent of the priesthood, there was a strong spiritual motivation among men and women to give themselves totally to God in consecrated virginity (cf. 1 Cor 7:32ff). While there is a certain common element in the theological validation for virginity and priestly celibacy, there are also elements specific to the minister of Christ which justify and authenticate priestly celibacy in view of his function as mediator acting *in persona Christi*, and of his spousal love for the Church which springs from his sacramental identification with the Eternal High Priest.

Although these separate vocational currents did undoubtedly inspire and support one another, their sources lie in different ascetical traditions. As Cochini concludes, while the call to virginity was grounded on the evangelical counsels and matured into the various forms of monastic and religious life, the discipline of priestly celibacy has its origin in a positive determination of the Apostles as tutored directly by Christ.[3]

As we have seen, the history of ecclesiastical celibacy in the West is not so much that of a slow evolution from the *lex continentiae* of the first millennium to the current discipline of priestly celibacy under the positive influence of the vocation to virginity. It is rather a development which was the consequence of Church authority, faithful to apostolic tradition, resisting the contrary current in different times and places, and, guided by the Holy Spirit, defining canonically the ascetical requirements most appropriate to the priestly condition and life-style. When opposition to the traditional discipline was fiercest, as at the time of the Gregorian reform and the Council of Trent, the response of those entrusted with guarding apostolic tradition was more specific and more definitive.

In our own time, when the discipline of priestly celibacy is suffering the most severe crisis in four hundred years, the response of the Magisterium has been equally definitive and courageous. The Vatican II decree *Presbyterorum ordinis* on the Ministry and Life of Priests (1965)[4], the encyclical *Sacerdotalis caelibatus* (1967), the document of the 1971 Synod of Bish-

---

3 Cf. ibid.   4 'By persevering in virginity or celibacy for the sake of the kingdom of heaven (cf. Mt 19:12) priests are consecrated in a new and excellent way to Christ (cf. 1 Cor 7:32–34). They more readily cling to him with undivided heart and dedicate themselves more freely in him and through him to the service of God and of men. They are less encumbered in their service of his kingdom and of the task of heavenly regeneration. In this way they become better fitted for a broader acceptance of fatherhood in Christ. By means of celibacy, then, priests profess before men their willingness to be dedicated with undivided loyalty to the task entrusted to them, namely that of espousing the faithful to one husband and presenting them as a chaste virgin to Christ (cf. 2 Cor 11:2). Moreover

ops,[5] the legislation in the 1983 Code of Canon Law,[6] and the apostolic exhortation *Pastores dabo vobis* of John Paul II (1992),[7] have not only affirmed the traditional teaching and discipline, but have added new and deeper theological reasons justifying celibacy as the state most appropriate to the nature and commitments of Christ's priests.[8] In the face of opposition and the spiritual blindness of a sensate culture, the temptation to take the easy way out and settle for optional celibacy is always very strong. Hence, it is a measure of the essentially supernatural character of the Church, and her permanent conviction of the apostolic origin of celibacy, that she has always had the grace and the courage to row against the current on this issue. Down through the centuries she has heard all the psychological, sociological, and functional reasons which seem to justify optional celibacy. Still, she has never felt that these arguments were adequate in themselves. Against the conventional wisdom, she has always grounded her conviction on supernatural faith in the promises of Christ, and has never

they are made a living sign of that world to come, already present through faith and charity, a world in which the children of the resurrection shall neither be married nor take wives (cf. Lk 20:35–36). For these reasons, based on the mystery of Christ and his mission, celibacy, which at first was recommended to priests, was afterwards in the Latin Church imposed by law on all who were to be promoted to holy Orders. This sacred Council approves and confirms this legislation so far as it concerns those destined for the priesthood, and feels confident in the Spirit that the gift of celibacy, so appropriate to the priesthood of the New Testament, is liberally granted by the Father, provided those who share in Christ's priesthood through the sacrament of Order, and indeed the whole Church, ask for that gift humbly and earnestly' (no. 16).   **5** 'Because of the intimate and multiple coherence between the pastoral function and a celibate life, the existing law is upheld: one who freely wills total availability, the distinctive character of this function, also freely undertakes a celibate life. The candidate should feel this form of living not as having been imposed from outside, but rather as a manifestation of his free self-giving, which is accepted and ratified by the Church through the bishop. In this way the law becomes a protection and a safeguard of the freedom wherewith the priest gives himself to Christ and it becomes "an easy yoke"' (Synodal document, *The Ministerial Priesthood*, Part Two, Section I, no.4 c).   **6** 'Clerics are obliged to observe perfect and perpetual continence for the sake of the Kingdom of heaven, and are therefore bound to celibacy. Celibacy is a special gift of God by which sacred ministers can more easily remain close to Christ with an undivided heart, and can dedicate themselves more freely to the service of God and their neighbour' (Canon 277, §1).   **7** 'The Synod does not wish to leave any doubts in the mind of anyone regarding the Church's firm will to maintain the law that demands perpetual and freely chosen celibacy for present and future candidates for priestly ordination in the Latin rite' (John Paul II quoting *Propositio* no.11 of the 1990 Synod of Bishops in *Pastores dabo vobis*, 29).   **8** Stickler points out that the fact of Rome recognising a different discipline in the East 'can scarcely be construed as official approbation of a change in the ancient discipline of celibacy' (*The Case for Clerical Celibacy*, op. cit., p. 81). cf. also Cholij, op. cit., pp 106–94.

doubted that the Holy Spirit can, and does, bestow this charism generously if it is asked for with humility

Vatican II, with its dogmatic constitution on Divine Revelation, has
reaffirmed with greater clarity than ever before the importance of 'the
Tradition that comes from the Apostles' (cf. no. 8) in the development of
the life of the Church. It is as a result of a comprehensive enquiry into this
Tradition, using all the assistance that theology, history, law, philology
and related sciences can provide, that scholars like Stickler, Cochini and
Cholij have affirmed the apostolic origin of the *lex continentiae*, and in this
way reinforce a doctrine which has frequently been articulated by Church
authority down through history.

Commenting on the 1979 Holy Thursday Letter of John Paul II to
priests, on his words about the link between priestly celibacy and the
language and the very spirit of the Gospel, Stickler concludes:

> Far from being a discipline of purely ecclesiastical origin, i.e., human
> and capable of derogation, celibacy is in fact a practice going back to
> Jesus himself and his apostles, even before it was made into a formal
> law. Thus does celibacy belong to the Tradition of the early Church
> as were many other articles of faith or discipline that became explicit
> and progressively took definite form as they were needed in accord-
> ance with the development of doctrine and Christian life, in which
> there have been frequent contestations and infractions.[9]

Down through the centuries the experience of celibacy in the Western
Church provides an abundance of reasons to attest to the appropriateness
of this charism for men called to the priesthood. In the East only celibate
priests were ordained to the episcopacy, and priests themselves, if ordained
as single men, could not marry subsequently.

Canon 13 of Trullo did not lay the foundation for a married clergy in
the Eastern Church. A married clergy had always existed to a greater or
lesser degree in the East, and, until well into the second millennium, in
the Western Church. Yet these clergy were required to live in perpetual
continence by a general law or custom of the church. While early church
documents demonstrate a marked preference for celibates, this did not
mean that the married clergy could continue begetting children. The preference in fact was for single men who were celibates over married men
who lived as celibates.

---

9 *Osservatore Romano*, 6 May 1979 (quoted in Cochini, op. cit., p. 45).

It was the Trullan legislation which established for the first time that secular clerics other than bishops should be free to exercise their conjugal rights apart from the times of service at the altar. This was a completely new innovation which, in Cholij's cogently argued thesis, undermined the internal consistency of the rest of the Trullan legislation for married clerics. It is his contention that the only intelligible reason why marriage should be prohibited to those already in orders is that ordination itself had, since apostolic times, brought with it the obligation to perfect continence. And the reason for the prohibition was essentially a practical one - the impossibility of consummating the marriage given that ordination required of the cleric a commitment to perfect continence. As regards the absolute continence of bishops, Trullo offered the same traditional reasons as that which applied to all clerics in the Western Church and in the early Oriental Church.

To justify the use of marriage for other clerics the Council of Trullo had to re-edit the ancient texts of the Carthaginian councils, although still retaining the link between continence and the celebration of the Eucharistic liturgy. In the Oriental Catholic Churches the introduction of strict celibacy was, as we have seen, a logical and necessary move to guarantee a daily celebration of the liturgy, the demand for which was growing.

One of the consequences of the Trullan legislation was that, about the eleventh century, marriage became mandatory for ordination as a secular priest, something which was contrary to apostolic tradition and ecclesiastical discipline during the first millennium. At root, the motivation for this legislation was to provide a solution for cases of unlawful concubinage among unmarried priests. The conviction had grown in the Eastern Church that only within the safety of the monastery walls could a life of strict celibacy be guaranteed, and this to such an extent that not only were unmarried men banned from the secular clergy, but priests and deacons who lost their wives were barred from exercising their ministry and in some cases were required to enter a monastery.[10]

Since the Middle Ages commentators have pointed to the discipline of clerical marriages in the East as demonstrating that celibacy is not demanded by the nature of the priesthood. Based on apostolic tradition and the witness of the first millennium in the Latin church it is clear that celibacy in the strict sense is not required by the essence of the priesthood. Nevertheless, the arguments in favour of an intimate link between the discipline of continence and the priesthood are cogent and consistent.

10 Cf. Cholij, op. cit., p. 198.

Even the mitigated Trullan legislation of temporary continence recognised this principle. The basic theological reason would seem to be the same as that which barred a cleric from entering marriage after ordination: the consecration of the body 'which originally always qualified and accompanied the reception of the sacrament of orders'.[11]

Many commentators, in trying to identify the basic reason for the discipline of clerical continence, have focused on the cultic or liturgical role of the priest, and as a consequence developed a Levitical theology of the priesthood to explain clerical continence. Cholij's opinion is that the Trullan discipline led in practice to a Levitical type ministry, which induced writers such as Aquinas to postulate only a 'fittingness' or 'convenience' argument for total continence.[12]

In recent decades, however, the theology of priesthood has placed a much greater emphasis on the Christological rather than the Levitical aspect of the argument. This is particularly the case in the Vatican II decree on the ministry and life of priests,[13] and Paul VI's encyclical on priestly celibacy (1967).

Still, it is perhaps in the writings of John Paul II that this particular characteristic has been most cogently developed in all its theological depth. With his very first encyclical, *Redemptor hominis* (March 1979), he gave notice of his deeply Christocentric vision of history, and in subsequent documents he has developed many aspects of this vision. In relation to priests, especially by means of his annual Holy Thursday Letters, he explored many aspects of their sacramental and ontological identification with Christ which gives them the capacity and the responsibility to always act *in persona Christi*.

His most complete statement of the Christological identity of the priest is articulated in the apostolic exhortation *Pastores dabo vobis* on the formation of priests (25 March 1992). It is here that the spousal dimension of the Catholic priesthood finds its fullest expression.

The priesthood in the tradition of the Church has always been considered as God's highest gift to man. If all are called to holiness, as Vatican II affirms,[14] it is hardly surprising that the Church would insist even more on the level of sanctity expected from her priests. Whenever and wherever the priesthood is perceived as 'consecration' in its fullest sense, where the priest is seen as acting always *in persona Christi* and reflecting fully in his life

---

11 Ibid., p. 199. 12 This was essentially the explanation given by Gratian, and St Thomas Aquinas (*S. Th., Supplementum* 53,3). 13 Cf. *Presbyterorum ordinis*, 14 in particular; also *Lumen gentium*, 10. 14 Cf. *Lumen gentium*, 42, and *Apostolicam actuositatem*, 4.

the spousal and exclusive love of Christ for his Church, it would seem that perfect chastity would have to be considered as belonging to the very structure of priestly ordination in order to make possible the full exercise of the gift received,[15] and to live that special intimacy with Christ to which the priest is called. The supernatural fruitfulness of this charism, witnessed to by the lives of so many exemplary priests down through history, confirms this affirmation. No small part of the immense spiritual paternity of men like Paul, Chrysostom, Charles Borromeo, the Curé of Ars, or Josemaría Escrivá was due to the fact that they gave themselves body and soul to Christ. There is no reason to doubt that in the future, in the supernatural enterprise of bringing the fruits of the Redemption to all mankind, the spiritual dynamic inherent in priestly celibacy will continue to play a key role.

FUTURE OF CELIBACY

What then should the priest do about the lack of labourers for the harvest in different   parts of the world today? How should he respond to the immense needs of evangelization, and the hunger for the Word and the Body of the Lord in particular countries at present? The Holy Father's reply is very clear and challenging. The priest, in imitation of the faith of the Church in her Redeemer-Spouse, needs to grow in confidence in the Lord of the harvest, and to leave behind his human doubting and timidity. This is a process which requires a new conversion every day, drawing pardon and strength from the sacrament of Reconciliation. It demands a constant returning to vocational grace, a serious prayer life, and a renewed commitment to answer Christ's call more faithfully.[16]

As we consider the moral climate of the world today and the wave of sensuality which seems to permeate so many areas, one could be tempted to have doubts about the future of a celibate priesthood. The Holy Father, in his 1982 Holy Thursday Letter, raises this very question as part of his personal meditation. 'Is it permissible', he asks the Lord, to doubt

---

15 Cf. 1 Cor 7:32–33 and 1 Cor 7:29. Stickler is led to the conclusion that celibacy is not merely suitable, but seriously posits the question of its being 'necessary and indispensable to the priesthood' (op. cit., p. 106). 16 Cf. Holy Thursday Letter, 1979, no. 10.

- that You can and will kindle in the souls of men, especially the young, the charism of priestly service, as it has been received and actuated in the tradition of the Church?

- that You can and will kindle in these souls not only a desire for the Priesthood but also a readiness to accept the gift of celibacy for the sake of the kingdom of heaven, of which both in the past and still today whole generations of priests in the Catholic Church have given proof?.[17]

John Paul II's reply is that we can never doubt the love of Christ and the power of the Spirit of Truth, which is greater than any human weakness and which 'preserves the Church's youth, continually renews her and leads her to perfect union with her Bridegroom'.[18]

He sees the commitment to celibacy as a 'kind of challenge that the Church makes to the mentality, tendencies and charms of the world, with an ever new desire for consistency with and fidelity to the Gospel ideal'.[19] But first, because celibacy 'includes a certain mystery' it is necessary to pray for the grace to understand it.[20]

At the close of his meeting with the presidents of the European Episcopal Conferences (December 1992), the Holy Father came back again to the question of celibacy. He pointed out that the value of this gift had been reaffirmed in the 1990 Synod of Bishops 'as an inheritance of the Latin Church for the good of her mission', and that this should give rise to faith and trust that 'the One who began this good work in us will bring it to completion' (cf. Phil 1:6). 'What is needed on our part, then', he continued, 'is full confidence in the divine Giver of spiritual gifts'. This confidence, he said, was especially important in countries where, due to increased secularisation, vocations were lacking. Indeed, he affirmed, it was difficult to avoid the impression that a specific strategy was at work to 'distance the Church from fidelity to her Lord and Spouse'. The Holy Spirit, however, would make it possible 'to overcome the spirit of this world and to see celibacy for the sake of the kingdom of God as a choice for life, against all human weakness and human strategies. We only need not to lose heart, or to create around this vocation and choice a climate of discouragement'. Fidelity, supernatural optimism, and ardent prayer were what were needed to win vocations to the priesthood even in the most unfavourable conditions.[21]

17 Ibid., 1982, no. 5.   18 Ibid., no.6.   19 Cf. Address, 17 July 1993.   20 Cf. ibid.
21 Cf. Address, 4 December 1992, in *Osservatore Romano*, 9 December 1992. In this con-

Praying ourselves, and getting others to pray, is the first and most important means to win the necessary priestly vocations to harvest souls for Christ. This is the strategy recommended by the Master himself (cf. Lk 10:2). But it cannot be just an occasional, anaemic petition. As we learn from the Gospel, effective prayer requires constancy (cf. Lk 18:1–8) and faith (cf. Mk 9:23), and a deep conviction about the generosity of our Father, who is also God (cf. Mt 6:25–33).

If there is solid formation in the faith, a generous spirit, and encouragement to respond to grace, vocations to the priesthood will always be forthcoming, based on confidence in the promises of Christ, and the effective action of the Holy Spirit in souls. Consequently, the nurturing and flowering of such vocations will come about when there is faith, and a deep conviction that Christ never abandons his Bride the Church.

The Pope finished off his address to the bishops with a heartfelt prayer of gratitude for the gift of celibacy:

> The Church thanks you, O divine Spouse, because from the most ancient of times it has been able to welcome the call to consecrated celibacy for the sake of the kingdom of God, and because for centuries she has preserved within herself the charism of priestly celibacy. We thank you for the Second Vatican Council and for the recent Synod of Bishops which reaffirmed this charism and have shown it to be the correct way forward for the Church of the future. We are aware of the fragility of the vessels in which we carry this treasure, yet we believe in the power of the Holy Spirit who works through the grace of the sacrament in each one of us. With all the more fervour we ask you to enable us to co-operate unfailingly with the power of the Spirit ...We pray that we may not fall into doubt or sow doubt in others, or become –God forbid! –supporters of different choices and of a different kind of spirituality for the priestly life

text it is of interest to note the comments of a German archbishop: 'The situation of the Church in Germany gives me an almost daily impression of *déjà vu*, since it seems to be following exactly what happened in the Church in Holland twenty-five years ago. In 1966, in the archdiocese of Utrecht, there were as many as twenty six ordained. In 1991, after a long number of years devoted to the debate about celibacy and without any new priests being ordained, there were again two ordinations. The example of Holland shows that the failure of a generation of bishops can decimate the Church. Consequently, it is time to state clearly what it is that, as fruit of uninterrupted Tradition, of Vatican Council II, and the Magisterium, and as the essential doctrine of the one, holy, catholic and apostolic Church, is no longer open to debate' (Archbishop Johannes Dyba of Fulda, in the *Frankfurter Allgemeine Zeitung*, 13 December 1992).

and ministry. For St Paul also says: 'Do not grieve the Holy Spirit of God' (Eph 4:30).[22]

The Vicar of Christ feels the need to make reparation for those who, for whatever reason, generate doubts about celibacy or who blindly propose a departure from traditional priestly spirituality. At the same time, there is great confidence in his affirmation of celibacy as 'the correct way forward for the Church of the future', because it is a gift of the Holy Spirit which is always generously bestowed.[23]

The history of celibacy in the Western Church demonstrates this fact. Even in times more challenging than our own, such as the sixteenth century, the Holy Spirit, working through a new generation of saints, recovered a situation which, humanly speaking, seemed irreversible, and made the charism of celibacy shine out once again as one of the treasures of the Catholic Church.

In John Paul II's recently published reflections on fifty years of priesthood, the very title of the book, *Gift and Mystery*, evinces the grandeur of the priestly vocation, that *admirabile commercium* between God and man. In it he reminds us that 'unless we grasp the mystery of this "exchange" we will not understand how it can be that a young man, hearing the words "Follow me!", can give up everything for Christ, in the certainty that if he follows this path he will find complete personal fulfilment'.[24] When we consider the human and supernatural richness of the life of John Paul II, we are not surprised that many have been inspired by this man to give themselves totally to Christ in the priesthood. With models like him to follow, the call of the Master will always be heard in the hearts of generous young men down through the centuries.

22 Address, 4 December 1992. **23** Cf. ibid. **24** Op. cit., p. 73.

Bibliography

I. DOCUMENTS OF THE MAGISTERIUM

Vatican Council II Documents:
Dei verbum, 18 November 1965.
Gaudium et spes, 7 December 1965.
Lumen gentium, 21 November 1964.
Optatam totius, 28 October 1965.
Presbyterorum ordinis, 7 December 1965.

Papal Documents:
St Pius X, Apostolic Exhortation, *Haerent animo*, 4 August 1908.
Pius XI, Encyclical, *Ad catholici sacerdotii*, 20 December 1935.
Pius XII, Apostolic Exhortation, *Menti nostrae*, 23 September 1950.
—— , Encyclical, *Sacra virginitas*, 1954.
John XXIII, Encyclical, *Sacerdotii nostri primordia*, 1 August 1959.
Paul VI, Encyclical, *Sacerdotalis caelibatus*, 24 June 1967.
—— , Synod of Bishops 1971, The Ministerial Priesthood.
John Paul II, Encyclical, *Redemptor hominis*, 4 March 1979.
—— , Encyclical, *Dives in misericordia*, 30 November 1980.
—— , Apostolic Exhortation, *Familiaris consortio*, 22 November 1981.
—— , Apostolic Exhortation, *Reconciliatio et paenitentia*, 2 December 1984.
—— , Encyclical, *Redemptoris Mater*, 25 March 1987.
—— , Apostolic Letter, *Mulieris dignitatem*, 15 August 1988.
—— , Apostolic Exhortation, *Christifideles laici*, 30 December 1988.
—— , Apostolic Exhortation, *Redemptoris custos*, 15 August 1989.
—— , Encyclical, *Centesimus annus*, 1 May 1991.
—— , Apostolic Exhortation, *Pastores dabo vobis*, 25 March 1992
—— , Encyclical, *Veritatis splendor*, 6 August 1993.
—— , Apostolic Exhortation, *Tertio millennio adveniente*, 10 November 1994.
—— , Encyclical, *Evangelium vitae*, 25 March 1995.
—— , *Holy Thursday Letters to Priests*, 1979, 1995.
—— , *Original Unity of Man and Woman: Catechesis on the Book of Genesis*, Boston, 1981.
—— , *Blessed are the Pure of Heart: Catechesis on the Sermon on the Mount and Writings of St Paul*, Boston, 1983.

——, *Reflections on* Humanae Vitae: *Conjugal Morality and Spirituality*, Boston, 1984.

——, *The Theology of Marriage and Celibacy: Catechesis on Marriage and Celibacy in the Light of the Resurrection of the Body*, Boston, 1986

——, *A Priest Forever*, Athlone, 1986.

——, *Priesthood in the Third Millennium: Addresses of John Paul II*, Chicago, 1994.

——, *Gift and Mystery: On the Fiftieth Anniversary of my Priestly Ordination*, London, 1997.

——, *Catechism of the Catholic Church*, Dublin, 1994.

Other Documents of the Magisterium

Congregation for the Doctrine of the Faith: *Instruction on the Ecclesial Vocation of the Theologian*, 24 May 1990.

Congregation for the Clergy: *Directory on the Ministry and Life of Priests*, 31 January 1994.

Congregation for Catholic Education: *A Guide to Formation in Priestly Celibacy*, 11 April 1974.

——, *Spiritual Formation in Seminaries*, 6 January 1980.

——, *Directives on the Formation of Seminarians concerning problems related to Marriage and the Family*, 19 March 1995.

Pontifical Council for the Family: *The Truth and Meaning of Human Sexuality*, 8 December 1995.

Pontifical Biblical Commission: *Interpretation of the Bible in the Church*, 15 April 1993.

2. OTHER BIBLIOGRAPHY

Michael Adams, *Single-minded: Aspects of Chastity*, Dublin, 1979.

ASTI: Guidelines for Professional Behaviour for Second-level Teachers, September 1995.

St Augustine, *Confessions*.

Jordan Aumann, *Spiritual Theology*, London, 1980.

Jean-Pierre Batut, 'The Chastity of Jesus and the "Refusal to Grasp"', *Communio* 24 (Spring 1997), pp 5–13.

Johannes Bauer, ed., *Encyclopaedia of Biblical Theology*, London, 1970.

K. Bihlmeyer and H. Tüchle, *Church History*, I, Westminster, 1968.

Allan Bloom, *The Closing of the American Mind*, London, 1987.

Robert Bolt, *A Man for All Seasons*, London, 1960.

Eugene Boylan, *The Spiritual Life of the Priest*, Westminster MD, 1959.

Francis J. Bowen, *Pioneers of the Faith*, London, 1938.

T.E. Bridgett, *Life of Blessed John Fisher*, London, 1890.

Cormac Burke, *Covenanted Happiness: Love and Commitment in Marriage*, Dublin, 1990.

Daniel Callam, 'Clerical Continence in the Fourth Century: Three Papal Decretals', *Theological Studies*, Vol 41, 1 (1980), pp 3–50.

Canons and Decrees of the Council of Trent, trans. H.J. Schroeder, Rockford, Ill., 1978.

G.K. Chesterton, *Autobiography*, London, 1937.

Roman Cholij, *Clerical Celibacy in East and West*, Leominister, 1988.

——, 'The *lex continentiae* and the Impediment of Orders' in *Studia Canonica*, 21 (1987) 391–418

——, 'Observaciones críticas acerca de los canones que tratan sobre el celibato en el Código de Derecho Canónico de 1983', in *Ius Canonicum*, 31 (1991) 291–305;

——, 'Priestly Celibacy in Patristics and the history of the Church' in *For Love Alone: Reflections on Priestly Celibacy*, Maynooth, 1993, pp 31– 52.

J. Coppens, ed., *Priesthood and Celibacy*, Milan-Rome, 1972.

St John Chrysostom: A treatise *On the Priesthood*. Translated by Rev Patrick Boyle CM, Westminster, MD, 1943.

Christian Cochini, *Apostolic Origins of Priestly Celibacy*, San Francisco, 1990.

Archbishop Desmond Connell, 'The Fruitful Virginity of Mary', *Position Papers*, no. 173, Dublin, May 1988, pp 149–58.

Hugh Connolly, *The Irish Penitentials: Their Significance for the Sacrament of Penance Today*, Dublin, 1995.

H. Daniel-Rops, *The Church of the Apostles and Martyrs*, London, 1963;

——, *Cathedral and Crusade*, London, 1963;

——, *The Protestant Reformation*, London, 1963;

——, *The Church in the Eighteenth Century*, London, 1964.

Avery Dulles, SJ, 'Religion and the News Media: A Theologian Reflects', *America*, 1 October 1994, pp 6-9.

Blessed Josemaría Escrivá: *Friends of God*, Dublin, 1981;

——, *The Forge*, London, 1988.

——, *The Way*, Dublin, 1968.

John Farrell, *Freud's Paranoid Quest*, New York, 1996.

F. Fernandez, *In Conversation with God*, I, New York, 1988.

St John Fisher, *The Defence of the Priesthood*, London, 1935.

Michael F. Flach, 'What Priest Shortage?', *Catholic World Report*, June, 1996, pp 36–41.

For Love Alone: Reflections on Priestly Celibacy, Maynooth, 1993.

Victor Frankl, *Man's Search for Meaning*, London,1964.

André Frossard, *Be Not Afraid!*, London, 1984.

Jean Galot, SJ, *Theology of Priesthood*, San Francisco, 1985.

Ramón García de Haro, *Marriage and the Family in the Documents of the Magisterium*, San Francisco, 1993.

R. Garrigou-Lagrange, *The Priest in Union with Christ*, Cork, 1961.

Gisbert Greshake, *The Meaning of Christian Priesthood*, Dublin, 1988.

Germain Grisez, *The Way of the Lord Jesus I: Christian Moral Principles*, Chicago, 1983.

John M. Haas, ed., *Crisis of Conscience*, New York, 1996;

———, 'The Sacral Character of the Priest as the Foundation for his Moral Life and Teaching', in *The Catholic Priest as Moral Teacher and Guide*, San Francisco, 1990.

Peter Harkx, *The Fathers on Celibacy*, De Pele, Win, 1968.

Manfred Hauke, *Women in the Priesthood? A Systematic Analysis in the Light of the Order of Creation and Redemption*, San Francisco, 1988.

R. Hesbert, *Saint Augustin et la virginité de la foi*, in *Augustinus Magister*, Congrés international augustinien II, Paris, 1954.

Dietrich von Hildebrand, *In Defence of Purity*, London, 1937;

———, *Celibacy and the Crisis of Faith*, Chicago, 1971.

Karl Hillenbrand, 'The Priesthood and Celibacy', in *Osservatore Romano*, 4 August 1993.

James Hitchcock, *Years of Crisis: Collected Essays 1970–1983*, San Francisco, 1985.

Philip Hughes: *History of the Church*, I, London, 1947;

———, *The Reformation in England*, II, London, 1954.

The International Theological Commission: *Le Ministère sacerdotal*, Paris, 1971.

Irish National Teachers' Organisation, *Guidance for Teachers: A Professional Response to Changing Times*, September 1996.

Stanley L. Jaki, 'Man of one Wife or Celibacy', in *Homiletic and Pastoral Review*, January 1986, pp.20–21;

———, *Theology of Celibacy*, Front Royal, Va., 1997.

Philip Jenkins, *Pedophiles and Priests: Anatomy of a Contemporary Crisis*, Oxford, 1996.

The New Jerome Biblical Commentary, London, 1989.

Paul Johnson, *The Quest for God: A Personal Pilgrimage*, London, 1996.

Walter Kasper, 'The Theological Anthropology of *Gaudium et spes*', *Communio* 23, Spring 1996, p.130.

Ian Ker, *John Henry Newman: A Biography*, Oxford, 1990.

Roch Kereszty, ' "Bride"and "Mother" in the *Super Cantica* of St Bernard: An Ecclesiology for our time?', *Communio* 20, Summer 1993, pp 415–36.

C. Knetes, 'Ordination and Matrimony in the Eastern Orthodox Church', *Journal of Theological Studies* 11 (1910), 348–400 and 481–513.

Enrique de la Lama, *La vocación sacerdotal: cien años de clarificación*, Madrid, 1994.

Ronald Lawler, Joseph Boyle, William E. May, *Catholic Sexual Ethics*, Huntington, IN, 1985.

Xavier Léon-Dufour, SJ, *Dictionary of Biblical Theology*, London, 1970.

St Alphonsus Liguori, *Dignity and Duties of the Priest*, New York, 1927.

Filippo Liotta, *La Continenza dei Chierici nel pensiero canonistico classico* (da Graziano a Gregorio IX), Milano, 1971.

John McAreavey, 'Priestly Celibacy', in *Irish Theological Quarterly*, 59 (1993/1), pp 22–43.

Diarmaid MacCullogh, *Thomas Cranmer: A Life*, London, 1996.

Bede McGregor and Thomas Norris, eds., *The Formation Journey of the Priest: Exploring* Pastores Dabo Vobis, Dublin, 1994.

Alasdair MacIntyre, *After Virtue: A Study in Moral Theory*, London, 1981.

L. F. Martin, 'When Clergy Marry: An Insider's View', in *Homiletic and Pastoral Review*, June 1997, pp 29–32, 45–47.

Maynooth Statutes, 1956 –*Acta et Decreta*.

Placid Murray, *Newman the Oratorian*, Dublin, 1969.

Michael Neary, *Our Hide and Seek God: Priesthood and the Word of God*, Cork, 1990.

Richard John Neuhaus, *The Naked Public Square: Religion and Democracy in America*, Grand Rapids, Mich. 1984.

John H. Newman, *Discourses Addressed to Mixed Congregations*, London, 1886;

——, *Apologia pro Vita sua*, London, 1886;

——, *Parochial and Plain Sermons*, VI, London, 1875;

——, *An Essay on the Development of Christian Doctrine*, London, 1875.

Aidan Nichols: *Holy Order: Apostolic Priesthood from the New Testament to the Second Vatican Council*, Dublin, 1990;

——, *Rome and the Eastern Churches*, Edinburgh, 1992.

Fernando Ocariz, *God as Father in the Message of Blessed Josemaría Escrivá*, Princeton, NJ, 1994.

Fernando Ocariz, Lucas F. Mateo Seco, José Antonio Riestra, *The Mystery of Jesus Christ*, Dublin, 1994.

Letters of Flannery O'Connor: The Habit of Being, ed., Sally Fitzgerald., New York, 1980.

Marc Ouellet, S.S., 'Priestly Ministry at the Service of Ecclesial Communion', in *Communio* 23 (Winter 1966).

The Oxford Companion to the Bible, Oxford, 1993.

The Diocese of Oxford: 'The Greatness of the Trust': *Report of the Working Party on Sexual Abuse by Pastors*, Easter 1996;

———, *Code of Ministerial Practice*, Pentecost 1996.

Josef Pieper: *An Anthology*, San Francisco, 1989.

Wanda Poltawska, 'Roots of Spousal Love', in *Osservatore Romano*, 28 September 1994;

———, 'Priestly Celibacy in the light of Medicine and Psychology', in *For Love Alone: Reflections on Priestly Celibacy*, Maynooth, 1993, pp 89–102.

Alvaro del Portillo, *On Priesthood*, Chicago, 1974.

Ignace de la Potterie, 'The Biblical Foundation of Priestly Celibacy' in *For Love Alone: Reflections on Priestly Celibacy*, Maynooth, 1993, pp 13–30;

———, *Mary in the Mystery of the Covenant*, New York, 1992.

John F. Quinn, 'Priest Shortage Panic', *Crisis*, October, 1996, pp 40–4.

Alice Ramos, 'Man and Woman, the Image of God who is Love' in *The Church at the Service of the Family*, Stubenville, Ohio, 1993 (Proceedings of the Sixteenth Convention of the Fellowship of Catholic Scholars, 1993).

Cardinal Joseph Ratzinger: 'The Nature of Priesthood', *Osservatore Romano*, 29 October 1990;

———, 'The Ministry and Life of Priests', *Homiletic and Pastoral Review*, August/September 1997, pp 7–18;

———, *The Ratzinger Report: Joseph Cardinal Ratzinger with Vittorio Messori*, Leominister, 1985;

———, 'Truth and Freedom', *Communio* 23 (Spring 1996), pp 16–35;

———, *Priestly Ministry: A Search for its Meaning*, New York, 1971;

———, 'Some Perspectives on Priestly Formation Today', in *The Catholic Priest as Moral Teacher and Guide*, San Francisco, 1990.

George W. Rutler, *The Curé D'Ars Today*, San Francisco, 1988.

———, 'A Consistent Theology of Clerical Celibacy' in *Homiletic and Pastoral Review*, February 1989, pp 9–15.

John Saward, *Christ is the Answer: The Christ-Centred Teaching of Pope John Paul II*, Edinburgh, 1995.

Matthias J. Scheeben, *The Mysteries of Christianity*, London, 1961.

Michel Schooyans, *The Totalitarian Trend of Liberalism*, St Louis, 1997.

Angelo Scola, 'The Formation of Priests in the Pastoral Care of the Family', in *Communio* 24 (Spring 1997), pp 56–83.

Michel Séguin, 'The Biblical Foundations of the Thought of John Paul II on Human Sexuality', *Communio*, 20, Summer 1993, pp 266–289.

Josef Sellmair, *The Priest in the World*, London, 1954.

Fulton Sheen, *The Priest is Not His Own*, London, 1967.

Janet Smith, *Why* Humanae Vitae *was Right: A Reader*, San Francisco, 1993.

Alfons M. Stickler: *The Case for Clerical Celibacy: Its Historical Development and Theological Foundations*, San Francisco, 1995;

——, 'The Evolution of the Discipline of Celibacy in the Western Church from the End of the Patristic Era to the Council of Trent', in Coppens, J. (ed), *Priesthood and Celibacy*, Milan, 1972, pp.503–97;

——, 'La continenza dei Diaconi specialmente nel primo millennio della Chiesa', in *Salesianum* 26 (1964) 275–302.

Federico Suarez, *About Being a Priest*, Houston, 1979.

Tad Szulc, *Pope John Paul II: The Biography*, New York, 1995.

Xavier Tilliette, 'The Chastity of Christ', *Communio* 24 (Spring 1997), pp 51–56.

Joseph Tolhurst, 'The Interchange of Love: John Henry Newman's Teaching on Celibacy' in *Irish Theological Quarterly*, 59 (1993/3), pp 218–25.

J.R.R. Tolkien, *Letters*, ed., H. Carpenter, London, 1981.

J. B. Torelló, 'Celibacy and Personality', in *Osservatore Romano*, 18 January 1973;

——, 'Las ciencias humanas ante el celibato sacerdotal', in *Scripta Theologica*, 27 (1995/1), 269–283.

Leo Trese, *A Man Approved*, London, 1953;

——, *Tenders of the Flock*, London, 1956;

——, *Sanctified in the Truth*, London , 1961.

Meriol Trevor, *The Pillar and the Cloud*, London, 1962.

Hans Urs von Balthasar, *The Office of Peter and the Structure of the Church*, San Francisco, 1986.

Pierre Veuillot, ed., *The Catholic Priesthood: Papal Documents from Pius X to Pius XII* (1903–1954), Dublin, 1962.

Karol Wojtyla, *Love and Responsibility*, London, 1981.

Index